A LITHGOW palooza!

101 Ways to Entertain and Inspire Your Kids

John Lithgow

A Broadthink Book

A Lark Production

A FIRESIDE BOOK
PUBLISHED BY SIMON & SCHUSTER
NEW YORK   LONDON   TORONTO   SYDNEY

Fireside
Rockefeller Center
1230 Avenue of the Americas
New York, NY 10020

Copyright © 2004 by John Lithgow

All rights reserved,
including the right of reproduction
in whole or in part in any form.

FIRESIDE and colophon are registered trademarks
of Simon & Schuster, Inc.

For information regarding special discounts for bulk purchases,
please contact Simon & Schuster Special Sales at 1-800-456-6798
or business@simonandschuster.com

Designed by Charles Kreloff
Illustrations by Elisha Cooper (www.elishacooper.com)
Photographs by Uli Rose

Manufactured in the United States of America

10   9   8   7   6   5   4   3   2   1

Library of Congress Cataloging-in-Publication data is available

ISBN 0-7432-6124-0

For Ian, Phoebe, Nate, and Mary, with my love

Acknowledgments

We had a palooza of a team. Much thanks to: Ariana Barth; Flynn Berry; Sulin Carling; Elisha Cooper; Allie and Matthew DiMona; George and Claudia Engelbrecht; Katrina Forbes; Seth Godin; Richard Grasso; Rachel Hoyt; Lauren Kanter; Charles Kreloff; Deirdre Maclean; Ezra Miller; Nate Morgan; Mark Ruhala; Pete Strupp; Trish Todd; Cooper, Doug, Spike, Orange Scarf, Angel, and Ickle Watts. The team was guided by the inexhaustible Lisa DiMona, Robin Dellabough, and Karen Watts, the true creators of this book. Finally, heartfelt thanks to Nancy Cushing-Jones, Cynthia Cleveland, and Barbara Weller, who heard me reminisce about my kids and said, "There's a book in this!"

Contents

Introduction

So what's a palooza? And what's it doing in the title of this book? Let me tell you.

I'm often asked, "What's the most fun you ever had on a project?" It would be a close call, and the contenders might surprise you. *Shrek*? *Harry and the Hendersons*? *3rd Rock from the Sun*? No. The most fun I ever had was with the most important people in my life: my children. The most fun of all? It would either be the cardboard-box castle I built for my younger son's birthday or the *King and I* puppet show my daughter put on with her girlfriends or the day-long sand castle I built with my big boy or our treasure hunt at the National Gallery of Art or the paper chase I engineered for eight teenage girls, the one that covered the entire campus of UCLA.

Those adventures were just a few of our paloozas.

Paloozas can be almost anything, but they all have several features in common. They don't cost much (some cost absolutely nothing). They are instigated or organized by parents but are quickly taken over by children. They may occasionally involve turning on a computer, a DVD player, or a VCR but never the television or a video game. They depend totally on the inexhaustible creativity, ingenuity, imagination, and sense of fun in young minds. They make use of all varieties of arts and crafts. They are equally amusing to both parents and children. And as much as they may inspire and entertain children, they may subtly, even secretly, educate them.

This book is crammed full of paloozas. One hundred and one of them, in fact. Its closest cousin is a cookbook, since we are essentially providing recipes. But our recipes are for good times, not good food (although lots of them involve cooking). Our categories follow the broad outlines of the various arts (writing, acting, dance, music, and art) but also include things to do in the kitchen, in the car, on vacations, in restaurants, on birthdays and holidays. Even household pets get their due. Many of the paloozas will strike you as wacky and wild, but think back to some of your best times when you were a kid. I bet you did some pretty ridiculous things in your day, and loved them.

I know what you're thinking. Did this man actually *do* all these crazy things with his kids? No, not nearly. In fact, my wife and I only did about 10 percent of them (that number doesn't include all my bright ideas that turned out to be disasters). I did, however, collect paloozas from lots of friends, and the process was exhilarating. Hearing parents describe their best times with their children is more surprising, delightful, and touching than any movie or play. The creation of the book was, in itself, the ultimate palooza.

No one ever cooks every single recipe

in a big fat cookbook. By the same token, it is virtually impossible to undertake every one of these paloozas. Don't even try. My intention is that, by leafing through this book, parents and kids alike might hit upon a few projects that capture their imagination. Let this book embolden you. Pick and choose, and blame all failures on me. When it's raining outside, when you've run out of birthday ideas, when an upcoming holiday fills you with dread, or when the sound of a video game is beginning to drive you mad, sit down with your kids and have a look. Who knows? My paloozas may spark another one that never even occurred to me. That's sure to be the best palooza of all.

Palooza Key

Each palooza features a summary sidebar that answers a few key questions about the palooza: Who can play? What do we need? Running time? And what's the budget?

Who can play?

advises age appropriateness. Paloozas are designed for age ranges from 3 to 6, 6 to 9, or 9 to 12. Some paloozas work for more than one age range (6–9 and 9–12); others could also be enjoyed by teenagers (those paloozas we describe as for 9 and up). If you see a palooza designated for all ages, it's great for the whole family.

What do we need?

describes the various materials you might use for the palooza.

Running time?

gives a rough estimate of the time involved to complete a palooza, from a few minutes to spread over an afternoon or even several days.

Budget?

indicates whether the palooza is free; almost free, depending on what materials you already have on hand at home ($); costs only a few dollars ($$); or could cost $20 or more, depending on how all out you go on the palooza ($$$). Many of the paloozas in this book can be free or almost free, if you're thrifty, creative with found materials, and use resources like the Internet and your local library to their full advantage.

the big
paloozas

Adopt-a-Soup Can

Hold on to your hats, this is a nutty palooza. But trust me, the kids will love it. Andy Warhol exalted sameness in his Campbell's Soup Can series. This palooza brings an individual can of soup to life and gives it a personality all its own.

What's the Palooza?

Choose a can of soup to adopt. Roam the soup aisle at the grocery store and read aloud the names of various kinds of soup. Pick a soup that tickles your fancy and bring it home to "live." Invent a name that suits your soup can's personality; think Beany Bacon, Alpha Beth Soup, Tommy Tomato, Charlie Chowder, and so on.

At home with the soup, make a birth certificate for it. Look at your own birth certificate as a sidelight. Include the soup can's name, date, time, and place of birth (date of purchase, and store name), and the name of its legal guardian (your name). Once the soup can is named and has proper documentation, invent the soup can's life story and personality traits. Then dress it accordingly.

To dress the soup can, carefully remove the paper label. Trace the outline of the label onto a piece of paper to make a can-sized "dress" pattern. Design and color the new dress (or pants, bathing suit, tutu, and so on) for the can using the pattern. Thinking of its personality, use the soup can's favorite colors and patterns. Stripes. Solids. Citrussy oranges and pinks. Businessy blues and grays. Don't forget to leave space to draw a face onto the paper. Outfit the can by taping on his new clothes. Add hair by attaching pieces of yarn to the top of the can with tape.

A soup can's accessories say much about his personality. Dress him up for a business meeting by adding a little necktie. Draw an umbrella and handbag for her. Or a baseball cap and glove for him.

What's your soup can like? She's a little bit shy, but loves Audrey Hepburn movies. He's always green with pea-soup envy. Does she socialize with other soups or prefer the company of mixed nuts? The idea is to make the can as interesting a character as possible. And to get her involved in your life! She comes to the table for meals. She helps with homework. She goes to ballet class and soccer practice. She may even go to school for show-and-tell. Be sure to tell how she got that dent below her ingredients list. It's quite a story.

Extrapalooza

Souper Can!

Souper Can is a soup-can superhero. He's got whatever powers you dream up for him. (And he's probably wearing a cape and lots of spandex!) Take photos or draw pictures of Souper Can doing outrageous superhero kinds of things. Use the photos or drawings to make a comic book of Souper Can's adventures. Souper Can lands on the roof of the dollhouse for an amazing rescue of a cat stranded on the second-story windowsill. Souper Can bravely cleans his plate of Mom's asparagus casserole. Souper Can discusses playground safety with the school principal. Souper Can looks under a child's bed with concern. Write funny captions or dialogue to go with the pictures.

Campbell's Soup Can Series

Pop artist Andy Warhol began to experiment with silk-screening images onto painted canvas in 1962, a technique that allowed him to repeat a subject numerous times. Images from popular culture—Brillo boxes, dollar bills, portraits of Marilyn Monroe, and the famous Campbell's Soup Can series, of course—are immortalized in his work. See www.warholfoundation.org for more about Warhol and his iconographic art.

Junk Garden

By planting in unusual objects, planting an entire garden in an old tire, or decorating a whole garden with quirky found objects, kids get to flex their resourceful and imaginative muscles. They also gain an appreciation for whimsy in the garden and for the earthly delights of a garden itself.

Who can play?
All ages, with supervision.

What do we need?
A little patch of good earth, child-sized garden gloves, watering can, trowel, and plants. Twine, stones or bricks to mark off the junk garden plot. And as many garden ornaments, aka junk, as you want (see suggestions, opposite). If container planting, potting soil and suitable pots.

Running time?
Foraging for garden junk can take ten minutes or a lifetime.

Budget?
$

What's the Palooza?

Create a junk garden by incorporating the odd and unusual in the backyard, family garden, or outdoor terrace by using household items—from metal buckets or work boots to red wagons and old chairs—as planters or garden decoration. One person's old frying pan is another's dream ornament for a patch of scarlet begonias. A toy truck displayed on a rock just so becomes an appealing garden sculpture.

Choose a patch of ground in your yard or garden that can be designated as the "junk garden." How big a patch of ground you choose depends on the size of your property, of course, and how much space you want to devote in the yard for the activity. A minimum of one square yard is plenty to start. Mark it off with stakes and twine, twigs, sticks, and stones, or other objects you gather for the garden border. Use seashells, wooden blocks, dominos, board game pieces, or even plastic race car tracks.

Once the border is defined, the junk garden is ready to be planted. Plant objects only or a combination of objects and plants. You may want to plant your objects first, so as to avoid trampling the plants. Or you may want to get impatiens or petunias in the ground first, so as to invent creative displays around them with found objects. You can also skip real plants altogether. Go wild "planting" colorful cups and saucers you've collected at yard sales or plastic juice cups. Dig a little hole in the ground and "plant" a cup so that it is sticking in the ground about halfway. Or paint wooden spoons bright colors and plant them as flowers in your garden. Plant action figures, plastic animals, Barbie, you name it.

Plant items from the kitchen or basement such as a yardstick, an old boot, measuring spoons, or flatware. Be artful about the planting and think of interesting ways to combine objects and plants. Use saucers as backdrops for small plants. Make a perch for birds out of an old spoon tied tightly to a twig with rubber bands. Tend the junk garden carefully and water frequently. Change or move the objects as you collect new items or simply to redesign the garden.

Extrapaloozas

Chair Trellis

Look for interesting old chairs at yard sales and antique stands. Choose a chair that has the patina of age or might be painted a favorite color. Position the chair in a spot that will accommodate the kind of plant you wish to grow, sun-, soil-, and water-wise. Ask your plant store for recommendations or choose a vine such as honeysuckle, sweet potato, passion flower, or a flowering bean vine, and train the vine to climb the chair. Voilà. Chair trellis.

Tire Garden

Use an old tire to make a raised bed. Fill the center of the tire with good soil and plant a tomato seedling in the center. Decorate the tire garden with Barbie shoes or marbles or other found objects. Then make tomato sandwiches in summer.

Junk Garden Themes

Choose a theme. Go all natural and use only twigs and stones, bird feathers, leaves, shells, moss-covered stones from a stream. Or make the garden dinosaurs-only. Cre-

Good Junk

Barbie shoes
Bowling balls
Chairs
Cups and saucers
Flatware
High-top work boots
Jelly jars
Mason jars
Mugs
Old watering can
Saucepans
Seashells
Sinks and bathtubs
Small toys
Teapots
Tinted glass bottles
Tire rims
Washtub
Wicker baskets
Wooden blocks
Wooden spoons

ate an imaginary universe in the garden using dollhouse furniture, "fairy furniture" made from items you collect (pipe cleaners, Popsicle sticks, toothpicks, old crayons), or twig tepees. Choose plants by theme, as well. Plant basil, lemon thyme, mint, dill, and lavender in a "nose garden." Plant snapdragon, tiger lily, catnip, and spider plants for a "zoo garden."

Container Planting

If it holds soil, and something will grow in it, it's a garden. Plant something wonderful in an old work boot. Or an old cast-iron frying pan. Or a little red wagon. Follow potting instructions for container planting from your favorite gardening book or rely on your own green thumb (paying attention to drainage, using good professional-grade potting soil, and so on), and plant to your hearts' content. Try lavender in the boot. Begonias in the wagon. Use yogurt cup liners (with a hole punched in the bottom for drainage) for planting in mugs you collect in thrift stores and yard sales. Have a mug garden collection.

Flowers for Your Garden

For immediate results in the flowerbed, plant seedlings or small plants from the nursery. Try annuals such as nasturtiums, petunias, impatiens, or verbena. Sunflowers are easy to plant from seed, and you can see growth almost daily. Green peas, lettuces, and pumpkins are fast-growing vegetables. Hollyhocks and daisies, two old-fashioned perennials, also mix well in a junk garden.

Storm King

Junk garden par excellence. This outdoor museum in New York State celebrates the relationship between sculpture and nature. Large-scale works by artists such as Alexander Calder, Richard Serra, Henry Moore, and Louise Nevelson adorn 500 acres of landscaped lawn, fields, and woods. See www.skac.org.

Bridges

I've never outgrown my sense of amazement at the sheer audacity of a bridge. The idea of spanning an enormous body of water while appearing suspended in air by a few thin steel threads is magical. No wonder children—and most adults—are endlessly fascinated by bridges.

What's the Palooza?

An exploration of bridges, mind-boggling and mysterious—think about them, design them, build them!

Make up a quiz entirely of questions about bridges: What is the longest bridge in the world? The highest bridge? The strongest bridge? The oldest bridge? What country has the most bridges? What are all the types of bridges? What are the great bridges of the world?

Once the quiz is finished, take a trip to the library or the Internet. In looking for quiz answers, you can find out about famous bridges around the world, the history of bridges, how bridges are built, what materials they're made from, and so forth. You can also find out about the dozens of types of bridges, including suspension, cantilever beam, cable, truss, swing, and arch, to name a few. Try to find an example of each kind of bridge in your search.

Now that you know something about bridges, start building bridges out of as many different common materials as you can think of: paper, sticks, stones, clay, blocks, Legos, wire, magnets, candy, cards, toothpicks, you name it.

Begin by sketching a simple bridge. Then decide what material would work best for that particular bridge design. An arched bridge might be built out of plasticine. A truss bridge could be made of Popsicle sticks, white glue or Scotch tape, and string.

Who can play?
All ages.

- - - - - -

What do we need?
Simple household construction materials, such as blocks, Legos, Popsicle sticks, string, thin wire, glue, tape.

- - - - - -

Running time?
As long or short as you like.

- - - - - -

Budget?
$

One of the simplest of all bridges is made of an 8½ x 11 inch sheet of paper and six books. Take the piece of paper and rest opposite ends on a stack of three books each. Here's where the mystery of science comes in: If you try to put a weight on this paper bridge, say a few pennies, it will collapse. If you fold the paper a few times, it magically holds the weight of the pennies.

If you're feeling ambitious, make a simple scale-model truss bridge, using toothpicks, glue, cardboard, and a marker. Go to http://www.yesmag.bc.ca/projects/bridge.html and follow the step-by-steps.

A terrific book all about build-it-yourself bridges is *Bridges! Amazing Structures to Design, Build & Test* by Michael Kline, Carol Johmann, and Elizabeth Reith. It's a great introduction to the whole wide world of bridges, with history, science, and lots of hands-on designing, building, and testing activities.

And check out www.pontifex2.com, featuring Pontifex II software, which allows you to build and test a bridge of your own design. Then you can use the 3-D graphics feature to view your creation from any angle, including "first person," where you're in the driver's seat of the test car.

Extrapaloozas

Travel Bridge

Start a "collection" of bridges by keeping a special bridge notebook in the car. Then, whenever the family drives anywhere, pay attention to every bridge, no matter how small, you cross. Try to catch the name of the bridge and include the town or state it's in, what body of water it spans, or if it covers a landform of some kind, such as a ravine. See if you can figure out what type of bridge it is, too: suspension? arch? cantilevered? Maybe you give yourself extra points for crossing an unusual bridge—a covered bridge, for example. But it's plenty of fun simply to keep a life-long list of bridges.

A Game of Bridge

Play an old-school game of bridge—London Bridge. Building bridges in the Middle Ages was fraught with suspicion because the bridge might disturb a place inhabited by devils and arouse their anger. In the original medieval game of London Bridge, being "caught" by the bridge was a way of separating players into devils and angels.

Two players stand face-to-face and clasp each other's hands high in front of them to form the bridge. Sing the words to the song as the other players walk or run under the bridge. To capture someone, the two bridge builders lower their arms whenever the verse reaches the words "My fair lady." Once every player has been caught, they divide in half, holding on to each other's waist to form a chain and play tug-of-war. (The tug-of-war symbolized the battle between good and evil—devils and angels.)

The Bridge at Beaugency

In 1936, James Joyce wrote a letter to his grandson, later published as *The Cat and the Devil*. Set in the French town of Beaugency, the mayor makes a pact with the devil, who vows to build a bridge over the Loire River—overnight! The story is fiction, but the town and bridge are real.

London Bridge

London Bridge is falling
    down,
Falling down, falling down.
London Bridge is falling
    down,
My fair lady.

Take a key and lock her up,
Lock her up, lock her up.
Take a key and lock her up,
My fair lady.

How will we build it up,
Build it up, build it up?
How will we build it up,
My fair lady?

Build it up with silver and
    gold,
Silver and gold, silver and
    gold.
Build it up with silver and
    gold,
My fair lady.

Gold and silver I have none,
I have none, I have none.
Gold and silver I have none,
My fair lady.

Build it up with needles and
    pins,
Needles and pins, needles
    and pins.
Build it up with needles and
    pins,
My fair lady.

Pins and needles bend and
    break,
Bend and break, bend and
    break.
Pins and needles bend and
    break,
My fair lady.

Build it up with wood and
    clay,
Wood and clay, wood and
    clay.

Build it up with wood and
    clay,
My fair lady.

Wood and clay will wash
    away,
Wash away, wash away.
Wood and clay will wash
    away,
My fair lady.

Build it up with stone so
    strong,
Stone so strong, stone so
    strong.
Build it up with stone so
    strong,
My fair lady.

Stone so strong will last so
    long,
Last so long, last so long.
Stone so strong will last so
    long,
My fair lady.

Repartee

Bashful. Buttoned up. Taciturn. Tongue-tied. Wouldn't you rather be the one they called *enlightening* and *effervescent, loquacious* and *mellifluous*? It's all a matter of exercising your conversation muscles—and having fun, of course. They don't call it "wordplay" for nothing!

Who can play?
Ages 9 and up.

What do we need?
Paper, pen, newspaper.

Running time?
Fifteen minutes.

Budget?
Free.

What's the Palooza?

Practice the fine art of conversation. It's not always easy to think of something to say, especially to someone you've just met. But there are simple ways to get a conversation started, and great ways to make it interesting.

The best place to start to explore conversation opportunities is around the dinner table at home. Usually the adults drive the dialogue, and it's easy to just let them do that. But you're tired of the "How was school? Did you do your homework?" dinner conversation you usually have. So take matters into your own hands. Throw a few provocative conversation starters out there and see what happens.

Ask questions. Choose one person to ask one question. Others around the table may want to answer the question as well, or the question may lead to another topic of conversation. Here are some ideas for questions to ask, but you should definitely think up some of your own:

> If you could live anywhere in the world, where would it be?
> What famous person would you like to meet?
> What is your earliest childhood memory?
> What were your favorite cartoons when you were a kid?
> If someone gave you $1,000 to spend in one day, how would you spend it?
> If you could be invisible for a day, where would you go and what would you do?
> How would you describe your perfect day?

Flash the facts. Share interesting pieces of information that are likely to spur conversation. For instance, did you know that no word in the English language rhymes with *month, orange, silver,* and *purple*? Or that the average person falls asleep in seven minutes? Or that an ostrich's eye is bigger than its brain? Collect tidbits like this from books and magazines that you read and use them to get people talking.

Use the news to stir things up. Did you see a story on the sports page calling your dad's favorite baseball player "trade bait"? Did you hear on the radio that the government says ketchup counts as a vegetable in your school lunch? Did you see a story about someone spotting a UFO? Share these kinds of "news" bites, and you're sure to spark lively debates about what's fact and what's opinion—or what's fact and what's fiction!

Know what you think. When you hear a news story or listen to a conversation, don't just let it go in one ear and out the other. Stop and ask yourself, "What do I think about that?" Pay attention to subjects and issues being discussed around you and try to work out your opinion on them. It's okay to have mixed feelings about something (on the one hand, on the other . . .) because

wit, n.: The natural ability to perceive and understand, a kind of genius; a keenness or quickness of perception; the ability to express clever or humorous verbal insights, often in the context of conversation.

bon mot, n.: A clever saying or witticism. From the French *bon* (good) and *mot* (word).

Great Wits

Benjamin Franklin
Mark Twain
Oscar Wilde
Dorothy Parker
Noel Coward
H. L. Mencken
James Thurber

■ ■ ■ ■

Bits of Wits-dom

At wits end: At the limit of one's mental resources; at a loss.

Battle of wits: A contest on which the outcome is determined by intelligence.

Great wits jump: To think alike.

Half-witted: Stupid.

Keep wits about him: Remains alert or calm, especially in crisis.

Scared out of his wits: Frightened to the point of incapacitation.

Lots of people act well, but few people talk well. This shows that talking is the more difficult of the two.

—Oscar Wilde
(1856–1900)

things are rarely crystal clear or black and white. Just try to know what you think and practice expressing it at the table. Who do you think would make a good president—and why? Do you think there should be a designated hitter in major league baseball—why or why not? Do you think that human cloning is possible—and if so, should it be allowed? The more you know about what you think, the more there is to talk about!

Extrapaloozas

Hi-Point, Lo-Point

You can play Hi-Point, Lo-Point with family and friends or people you've just met. Start by sharing the hi-point, or best moment, of your day. Then describe the lo-point, or least pleasant part of your day. Hi-point? I got an A on my science test. Lo-point? My sandwich fell on the floor at lunch. Get everyone to share their hi-points and lo-points. Compare stories—who had the highest hi-point and the lowest lo-point? Play hi-point, lo-point every night at dinner and soon you'll have a Hi-Point, Lo-Point Hall of Fame. And shouldn't the person with the lowest lo-point not have to do dishes?

Conversation Piece

A conversation piece is an object that is so unusual and provocative that people can't help talking about it. It doesn't matter whether it's shocking or beautiful or rare or bizarre, as long as it arouses interest. If you are in someone's home and you see a skull on a bookshelf, for instance, or an elegant orchid on a table, you can be sure these are meant to be conversation pieces. Sometimes people dress in an extreme or unusual manner in order to *be* a conversation piece. Or they'll wear a startling piece of jewelry or over-the-top hat. Conversation pieces command attention, to be sure, but they don't guarantee that sparkling conversation will happen. That's still up to you.

It's About Time

It's hard to imagine getting through a day without our alarm clocks, wristwatches, and wall clocks. But ancient societies experienced and measured time in completely different ways (and they did just fine, didn't they?). This palooza explores some aspects of time we rarely take the time to think about.

What's the Palooza?

Devote a day to the exploration of time, and see what it would be like to live without our modern mechanical clocks at all. Before the late fifteenth century, mechanical clocks as we know them did not exist. But people came up with other ingenious ways to measure time. We've all heard of hourglasses and sundials. But there were also fire clocks, which were made of a burning candle with lines marking each hour, or even an incense stick that burned at a steady rate. Water clocks measured time by the flow of water through a small hole. In some of the most primitive cultures, time has been measured in vague but concrete approximations—people would talk of "the time it takes to cook a pan of beans" as a unit of time. And, of course, without reliable tools for measuring time, the sun acted as the biggest indicator of time.

Make a sundial before the day you will spend thinking about time. You will need a large piece of heavy paper or cardboard, a short pencil, a small amount of clay, and a watch. Place the pencil point down in the center of the cardboard, using the clay to secure it firmly. On a clear, sunny day, put the cardboard outside soon after the sun rises, making sure to put it in a spot that will not be obscured by shadow during any part of the day. If necessary, the cardboard can be held in place with small stones or a brick. At every hour until sunset, mark the place on the cardboard where the end of the pencil's shadow lies

The long, unmeasured pulse of time moves everything

—Sophocles
(495–406 B.C.)

and the current time. Be careful not to shift or disturb the cardboard, or your measurement will be inaccurate.

The next day (which should probably be a Saturday, Sunday, or other no-school day), rise with the sun—or whenever your own biological clock tells you to—and let the fun begin! Unplug, put away, or cover up all your clocks, and use your sundial instead.

Over the course of the day, see if anyone in the family *really* has a good sense of time. One at a time, have each person lie down on the floor and close his eyes and start the stopwatch. Whenever he thinks one minute, or two minutes, or five minutes have passed, he stops the stopwatch and checks the amount of time that really passed. Write down each person's name and how many minutes he *actually* spent lying on the ground. Whoever gets the closest to ten minutes wins the Natural Time-keeper Award.

Mostly what you'll discover is how out of touch everyone's sense of time really is. Try to brainstorm the various ways that you can measure the passing of the day without looking at a clock or watch.

Talk about units of time drawn from the details of your day-to-day life: how about the time it takes the answering machine to pick up? The time it takes to lock the front door? See if you can incorporate these time units into your everyday conversations, such as, "Dinner will be ready in the time it takes to walk around the block." And then walk around the block, because that's a good idea, anyway!

At the end of this day of primitive timekeeping, it might be hard for you to decide whether you are lucky or unlucky to live lives where time is precise to the second. Does it make your life more organized or more frenzied? Would it be possible to abandon our traditional perception and measure of time completely? Never look at a watch or even your sundial? Imagine time not as cyclical, rather as one long line into the future without any measure but the quality of how you spend it. Read a good book until your eyes get tired. Then take a lovely nap until you wake up. Eat when you are hungry. Take a bath when it would feel good. Shaking off some of our micro-measurements of time would at least be a relaxing vacation!

Extrapaloozas

Time Management Race

Set up relay teams, with one or more persons in each. Create a "course" of household or other tasks like loading or unloading a dishwasher, making and packing lunch for school, making a bed, and so on. Guess how long it will take to complete the tasks. Use a stopwatch to time the tasks. Closest guess to the correct time wins.

Reinvent the Calendar

How would you organize the 365 days of the year into smaller units or make your year have fewer than 365 days? What day will be the start of your calendar? What would you call the days, weeks and months? Maybe your "days" only come in pairs—Even Day and Odd Day. What are the special days on your calendar? Will the calendar correspond to the phases of the moon or changes in season, or will it be organized by something random, like whenever someone loses a tooth?

Theories of Time

- - - - - - -

The flow of time is one of the hardest concepts to grasp. Over the course of history, there have been countless intriguing theories about time, some more credible than others.

Hindu tradition says that the earth sits on the backs of four elephants that stand on the shell of a giant turtle. The elephants walk in circles, causing the changing of the seasons.

Ancient Greeks thought of time as the ultimate force of judgment that would right all wrongs.

Ancient Egyptians, as in many cultures, thought of time as cyclical. They thought the world would collapse into chaos and then begin anew.

Sir Fred Hoyle, a twentieth-century astronomer, theorized that although time seems to move from the past to the future, every moment in time actually exists simultaneously. All that changes is our perception of which moment we are in.

Albert Einstein's general theory of relativity, which connects space and time inseparably, suggests that a black hole could actually make travel through time possible (although building a machine that would enable us to do this is an ongoing challenge!).

Labyrinth

I never knew that mazes and labyrinths are not the same until I happened to be invited to the home of a friend who had a full-sized labyrinth on her property. As we walked it together, she explained that a labyrinth only has one path: you walk in toward the center and out again the same way. Mazes are meant to be confusing, full of dead ends and blind alleys, high walls or hedges, and twists and turns. Labyrinths are less frustrating but equally mysterious to a child, which is why they make a great palooza.

Who can play?
All ages.

What do we need?
Paper, pencils,
markers, crayons.

Running time?
Thirty minutes.

Budget?
$

What's the Palooza?

Learn how to draw your own labyrinth. First, look at the examples of the labyrinths, opposite, which are the two most common types out of hundreds of variations. Labyrinths have a rich and varied history; they've been found on Greek coins and clay tablets, Roman mosaics and pottery, Swedish coastlines, medieval European cathedral walls and floors, Native American baskets and cliffs, Peruvian sands, Indian dirt, and English village greens.

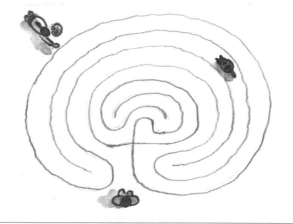

Begin with the simplest labyrinth of all, the three-path (three-circuit). Look at the "seed pattern" below and copy it on a piece of paper at least 8½ by 11 inches. It's better to draw the seed pattern in the bottom half of the paper. Then it's a matter of connecting the dots and lines, as illustrated below. Once you've drawn your own, you can "walk" the labyrinth by tracing the path with either your finger, a pencil eraser, or a crayon or marker. (This is great to do in a restaurant with crayons and paper tablecloths.) It might take a few practice labyrinths before you get the hang of drawing the lines evenly enough to make nicely spaced paths, but that's part of the process.

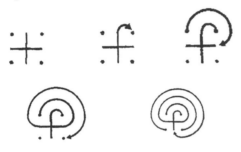

After you're comfortable with the three-circuit labyrinth, you can try the seven-circuit, as illustrated below.

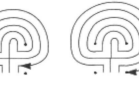

Chartres Cathedral

The beautiful, twelfth-century, forty-foot labyrinth on the floor of the cathedral at Chartres in France is made of 272 marble tiles or pavers, the average number of days a woman is pregnant. Its center is shaped like a flower with six "petals" and has been copied around the world by labyrinth designers.

Online Finger Labyrinth

To experience finger-walking a labyrinth, you can try this interactive Web site:

www.gracecathedral.org/labyrinth/interactions/index.shtml

Solvitur ambulando
(It is solved by walking).

Labyrinth Locators

- - - - - -

You can find a list of nationwide labyrinths in the book *The Way of the Labyrinth* by Helen Curry. Or check the following Web sites to find your nearest full-sized labyrinths open to the public:

www.labyrinthsociety.org/html/locator.html

www.gracecathedral.org/labyrinth/new locator/newdb/

Extrapalooza

Sand and Land Labyrinths

Once you know how to draw a labyrinth with pencil and paper, you're ready for a larger canvas. Any wide open, level ground outdoors makes an excellent place for a three- or seven-circuit labyrinth with paths lined in small stones or rocks. If you're ambitious and energetic enough, make it really large and invite friends to walk it.

Your own backyard has labyrinth potential: try a simple three-circuit labyrinth by marking with chalk then cutting the pattern in the grass with a lawn mower. Driveways and sidewalks are great for chalk labyrinths of any size.

Next time you're at the beach, make labyrinths in the sand, using either a stick, your hands, a shovel, or even your feet.

Left-Hand Man

About 10 percent of the world's population is left-handed, and no one knows why. In some cultures, left-handedness is taboo, and left-handed children must write and eat with their right hands as if true righties. Lefties today are met with fewer cultural prejudices, but they truly do live in a world made for right-handed people. This palooza lets children explore the curious asymmetry of their own bodies and the inherent right-handedness they might never have noticed in everyday objects.

What's the Palooza?

Devote a day to left-handedness. Righties try to make their way through the day using their left hands the way they usually use their right hands. If you want to be really authentic, do it on August 13, International Left-Handers' Day. You'll realize how well trained our preferred hands really must be to do everyday tasks. Eating with a fork with your opposite hand feels awkward and can be messy. And writing with your opposite hand—well, for most people, it's just sloppy. You'll notice right away how automatically you use your right hand when dashing to pick up the phone or flip on the lights. As hard as it may be to switch for the day, you'll discover how hardwired you are to your handedness.

Explore the house and study all the little things you never noticed were intended for right-handed people. Wear your watch on your right wrist (as most left-handers do). It's hard to change the time without taking the watch off—the knob is on the wrong side! Play a game of cards with a standard deck. You'll notice that if you fan your cards in the left hand, you can't see the numbers. Now try writing in a spiral notebook. Ouch! Those

Who can play?
Ages 6 and up.

What do we need?
Just a pair of hands, pencils and paper, and a houseful of everyday objects to examine.

Running time?
Over the course of a whole day.

Budget?
Free.

The term *southpaw* was coined in Chicago, where in one ballpark, the diamond was positioned so that pitchers faced west. If the pitcher was a lefty, the hand that he used to throw the ball was toward the south. Curiously, America's pastime is one arena in which lefties reign supreme. At any given time, there is a disproportionate number of left-handed professional baseball players. Left-handed batters actually have an advantage in baseball—when they're up to bat, they're a half step closer to first base. Try playing a game of Wiffle ball batting left-handed. Or even a game of kickball, kicking left-footed.

books are definitely made for right-handed writers. Use a pencil to write. You'll see that our writing system, which reads from left to right, causes your left hand to get smudged with graphite as it continually rubs over what's just been written. Try using scissors or a can opener with your left hand. See how they're made just for righties? Make a list of all the things you can think of that favor the right hand. Even better to discover the rare objects that are easier to use with your left hand (a toll booth is one example).

Extrapaloozas

The Right Way

Here's where the 10 percent of you who are left-handed try to see how the other 90 percent live. You'll struggle with awkwardness when writing and doing other ordinary activities, just the way the righties do when trading places with you. Look for all the little ways to work with your right hand—buttoning your shirt, tying your shoes, buttering your bread. You can gripe every other day of the year about tools and equipment being right-handed—today's your day to live in the lap of right-handed luxury.

Leonardo da Lefty

Being a lefty isn't only about getting ink smudges all over your hand when you write. It means that you're wired differently—the right hemisphere of your brain, instead of the left, is the dominant one. Left-handed—and thus right-brained—people tend to be creative and visually oriented, with exceptional spatial abilities. Whether you're left- or right-handed, stimulate the right side of your brain by looking closely at left-handed art. Examine the masterpieces of Michelangelo, Leonardo da Vinci, and Raphael and see if you find some quality or tendency of their work in common. Look at the works of Picasso and van Gogh and think about how the way their brains worked—as well as their talented left hands!—helped them develop such unique styles of painting. Look up the drawings of M. C. Escher, which demonstrate the incredible spatial sense found among many left-handed people. Give the right hemisphere of your brain a real workout by trying to draw spatially impossible shapes and staircases leading nowhere. Go to www.artcyclopedia.com to view works by these and other artists.

Handedness, Footedness, and Everything Elsedness

Handedness isn't the only thing that's asymmetrical about our bodies. Most people have a dominant foot, ear, and even eye, which may not be on the same side as their dominant hand. Here are some tests to figure out which side is dominant for each body part.

Feet: Which foot do you use to kick a soccer ball? Which leg is on top when you cross your legs?

Eyes: Cut a hole the size of a dime in a piece of paper. Choose an object in the room and hold the paper at an arm's length away, looking at the object through the hole. Now slowly bring the paper up to your face while continuing to look at the object. When the paper is touching your face, which eye is looking through the hole?

Ears: Which ear do you hold the telephone up to?

Hands: I'm sure you know whether you are left-handed or right-handed, but it is still fun to observe the characteristic traits of handedness. Line your two thumbs up against one another. The nail on the thumb of the dominant hand should be the slightest bit broader. Now clasp your hands. The thumb on top should belong to the dominant hand. With your dominant hand, draw an X and circle it. Righties tend to draw circles counterclockwise; lefties tend to draw them clockwise.

Left-Handed Legends

James Baldwin
Ludwig van Beethoven
Napoleon Bonaparte
Julius Caesar
Lewis Carroll
Charlie Chaplin
Bill Clinton
Benjamin Franklin
Mahatma Gandhi
Judy Garland
Vincent van Gogh
Whoopie Goldberg
Jimi Hendrix
Jack the Ripper
Joan of Arc
Paul McCartney
Michelangelo
Marilyn Monroe
Pablo Picasso
Colin Powell
Raphael
Babe Ruth
Mark Twain
Leonardo da Vinci
H. G. Wells

Imaginary World

It takes a special gift of imagination to invent a whole world, fully realized inside your head. A child absorbed in the tiny details of their imaginary world is a wonder to behold.

Who can play?
Ages 6 and up, with supervision as necessary.

What do we need?
A shoe box, shirt cardboard, scissors, glue (or glue gun), sticks, bark, pinecones, moss, leaves, acorns, or other tree seedpods.

Running time?
A couple of hours.

Budget?
$

What's the Palooza?

Build a fairy house! Among the most enchanting inhabitants of an imaginary world are the fairies. And while fairies certainly make it their business to stay out of sight, you can make your yard or front step or windowsill a welcoming place for these sly, shy creatures by making a house for them featuring all the fairy creature comforts.

Start with a lidded shoe box (the smaller, the better), so you can lift the "roof" off your house to arrange and decorate inside. Cut holes (in any whimsical shape) for windows—fairies like natural, dappled light, so be sure to allow for a window on each wall. Cut a door opening at the front of your house, leaving one long side attached as the hinge side of the door. You may also want to make a back door, for a quick escape.

Take the top off your shoe box to work on your roof. You can have a flat roof decorated with leaves or bark, perhaps with a chimney or two made of twigs and bark. Or you can construct a pitched roof, by creating A-frames out of two six-inch twigs affixed with glue. Three or four A-frames ought to be enough support for your roof. The roof can be constructed of shirt cardboard cut to fit your A-frames, then decorated with leaves or bark like shingles. Or you can skip the cardboard and make the roof out of big pieces of bark, carefully glued to the

A-frames. A twig chimney would be a nice touch. Be sure to glue the roof securely to the top of the shoe box at the bottom of each A-frame twig. Let this dry thoroughly before handling.

Back to the house. Find bark or leaves or evergreen fronds to glue to your house like big shingles. Leave enough clearance at the top of the house so you can set your roof on top. Use small twigs for window mullions; skeleton leaves hung just inside the window make nice curtains.

Speaking of curtains, what else is inside your fairy house? An area rug or wall-to-wall carpet made of moss? Perhaps there is furniture made of Popsicle sticks and bottle caps. Tablecloths made of flower petals. A handsome fireplace of chunky little rocks. Bowls or sconces made of acorn caps. A seedpod couch. A wall mirror made of a piece of mica. Use thick twigs as beams in the corners or across the ceiling (the underside of the shoe-box top/roof). Wander around outside gathering interesting small things and imagine how a tiny person might make use of them. The cozier and homier your fairy house, the better for your fairies.

Nestle your house in a quiet, rumpled spot in the backyard or tucked behind a pot in the garden. Because fairies need to wash and dry their delicate wings, be sure to provide a little pool for bathing, perhaps made from a shallow saucer, and a nice flat stone for drying in the sun. When you're not looking, of course.

You can also set your fairy house on the sill of an open window, where the fairies can spot it. Hang a garden chime made out of old silverware nearby—fairies love the tinkling sound when the wind blows.

Extrapalooza

A Whole New Rock

Scientists are always discovering new things in the universe. What if you could "discover" a whole planet and its population? What is your discovery called? Where is this planet in relation to your own? Does it have grav-

Good Books

There are wonderful books that describe all kinds of elaborate imaginary worlds. For older kids, there is Mary Norton's *The Borrowers,* which may be the classic story of "little people" living among us. *Gulliver's Travels* by Jonathan Swift tells of Lemuel Gulliver's adventures among the tiny people of Lilliput. C. S. Lewis invites us to step through the wardrobe in the attic into the imaginary world in *The Chronicles of Narnia.* And Lewis's friend and colleague J. R. R. Tolkien invented the granddaddy of all imaginary worlds when he published *The Hobbit* and the *Lord of the Rings* trilogy. For younger kids, there's a wonderful adapted version of *Alice's Adventures in Wonderland* by Lewis Carroll, illustrated by DeLoss McGraw. There's also *The Wizard of Oz* by L. Frank Baum, illustrated by Charles Santore and *Peter Pan* by J. M. Barrie, illustrated by Trina Schart Hyman.

ity? What grows there? What are the inhabitants called? Maybe they're not "people," maybe they're "Ackz." What are their common physical features? How do they move or breathe? What do they eat? Can they see, hear, and smell, or do they have other senses we've never heard of? What language do they speak? What do their families consist of? Do they wear clothes?

Once you've thought a bit about these questions, try to fully imagine someone from this planet, perhaps someone just your age. Name him; imagine his family, his home, his history. Does he go to school? Does he have a pet? What is it? You ride a bike—how does he get around his neighborhood? Name and describe his friends.

You can daydream for days about this planet and the beings you invent. Think about keeping a diary of this imaginary world. Write snips of dialogue using bits of alien language they speak. Think of adventures your young boy might have. Draw the planet. Draw a building or a vehicle on that planet. Draw the young boy you imagined. Draw his family. The more detail with which you imagine this planet and its inhabitants, the more real they will become! Go to www.space.com/spacewatch to get ideas about where your planet might be and what it might be called.

Photo-Essay

The photo-essay is a very twentieth-century form of expression that first came into prominence with the launch of *Life* magazine in 1936. Publisher Henry Luce assembled some of the most talented photographers working at the time to create a magazine where the stories would be told through photographs. Photo-essays uniquely show how life really is composed of small moments and intimate expressions—and give us an opportunity to appreciate them.

What's the Palooza?

Create a photo-essay that tells a story by presenting carefully chosen, unposed photographs. You are the visual storyteller, taking several photos of your subject, from which you select the best, most interesting combination of photos to create your essay. Your subject can be an exciting event, like a space shuttle takeoff, or a historic event, like a big protest rally in Washington, or an ordinary event, like a visit to the dentist. It can be a story of a time and a place, like a day-in-the-life at a roadside fireworks shack on the day before the Fourth of July.

Whatever your subject, try to take photos that are natural, unself-conscious, almost ordinary in their matter-of-factness. You are a quiet observer of the goings-on, catching small moments that will help you tell your story. A photo-essay about your sister's dance performance might begin with a shot of her leaving her house or arriving at the theater. Instead of a perfect posed shot of her in her tutu, you catch her in front of a mirror with bobby pins in her mouth, as she scrambles to pull her hair up into a bun. You might also have a shot from the wings, where you show a calm, bored audience

Who can play?
Ages 9 and up.

What do we need?
Camera, film, cardboard or foam mount board.

Running time?
A day or more to take photos, get film developed, and assemble and display essay.

Budget?
$$

waiting for the performance, in contrast to the chaos backstage or in the wings. At the end, we see our dancer accepting a bouquet of flowers, happily embracing her proud grandmother, or asleep in the car, tutu and all.

Create an essay on a day in the life of someone you know. Other subjects for a photo-essay could be your family vacation, the construction (or demolition!) of a building, a sporting event, the hunt for a perfect Christmas tree, a visit to your big sister at college. It can be anything that bears a thoughtful, close look at the details that make up the whole.

Be sure to have plenty of film available because you'll need to take quite a few photographs to get enough of just the right shots to make up your story. Digital cameras are great, because you know on the spot if you have a good picture, so you don't have to develop a lot of so-sos. But any kind of camera is fine as you explore the art of photographic storytelling.

Once your pictures are developed, spread them out on a table and try to identify the few that vividly indicate what happened. Be on the lookout for little telling details—unexpected expressions on people's faces, sub-

Gordon Parks

After Gordon Parks viewed newsreel footage of the Japanese bombing of the U.S. gunboat *Panay*, he became "determined to become a photographer," and bought his first camera, a $7.50 Voigtlander Brilliant. He was the first African-American to do photographic work for *Life* magazine, where his unflinching photo stories of poverty in Harlem and Latin America and the civil rights movement in America were as vivid and compelling as stories he photographed of the Paris fashion shows, a Spanish bullfight, Duke Ellington, and Muhammad Ali. Parks brought an honesty and a curiosity to everything he photographed. Look at *Half Past Autumn: A Retrospective* to see a wonderful collection of his work put together by the Corcoran Gallery in Washington, D.C. And go to www.masters-of-photography.com/P/parks/parks.html to see a terrific array of his photographs.

tle body gestures, an odd feature of the physical surroundings. These details are what will make your photos distinctive, and tell more of the story than even words might have.

After you've chosen your photos, mount them in order on cardboard or dry-mount board with glue or spray adhesive. Then title and date your essay. Once you've created a photo-essay, you'll enjoy certain experiences by wondering how you'd tell the story in photos!

Extrapalooza

Small Time, Big Time

Practice the art of the photo-essay on very small, simple events. An essay on the school flag being raised. Or someone buying an ice cream cone. Or your dad reading the morning newspaper. Shooting these short, uncomplicated events will sharpen your eye for the juicy details of the bigger events you may want to describe in photos.

The camera is an instrument that teaches people how to see without a camera.

—Dorothea Lange
(1895–1965)

Black and White vs. Color

Color photos can be splendid, but many photographers believe that you can only appreciate what you're really seeing in a photo when it's shot in black and white. When looking at a black-and-white photo, your eye isn't distracted by color and instead is drawn to the smaller details you might have missed otherwise—slight facial expressions, small gestures, the physical relation of one element in the photo to another. Experiment taking photos in black and white as well as color and see which suits your style.

Board Game

You've probably been playing board games for most of your life without much considering how they are invented and constructed. When you create your own game, you begin to understand what makes a game tick—and fun to play.

What's the Palooza?

Rework or recycle an existing game—or invent something totally new. First, choose a theme, the topic or subject your game is built around. The theme of Clue is murder mystery. The theme of Battleship is naval war strategy. Think of a subject that interests you. Do you like horses? Maybe your game will be a horse-race game, with different breeds and great horse names, racing around the board to the finish line. Maybe you're a history buff—Revolution might be all about heroes and villains and battles of the Revolutionary War.

What's Your Goal?

There are two basic board games. In strategy games like Monopoly, the goal is to gain control of the board by capturing or blocking the opponent's pieces, overpowering the opponent with your pieces, or trapping (and eliminating) your opponent. In race games like Candyland, you start at one point on the board and try to beat your opponent using the same or different paths to a finishing point.

Once you figure this out, you can determine what moves your game along—dice, cards, a spinner, a timer. Or invent your own combination of mechanisms: the player rolls the die and only has a certain amount of time to figure out his options.

Decide how the players will interact with the game. Create identity pieces for each member of your family, either place cards with each of their pictures on them, or pieces that have some connection to the person—a little plastic horse for your sister, a miniature telephone for Mom, a car for Dad. You may design and create cards if your game calls for them—unlined index cards will do the trick.

Game Glossary

Below are some quirky terms board-game developers use to describe types of games, game features, or certain qualities of game players.

Analysis paralysis: When a player or players' overanalysis of a move or possible outcomes increases the downtime in a game to an undesirable level.

Beer and pretzels game: A game so random and silly that long-term strategies are not possible, played mainly as a humorous distraction rather than as a genuine competition.

Bits: The assorted physical components of a game, including pieces, cards, timer, turner, dice, and so on.

Dice-fest: A game that uses lots of dice to propel the game. Also refers to a game that has a very random quality because the dice are so important to the outcome.

Downtime: The time a player or players spend doing nothing while waiting for other players to finish their turns.

End-game: The final stage of a game, which is when the ultimate winner is decided. Strategies used during this stage of a game are often very different from strategies used at the beginning of the game.

Fiddly: A term used to describe lots of fussy parts and details to each turn, which tends to bog down the pace of the game.

Gamer: A person who likes to spend his free time playing games.

Gamey: Describes a practical feature of a game that seems unnecessary or trumped up.

Going nuclear: Deciding to give up on your own standing in a game in order to destroy or harm another player's chance of winning.

Heft factor: An admiring term referring to the physical weight of a game, usually describing the quality of the bits and board.

Kingmaker: A player who is himself in a losing position, but whose actions have the power to decide the winner of the game.

Replay value: A game's ability to continue to be entertaining after several playings.

Rules lawyer: A gamer who is obsessed with the interpretation of the rules, to the point of diminishing other players' enjoyment of the game.

Zero-sum: Common in two-player games, this term refers to the quality of a game that suggests that everything good that happens to one player is necessarily bad for another.

The Details!

Before you design your board, think about how many people can play. Make enough cards or pieces for more than two players even if you're working on a game for only two players—it will be frustrating later if you try to play your game with more than two people and don't have enough cards and pieces.

What rewards and hazards will make your game interesting, and work with your theme? A piece of gold collected when you land on one square; a spell in the quicksand when you land on another? Are there things that can turn the game upside down or suddenly put someone who was losing in a winning position? Life is filled with surprises—your board game should have some, too!

The Board

Think about how your board will look and work. Maybe you want your board to reflect a route that snakes from one point to another. You might adapt the chessboard design in a clever way. Your board could be round—or 3-D! Maybe you've created a game where the players work their way up and down more than one level.

The point is, the board for a board game can be anything you want it to be. Look at all the boards in your family's game cupboard for ideas, and recycle the boards and pieces for your own game.

To use an old board as the foundation for your board game, cut and glue sturdy paper to fit the old board. Sketch ideas for your board design on another piece of paper, then pencil it out on your actual board. Use

markers or crayons to draw the features; you can also use stickers, or even images cut out from magazines—imagine a basketball board game with the squares decorated with *Sports Illustrated*–style pictures of your favorite professional players.

The Name of the Game

Good games always have names that are either entertaining and vaguely descriptive (Pictionary, Smart Mouth, Boggle) or use a word that's part of the vocabulary of the game (Uno!).

If you've created a game where every square on the board is a famous painting, the game might be called simply Museum. That horse-race game? Maybe it's called By a Nose.

Remember that your game is a work in progress that you can test and refine and change as much as you like. The only way to see if your game is working is to play it—a lot.

Extrapaloozas

New Old Games

If you're more of a reinventor than an inventor, try to put a twist on a game that already exists. Make your own deck of cards with photos of friends and family—even pets!—standing in for the usual king, queen, jack, and ace of the standard deck of playing cards. Make your own chess pieces out of Sculpey. Or use small plastic figures in place of the usual chess personnel—a mixed squad of plastic dinosaurs or army men would work. Make a mancala game out of old buttons. Or make your Monopoly game local—change the standard streets and landmarks to streets and landmarks from your own town!

Box It Up

To create a box for your game, use a sturdy, plain gift box you can design and decorate. If your game is an odd size, you can buy non-standard-sized plain gift boxes at paper goods stores. Create a logo for your game that appears on the box. Draw scenes from your game to "market" the appeal. That safari game might have a giant snapping crocodile featured on the box. Mark the name of the game on all sides of the lid, so you can tell what it is in a stack of games. Store pieces and/or cards in small, reclosable plastic bags. And make sure to include the directions and rules, either on a card (laminate it if you can, because it will get a lot of use!) or written on the inside of the lid. Make your directions simple and clear. Explain the game step by step, in logical order, being very precise with the words you choose. If you're sloppy with the language in the rules and directions, arguments are sure to happen! Test the rules on your friends and family to be sure they are easily understood. And don't forget to include a list of materials or parts of the game at the beginning of your directions, so the players know what they should be playing with.

The Real Estate Game

Monopoly was first known as "The Landlord's Game." It was based on serious economic principles and was meant to teach about property ownership. In 1910, some college students turned the game into a more popular version close to what it is now. In 1933 a man named Charles Darrow copyrighted the game called Monopoly and began making the game to sell. He created boards out of old tablecloths and hand-painted the properties on the cloth. He scavenged around for little trinkets to use as game pieces. The game became popular very quickly, and in 1935 Parker Brothers bought the rights to produce the game. The rest, as they say, is history. The game has been produced in fifteen languages, and more than 100 million sets have been sold around the world. Special editions of the sets are abundant, ranging from Monopoly Elvis edition to Monopoly Harley-Davidson edition. And the game has been made of everything from chocolate to solid gold.

Sensation

Actors often use a technique called *sense memory* when they want to re-create the sensory impression of a particular experience in their acting. The idea, as practiced and encouraged by legendary director and acting coach Lee Strasberg among others, is to take note of what you experience in everyday life by using all five senses and to commit those impressions to memory. This palooza is a bit of a twist on Strasberg's sense memory exercises and Blindman's Bluff.

What's the Palooza?

Explore the idea of trusting your senses and developing your sense memory.

Trust Walk (Ages 6–12)

One player is blindfolded and then led around a familiar room or area by another player, "observing" objects and spaces in the room with all available senses. Before tying on the blindfold, have the trust walker take in the room by sight. If it's the player's bedroom, look at the objects on the desk and bookshelves. What's on top of the bureau? Where are the windows, closet doors, toys, and other belongings? Tie the blindfold on and through a combination of both leading the player to an object and simply placing objects in hand, have the player make guesses as to what he is touching. Challenge the player to search the objects for clues that engage his memory. For instance, you put a book in the player's hands. That's easy, it's a book. But which book is it? The player has to think about the book in his hand—is it hardcover and heavy or paperback and small? The player also has to think about which books are in his

---

Who can play?
All ages, depending on the game.

- - - - - -

What do we need?
A scarf or bandanna that may be used as a blindfold. Sensory objects of all kinds.

- - - - - -

Running time?
Thirty minutes to an hour.

- - - - - -

Budget?
Free.

room. When he feels the book carefully for details, he notices a dog-ear at the bottom corner of the cover. Oh! That's Wringer, which he fell asleep reading last night, causing the bend in the cover.

Move the game to another area that the player has not had any time to "take in" beforehand. Is there a noticeable difference in the number of objects the player is able to identify? Use other senses besides touch. Are there objects that can be identified by smell or sound? Finally, extend the trust walk throughout the remainder of the house or even out of doors. Can he guess where he is? Can he identify objects, sounds, and smell? Reverse the player and leader roles. Talk about the idea of trusting your senses. How about trusting your leader? When you remove the blindfold you will realize more fully and appreciate all over again the colors, sizes, and shapes of the things around you, and your attention to the details in your surroundings will be sharpened.

Sense Memorizing (Ages 9–12)

Think about what happens when you're really hungry and someone mentions your favorite food. Your mouth might start to water because you have a vivid memory of how that food tastes. You have a sense memory for your favorite food, and your mouth is responding to that memory. Actors use sense memory to create realities in their scenes, training their senses to be heightened and aware so that when they are called upon to be or do a certain thing as part of a role, they are able to make it believable. The idea is that if the actor believes what he's doing on the stage is real, the audience will also believe it is real.

Whatever you're doing right now, decide to notice and "memorize" as many fleeting sense experiences as you can. A car passes by. You put your elbow down on the table. The phone rings. You take a bite of an apple. After you experience the real sensation, try to re-create what it felt like again a moment later. Can you close

I shut my eyes in order to see.

—Paul Gauguin
(1848–1903)

your eyes and re-create the feelings of the following situations using your sense memory?

Jumping into a swimming pool
Making a snowball without your gloves
Lying on the beach in the sun
Picking up a glass of ice water
Sipping ice water

Extrapalooza

Blindman's Bluff
(the original, suitable for all ages)

Stand in a circle. One player gets to be the blind man first and stands in the middle of the circle, blindfolded. The blind man is gently spun around three times and let go to walk toward the other players. Upon reaching a player in the circle, the blind man tries to guess who it is by feeling the other player's face, hair, clothes, and so on. Guess correctly, and you're no longer the blind man. Switch places with the player you've identified. Play continues until everyone has had a turn at being the blind man.

The Method, n.: Also called the Stanislavski Method, after Konstantin Stanislavski, founder of the Moscow Art Theater, 1898. A theory and technique of acting in which the actor identifies with the character to be portrayed and acts the part in a naturalistic and highly individualized manner. Sense memory techniques used by contemporary actors such as James Dean, Al Pacino, and Dustin Hoffman may have originated in Stanislavski's teachings.

On a Roll

Papier de toilette. Carta igienica. Toilettenpapier. Papel de tocador. Toilet paper by any other name is still just toilet paper. And you probably have plenty of it at home. If not, well, ahem, you might want to go out and get some, especially for this palooza.

What's the Palooza?

I nvite the humble roll of toilet paper to come out and play. The wildly popular performance artists, Blue Man Group, have a rousing finale to their show that involves toilet paper. I don't want to spoil the experience for those of you who've never seen them perform, but I can tell you at least this much: the piece involves seemingly endless streams of toilet paper and lots of audience participation. And it puts a big grin on your face. This palooza celebrates T.P. and promotes an entire afternoon's worth (or better yet, a sleepover party's worth) of toilet-paper-themed activity. You can play this palooza alone, with a parent or sibling, or with three or four others in a small group. One small but important piece of advice: dispose of the paper in the garbage, don't flush it—no one wants to gum up the works with too much *papier*!

Toilet Paper Wrap Art Ages (9–12)

Christo and Jeanne-Claude are artists famous for wrapping familiar objects in fabric to create sculpture that draws our attention to the objects in a new way. They started out in the 1960s wrapping small things—bottles, cans, packages, doorways—and moved on to much bigger things. They wrapped one of the famous bridges in Paris, the Pont Neuf, in woven nylon and rope (*The Pont Neuf Wrapped*, Paris, 1985). They wrapped the Reichstag in Berlin (*Wrapped Reichstag*, Berlin, 1971–1995). They wrapped trees with fabric and twine in Switzerland

(*Wrapped Trees*, Project for the Foundation Beyeler, Collage, 1997). One gets the feeling that Christo and Jeanne-Claude view everything they see in the world in terms of how it might be wrapped!

Use toilet paper to create your own wrapped art à la Christo and Jeanne-Claude. Look for objects of unusual shapes and sizes to wrap. Wrap a table lamp (unplugged, of course). Wrap the television set (do this on TV Free week?). Wrap old toys or your bike. Try to wrap objects in different ways. Wrap tightly, swathe loosely, drape. Soon you will understand what intrigues Christo—when an object is wrapped, how is it then perceived, on its own and in relation to what's around it? Does it seem to you to lose definition or to gain new qualities that you are seeing for the first time?

You can also do a human wrap, which Christo did with his 1962 *Wrapping a Girl* in London. Arrange someone in a pose and then wrap him with toilet paper. You see the human form in a different way when you hide the obvious details. You begin to appreciate the shape and the scale of the human body. Take photos of your creations. Create names for your wrapped artworks. Display them. See www.christojeanneclaude.net for pictures and descriptions of the works of Christo and Jeanne-Claude.

The Toilet Paper Web (Ages 6–12)

Players stand in a circle as far apart as the room allows. One player starts by holding on to the first couple of sheets of toilet paper and tossing the rest of the roll across the circle to another player. The second player catches the roll and, careful not to break apart the toilet-paper streamer, holds on to the end sheets before tossing the roll on to a third receiver. Play continues with the roll being tossed across the circle from player to player without breaking the stream, creating a web of toilet paper. Once the roll is

Gates

In February 2005, Christo and Jeanne-Claude will install *Gates* in New York City's Central Park. This work will consist of 7,532 arched gates that wind through the park, draped in more than a million square feet of fabric. It will take hundreds of people five days to install the gates, and it will take one day for the fabric panels to unfurl across the gates. Gates will remain in place for sixteen days, and as with all of Christo's work, all of the materials will be recycled.

completely used, play continues with yet more rolls of toilet paper, or, if the web is sufficiently big and strong, it becomes a kind of parachute. Raise the web parachute up and down, walk or skip around in a circle holding on to it, toss lightweight toys or objects into it—a ball, comb, a small stuffed animal—and toss them up and down. Raise the web up high. Let go of it and let it fall on top of everyone. Or raise it up and take turns running underneath it, changing places in the circle with another player. When ready to dismantle, see how many objects you can toss into the middle of the web before it breaks.

Toilette Couture (Ages 9–12)

Paper dresses were a huge fad in the 1960s. The Scott Paper Co. is actually credited with making the first paper dress in 1966 as a promotional item for its "Color Explosion" toilet paper and paper towels. Design and make toilet-paper dresses. Ball gowns. Miniskirts. Tight, Dietrichesque dresses impossible to walk in. Make accessories, like neckties, turbans, jewelry, shoes, scarves, belts, aprons. Have a fashion show. Or stage a photo shoot, as if creating a fashion spread for a magazine.

Invent-a-Saurus

Mix a fascination with wildlife, natural history, dinosaurs, and other creatures with the challenge of concocting your own imaginary animals and you get a palooza worthy of Michael Crichton.

What's the Palooza?

Invent your own land before (or after?) time. Create your own creatures and draw them, label them, categorize them, write a field guide for them. Cross dinosaurs you know (triceratops, tyrannosaurus, stegosaurus, brontosaurus) with other animal categories (mammals, reptiles, rodents, crustaceans, birds, fish) and see what you get. Have dinosaur picture books on hand as references, as well as an illustrated animal encyclopedia. Make lists of favorite dinosaurs and favorite animals and start making imaginative combinations that are fun to illustrate.

Take the Chinese menu approach and choose from different columns:

Column A	Column B	Column C	Column D	Column E
DINOSAURS	MAMMALS	BIRDS	REPTILES	FISH
Brachiosaurus	Elephant	Ostrich	Crocodile	Angelfish
Diplodocus	Rhinoceros	Owl	Gecko	Blowfish
Iguanodon	Tiger	Parrot	Lizard	Eagle ray
Stegosaurus	Whale	Swan	Snake	Jellyfish
Triceratops	Zebra	Turkey	Tortoise	Seahorse

Mix and match the dinosaurs and animals to invent fantastical species. Stegojelly. Tricerasnake. Iguanoturkey. What would these dinorific animals look like? Are they big? Miniature? Outline the creations first in

Who can play?
Ages 6 and up.

What do we need?
Pencil, paper, eraser, markers, crayons, colored pencils or watercolors. Pictures of dinosaurs and other animals from books and magazines.

Running time?
Thirty minutes (or hours, over time).

Budget?
$

dinosaur (di-no-saur), n.: 1. An extinct, chiefly terrestrial reptile that lived in the Mesozoic era. 2. A person or thing that is hopelessly out of date or incapable of adapting to change. Note: Zoologist Sir Richard Owen coined the name dinosaur from the Greek dinosauria, which means "terrible lizard."

pencil, getting the basic shape down on paper. Then fill in detail. Is it scaly or smooth-skinned? Muscular? Does it have hair? Or feathers? If it has wings, can they flap? What do the teeth look like? Check out illustrator Robert Jew's *Lizard Head*, a painting of an iguana so realistic you can see every bump on the lizard's skin (www.aca demic.rccd.cc.ca.us/~art/jew.htm). Think about your invent-a-saurus's features in this kind of up-close-and-personal detail.

When your drawing is complete, go over your pencil marks with markers, crayons, or colored pencils. Because no one really knows what color dinosaurs were, you can use any color or combination of colors you can imagine. Play with stripes, spots, or swirls. Use fluorescent colors or crayons with shimmers and sparkles. In his painting *The Yellow Cow*, artist Franz Marc uses brilliant, dreamlike colors to get us to look at the familiar cow in a new way. Pull out all the stops on color and patterns as you create your finished work.

Extrapaloozas

Home Sweet Home

Imagine your creature's habitat and then create it. Is it a jungle? A desert? A woodland? Maybe it's a city with tall buildings and buses and elevated trains! What's the weather like? What does the vegetation look like? Is it marshy? What kinds of plants?

You can draw the environment to scale on a large piece of paper, then cut out your creature drawings and place them in their habitat. Better yet, create a natural-history-style 3-D diorama environment for your 'saurus. Get a big shoe box or other box and turn it on its side. Paint a background and foreground. Glue on bits of moss for groundcover or cotton balls for clouds. Use twigs or stones from outside to make your environment realistic. Then arrange your cutout creature inside this lifelike environment. Make up stories about the creature. Does he roam in herds like the iguanodon? Or is he a lone ranger like T-rex? Is he a predator? Herbivore? Does he swim? Fly? What if humans entered the picture? Have your creature interact with other creatures you invent in his natural habitat.

Field Guide

Use a school composition notebook to make a field guide of your own for your invent-a-saurus creations. Draw and label your creatures in the pages of the notebook, or make pockets inside the notebook to house the creatures you've drawn and cut out with scissors. Make notes in the field guide about the creatures' feeding patterns, mating habits, herding instincts, and defense mechanisms. Note color and size differences between males and females.

Good Books

Some terrific dinosaur books loaded with invent-a-saurus ideas include *National Geographic Dinosaurs* by Paul Barret and Raul Martin, *American Museum of Natural History: On the Trail of Incredible Dinosaurs* by William Lindsay, and *Walking with Dinosaurs: A Natural History* by Tim Haines. See also James Gurney's beautiful *Dinotopia* and its sequels, which imagine a fantastic world where dinosaurs and humans coexist. And absolutely check out *The Wildlife of Star Wars: A Field Guide* by Terryl Whitlatch and Bob Carrau for inspiration when invent-a-saur-ing. This is a gorgeous, lavishly illustrated book about the imagined wildlife of *Star Wars*.

Starry Night

This palooza directs our gaze to the sky in search of the art and poetry there.

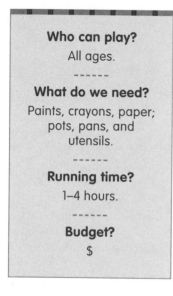
What's the Palooza?

Explore the nighttime sky and find the art in the stars. Translate what you see into images and words.

Take a look at Vincent van Gogh's *Starry Night* on www.vangoghgallery.com. This famous painting isn't an exact representation of the stars, but an expression of how they made van Gogh feel. It's a swirling tempest of a nighttime sky. Look at other van Goghs, like *Starry Night over the Rhone* or *Road with Cypress and Star*. What did he see when he looked at the night sky that took this distinctive form in his paintings? What do *you* see in the stars?

Start with a little stargazing. Choose a good viewing place and time: a clear night far from a city. If you live in a city, save this palooza for when you're on vacation, or hop in the car and drive to where the city glow won't disturb your view.

Turn off all yard lights and inside lights, then go outside with a pair of binoculars. Let your eyes get used to the dark while you're setting up—it can take up to ten minutes for your eyes to fully adjust to the darkness. Spread a blanket on the ground, lie down on your back, and look up.

You've seen stars so often that you stop noticing them. Try now to really look at them. Let the sky full of stars wash over you and surround you. Think about the stars in relation to your five senses. What do they look like to you? Jewels? Pinpricks of light? Observe how they're grouped, how they shine. Note the words that come to mind about what you're seeing.

If stars were music, what would it sound like? Some-

The Constellations

Here are the eighty-eight constellations recognized by the International Astronomical Union:

Andromeda—Princess of Ethiopia
Antilia—The Air Pump
Apus—The Bird of Paradise
Aquarius—The Water Bearer
Aquila—The Eagle
Ara—The Altar
Aries—The Ram
Auriga—The Charioteer
Boötes—The Herdsman
Caelum—The Chisel
Camelopardalis—The Giraffe
Cancer—The Crab
Canes Venatici—The Hunting Dogs
Canis Major—The Big Dog
Canis Minor—The Little Dog
Capricorn—The Goat
Carina—The Keel
Cassiopeia—The Seated Lady
Centaurus—The Centaur
Cepheus—King of Ethiopia
Cetus—The Sea Monster
Chameleon—The Chameleon
Circinus—The Compass
Columba—The Dove
Coma Berenices—Berenice's Hair
Corona Australis—The Southern Crown
Corona Borealis—The Northern Crown

Corvus—The Crow
Crater—The Cup
Crux—The Southern Cross
Cygnus—The Swan
Delphinus—The Dolphin
Dorado—The Swordfish
Draco—The Dragon
Equuleus—The Little Horse
Eridanus—The River
Fornax—The Furnace
Gemini—The Twins
Grus—The Crane
Hercules—Hercules
Horologium—The Clock
Hydra—The Sea Serpent
Hydrus—The Water Snake
Indus—The Indian
Lacerta—The Lizard
Leo—The Lion
Leo Minor—The Lion Cub
Lepus—The Hare
Libra—The Scales
Lupus—The Wolf
Lynx—The Lynx
Lyra—The Lyre
Mensa—The Table Mountain
Microscopium—The Microscope
Monoceros—The Unicorn
Musca—The Fly
Norma—The Square
Octans—The Octant
Ophiucus—The Sepent Bearer
Orion—The Hunter

Pavo—The Peacock
Pegasus—The Winged Horse
Perseus—Perseus
Phoenix—The Phoenix
Pictor—The Easel
Pisces—The Fish
Pisces Austrinus—The Southern Fish
Puppis—The Stern
Pyxis—The Pass
Reticulum—The Reticle
Sagitta—The Arrow
Sagittarius—The Archer
Scorpius—The Scorpion
Sculptor—The Sculptor
Scutum—The Shield
Serpens—The Serpent
Sextans—The Sextant
Taurus—The Bull
Telescopium—The Telescope
Triangulum—The Triangle
Triangulum Australe—The Southern Triangle
Tucana—The Toucan
Ursa Major—The Great Bear
Ursa Minor—The Little Bear
Vela—The Sails
Virgo—The Virgin
Volans—The Flying Fish
Vulpecula—The Fox

thing light and tinkly, from the high end of the piano? Or complex and dramatic, a symphony of sound? Do stars have a scent? Have you ever tasted anything that reminds you of stars? If you could reach up and touch the stars, what would they feel like? When you get back inside, jot down any impressions you had while looking at the stars and any words that describe them. Think about colors, shapes, sounds, tastes, textures; use nouns, verbs, adjectives, adverbs.

Now, follow in van Gogh's footsteps and draw or paint a picture of the stars. Use the words you wrote down to decide what you'd like to express about the stars. You can use any colors and put the stars in any context. Perhaps when you think of the stars, you don't see a big sky filled with millions of tiny lights, but instead you imagine stars reflected in your own eyes. Maybe you'll paint only one star—the brightest, or the one that most held your attention. Create a series of pictures, exploring different perspectives and forms, using different media, and hang them all together as a portrait of the stars.

Try writing some poetry about the stars. Start with a simple haiku, a nonrhyming poem that has three lines and seventeen syllables. The first line has five syllables, the second line has seven syllables, and there are five syllables in the third. Look at your star word notes and see if there are some that seem to connect well. For example,

Bright stars glimmering
Against the dark sky at night
Are smiling at me.

Now play with what you've written to explore your impression in another way:

Bright lights simmering
In a dark pot of star soup
Want to lick the spoon?

Extrapaloozas

The Ultimate Game of Connect-the-Dots

Constellations are groups of stars that appear to form a recognizable pattern. Go to www.skymaps.com to download a free map of this month's sky. Search for the constellations that are best seen during this month. Once you get the hang of finding the constellations, make up your own.

Go stargazing and let your imagination run wild. Does that group of stars look like a rose? Another group might look like a buffalo. Now, name your constellation. Name it after yourself—Rachel's Ring or Heather's Hat. Or give it a more poetic name, like Flower with Wilting Leaves or Erupting Volcano. Sketch your constellations and make a guide to *your* night sky.

Star Mythology

People have looked at stars and made up stories and legends about stars for thousands of years. Some myths use the stars to explain things on Earth; others try to explain how the stars got up into the sky in the first place. Ancient Babylonian mythology described stars suspended on strings that were pulled up in the daytime and let down at night.

According to Navajo myth, the stars came to be scattered across the sky when First Woman carefully took jewels (stars) from a blanket and arranged them in the sky to spell out the laws for the people. Coyote offered to help her, but soon became frustrated with the enormity of the job. Coyote tossed the remaining stars into the sky, destroying First Woman's message and throwing the world into chaos.

Make up your own myth about the stars. Tell stories using the constellations that you invented. Maybe the myth about your Rocking Chair constellation explains how it was put in the sky for weary space travelers to sit on in while in space. Or tell a fantastic story about how the stars came to be in the sky. Your story can be as offbeat or unusual as you want it to be.

When I have a terrible need of—shall I say the word—religion, then I go out and paint the stars.

—Vincent van Gogh
(1853–1890)

Palio

This ancient horse race is run every summer in Siena, Italy—oh, the wild mix of history and loyalty and passion and color! Every bit of cunning and sneakery is at work, which is what makes it a perfect palooza—a contest of creativity and wit and will.

Who can play?
Ages 6 and up.

What do we need?
The components of any games you concoct for your Palio. Ingredients for your *contrada* dish. For your logo, butcher paper and markers. For your uniforms, plain white T-shirts and markers. For the banner, an old pillowcase or plain fabric, fabric paint or permanent markers, scraps of different colored fabric and bric-a-brac, fabric glue, and a dowel.

Running time?
For the Palio itself, an afternoon or evening. The planning and cooking might take place over a week.

Budget?
$–$$

What's the Palooza?

Create a feverish contest between immediate family members, relatives within an extended family, or families in your neighborhood. The Palio, or "the banner," has been run every summer since the 1200s in Siena, Italy, a hilly city surrounded by walls and towers meant to protect it from the brutal attacks of enemy republics. Who knew that the battle inside the walls was the one to watch? The Palio is a horse race that is run among the city's official neighborhoods, or *contrade*, and it is a spectacle beyond belief. Every neighborhood has a symbol (the Ram or the Unicorn or the Eagle, for example), and everyone who lives in that neighborhood devotes all their intelligence and energy into fielding a capable horse and jockey for this annual race through the town's Piazza del Campo, on a rough dirt track, with rubbery rules that allow for last-second trickery and treachery. What fun!

Teams. Start by designating teams. If you're a small family, maybe each member of the family is a team and can invite a friend from outside the family to join him. Or you can pair up within the family, or have entire families be single teams. Choose a symbol for your team that represents the strength or virtue you'd like to stand for. You can use the Italian symbols for inspiration or make up your own: A lion, for strength and valor. A rabbit, for speed and agility. A pyramid, for mystery and longevity. Choose team colors and create a logo for your team with markers

The Seventeen Contrade and Their Mottos

Onda (the Wave), "The color of the sky, the might of the sea."

Valdimonte (the Ram), "Under my blow, the great wall crumbles."

Nicchio (the Shell), "It is the red of the coral that burns in my heart."

Leocorno (the Unicorn), "The weapon I bear in my brow can heal and can wound."

Torre (the Tower), "Power as well as might."

Giraffa (the Giraffe), "The higher the head, the greater the glory."

Bruco (the Caterpillar), "My name stands for revolution."

Civetta (the Owl), "I see in the night."

Lupa (the She-Wolf), "The symbol and honor of Siena and its people."

Istrice (the Porcupine), "Only in defense do I use my quills to wound."

Drago (the Dragon), "The ardor in my heart becomes flames in my mouth."

Oca (the Goose), "A call to arms."

Selva (the Forest), "The first Forest in the Field."

Aquila (the Eagle), "The beak, the talon, and the wing of the Eagle."

Pantera (the Panther), "The Panther roared and the people stirred. My pounce knocks down all obstacles."

Chiocciola (the Snail), "With slow and heavy step, the Snail enters the field to win."

Tartuca (the Tortoise), "Strength and perseverance I harbor."

on butcher paper. This will be your team flag and the image that appears on any other team or fan paraphernalia you want to create—T-shirts, hats, coffee mugs, bobble heads. Write a team motto!

Palio Maestro. One adult has to be the conductor of this little orchestra we call Palio. He collects ideas for the games from all the teams, creates the games (maps out races, devises rules, writes questions, and so on), then conducts the games. And after all that hard work, he is then treated royally at the Palio Gala. A fun-loving uncle, grandma, or family friend would be ideal for this job.

Banner. Decorate a pillowcase or a plain piece of fabric with each team's logo to create the winner's banner for the Palio. Use paint and scraps of fabric; incorporate logos with other colorful patterns. Get fancy! This is the fiercely fought for, much-coveted prize.

Food. Each team chooses a recipe for their signature dish. It can be themed, like a carrot cake or carrot casserole for the Rabbit team. Or it can be just a distinctive dish for which the team will be known. Each team should prepare their recipe to serve at the Palio Gala at the end of the contests.

Contests. Create a series of four or five games that are a mix of contests of physical skill, knowledge, and resourcefulness. A relay race that snakes a crazy route through your neighborhood—with a banana for a baton. A tricky combination of a spelling bee and trivia quiz. A persnickety scavenger hunt for items involving the five senses—and all beginning with the letter "P." A complicated game of international hopscotch. Assign each contest a certain number of points to be distributed among the teams. For instance, a the winner of a 20-point contest might receive 10 points, second place gets 5 points, third place gets 3, and last place gets 2. And make sure your games take into account the variety of ages of players a trivia/spelling challenge for an adult, for example, would be more difficult than for a nine-year-old. Take the time to create games that are clever and surprising—or just plain nutty. After all the games are played and points tallied, a winner is declared.

Palio Gala. After the winning team proudly takes possession of the banner, all teams retire to the Palio Gala, where each team's special food is served. Turn this into a festive banquet. Decorate the table with each team's colors and logo. Serve fizzy punch and Day-Glo desserts. Good music is a must. Take pictures of the winning team with the banner for your Palio scrapbook, where you'll also stow photos and details of the annual Palio.

performance
paloozas

Tableaux Vivants

The Victorians endlessly entertained themselves with tableaux vivants, or living-statue scenes, depicting classical paintings or allegories or moments in history. Elaborately costumed tableaux were the entertainment centerpiece of many a high-society ball, while simpler though no less inventive versions were created every night in ordinary homes. This is a thoroughly modern take on a classic Victorian amusement.

What's the Palooza?

The twist to this palooza is that you won't be acting out a scene, but rather staging a shot, kind of like dramatic freeze tag. Choose a scene or theme to depict, forage in closets for costumes and props, then create the picture. Think of scenes from your favorite books or movies, from the breakout in *Holes* to the melting-witch scene in *The Wizard of Oz*. Or re-create a famous image, say Emanuel Gottlieb Leutze's *Washington Crossing the Delaware* or Auguste Rodin's *Thinker*. Or explore a theme more abstractly, like a series of tableaux depicting the four seasons. The French might depict *liberté*, *equalité*, *fraternité*. You might depict great moments in baseball history!

Another approach is to skip the costumes and props entirely and depict a scene very simply, relying only on the staging and dramatic execution. You don't need to be dressed like Washington crossing the Delaware and standing in a boat to stage a wonderful, evocative—or even funny—tableau of that scene. Every figure could be precisely, unmistakably arranged in the scene—all wearing pajamas, or with Washington wearing a cowboy hat. There's no end to the simple, witty variations you can create.

Take turns being the director, placing subjects in their positions, adjusting props. Create one elaborate tableau or several tableaux, as time and resources allow. Finally, take a photograph of each tableau to memorialize the creation, and perhaps keep them in an album of family tableaux.

Extrapaloozas

Tableaux Photographs

Photography was as much a passion for Lewis Carroll as his writing, and he was a master of the tableau photograph. Based on the live tableaux vivants so familiar in his time, he'd arrange and photograph costumed sitters in historical or allegorical scenes, playing elaborately with his idea of the photograph as still theater.

You have all the same tools at your disposal as Mr. Carroll did—vivid imaginations, willing subjects, closets full of potential costumes, and a camera to capture the staged moment. There's a wonderful opportunity to explore the dynamics of staging such a scene, especially within the frame imposed by a photograph.

Nineteenth century photographer Julia Margaret Cameron also staged photographic tableaux, though more often focused on a single figure, usually a woman depicting some ideal such as holiness, or nature, or pure-hearted love. Her subjects are ethereal and her photographs evocative. Modern photographer Cindy Sherman uses herself as the sitter in her own photos, casting herself as a wild range of characters, both historical and symbolic. You can create this more personal tableaux photography choosing individual human

Costumes and Props

Besides the usual raid of the attic, check out the linen closet. Old sheets can be elegantly draped with Grecian flair, dramatically thrown about the shoulders as a cape, or arranged around the waist for the princess-ball-gown effect. The coat closet will yield hats, umbrellas, canes, and boots. The broom closet can offer a mop to serve as a horse. Use clear plastic wrap, tinfoil, paper grocery bags, or garbage bags to help craft a costume. And don't forget the secondhand stores, where you'll find the makings of many a terrific costume.

subjects, from Henry the Eighth to Mona Lisa to Amelia Earhart, and staging a photograph based on a familiar image (a painting or photograph) of the character. The point, of course, is to enlist enough visual touchstones, from a familiar pose to clothing to expression, to evoke the spirit of the familiar.

Holiday Tableaux

Turn any holiday scene into a performance or photographic tableau. Stage a great Christmas scene and use the photo for the cover of your holiday card. Or a Valentine scene as a one-of-a-kind Valentine. Stage Saint Patrick's Day. Or the first Thanksgiving. Even the signing of the Declaration of Independence for the Fourth of July.

Mrs. Fisher . . . had decided the tableaux vivants and expensive music were the two baits most likely to attract the desired prey, and . . . induced a dozen fashionable women to exhibit themselves in a series of pictures which, by a farther miracle of persuasion, the distinguished portrait painter, Paul Morpeth, had been prevailed upon to organize.

Lily was in her element on such occasions. Under Morpeth's guidance her vivid plastic sense, hitherto nurtured on no higher food than dress-making and upholstery, found eager expression in the disposal of draperies, the study of attitudes, the shifting of lights and shadows. Her dramatic instinct was roused by the choice of subjects, and the gorgeous reproductions of historic dress stirred an imagination which only visual impressions could reach. But keenest of all was the exhilaration of displaying her own beauty under a new aspect: of showing that her loveliness was no mere fixed quality, but an element shaping all emotions to fresh forms of grace.

—Edith Wharton, *The House of Mirth*

Canned Film Festival

This is a great weekend palooza that requires creativity and teamwork—the key, as it happens, to all great movies.

What's the Palooza?

Plot, script, film, and screen a short film of a story created around three randomly chosen props. Get a small group of people together for this palooza, including siblings, friends, or parents.

Props and story. Have one person go around the house and choose three unrelated objects around which your film's story will be built. Let's say you've got a wig, a notebook, and an eggbeater. Brainstorm the kind of story you could create with these props. Is it a mystery, where a stranger in a wig murders the mailman with an eggbeater, and leaves behind only her journal as a clue to her motive and identity? Or is it a comedy about a day in the life of a woman who uses her journal to spin zany fantasies that let her escape her stifling life as a housewife? What kind of drama might these props allow?

After a rollicking bit of backing and forthing, your group will land on a genre and a basic story. Let's say it's the comedy.

Characters and cast. Invent a simple set of characters to enable the plot you've hatched, two or three main characters at most, and perhaps a few extras. Create a profile for each of the characters to give a sense of who they are and how they might interact with each other. Give them a little bit of a history to help you imagine them. The characters in our example might be the housewife, her somewhat bratty son, and her kindly but oblivious husband. A minor character might be the washing machine repairman, who rings the doorbell in the middle of the day, interrupting her fantasy of winning the New York marathon. There might be a few kids who are extras, perhaps teammates on the son's soccer team.

Sketch a script. Write a detailed script of all the action, dialogue, and director's cues for your story. Since this is a day-in-the-life tale, you'd start your story in the morning, maybe when she's feeding her family breakfast (making them eggs with the eggbeater!) and getting them off to school and work.

Maybe there would be some conversation at the breakfast table, the kind that would tell something about their relationships and just how bored or distracted the mom is. Perhaps at a stoplight on her way home from dropping her son off at school, she looks down at her journal on the passenger seat and begins daydreaming about being a race car driver. And so the day would go, punctuated by moments of boredom that dissolve into nutty fantasies that are then interrupted by real life. She's a race car driver, then a scientist, a

Film Talk

Bandy these words about with aplomb, and you'll be yelling "Action!" in no time.

Adaptation	Clapboard	Flop	Shoot
Aerial shot	Cliffhanger	Footage	Shot
Antagonist	Climax	Frame	Slapstick
Antihero	Closeup	Green-light	Sleeper
Art house film	Continuity	Indie	Slow motion
Audio	Credits	Lead	Soundstage
Auteur	Crew	Legs	Sound track
B movie	Critic	Location	Special effects
Backdrop	Cut	MacGuffin	Split screen
Behind the scenes	Cutaway	Narration	Stand-in
Billing	Director's cut	Premiere	Storyboard
Biopic	Dissolve	Producer	Stunt double
Bit part	Dolly	Production value	Supporting player
Black comedy	Dub	Reel	Take care
Blooper	Editing	Remake	Trailer
Body double	Establishing shot	Retrospective	Treatment
Box office	Extra	Running time	Voice-over
Cameo	Fade	Score	Walk-on
Casting	Film noir	Screenplay	Wrap
Character actor	Flashback	Screen test	
Cinema verité	Flash-forward	Sequel	

marathon runner, a super-spy (wearing the wig for a disguise, of course), a chef at a five-star restaurant, and so on. Fast-forward to the end of her day, when she's exhausted from all her adventures, and her family wonders why she's so tired. "What's she been doing all day?" Map it out right, and all this will happen in a matter of ten or fifteen minutes on film.

Costumes. Keep costumes simple, using clothes and stuff from around the house. This is a comedy, and Mom wearing a football helmet for a race car helmet is funny. Mom running down her own driveway to cross the finish line in the marathon is funny. Mom wearing a toque and barking orders at the kitchen help (the extras) is funny.

Spielberg Did It, and You Can, Too!

Hollywood director Steven Spielberg was an obsessive amateur filmmaker as a child growing up in Scottsdale, Arizona. Inspired by action movies and westerns he'd see every Saturday afternoon at the movies, he'd direct his family, friends, even his Boy Scout troop, in short films. He won first prize in a film contest for a forty-minute war movie called *Escape to Nowhere* at the age of thirteen. *Amblin,* the twenty-four-minute movie he made while studying film and English at Cal State Long Beach, landed him a long-term deal to direct movies for Universal Studios, making him the youngest contract director in Hollywood history.

Film it. The more carefully you map out your scenes, the smoother your filming goes. This doesn't mean you don't improvise and make changes along the way. If a scene doesn't work, it doesn't work, and you make up something else. You can edit, of course, but just have fun. Think of your movie as if it's a little sketch you can tinker with until it suits you. And if it doesn't, do it again!

Screen it. Here's where the festival part comes in! Pop some popcorn and set up for a family-and-friends screening of your little opus. You'll watch it over and over, just to see what you got right, what was hilariously botched, and what you want to try again. And now you've got the bug.

Extrapalooza

Le Palme d'Or

Make it a real filmfest contest. Give two or three teams of filmmakers/actors different sets of props and script and film different movies for your voting audience. Or give them the same props to create and film different stories. Or give them three randomly chosen words from a dictionary around which to invent a story to film. Have the audience at your screening vote for best film.

Soliloquy

As a palooza, soliloquy is an opportunity to relish language and the power of a dramatic speech.

What's the Palooza?

Memorize one of Shakespeare's great soliloquies or another dramatic monologue. Consider, for example, Romeo's nocturnal soliloquy in the orchard scene from *Romeo and Juliet*:

He jests at scars, that never felt a wound.
[Juliet appears above at a window.]
But, soft! what light through yonder window breaks?
It is the east, and Juliet is the sun.
Arise, fair sun, and kill the envious moon,
Who is already sick and pale with grief,
That thou her maid art far more fair than she:
Be not her maid, since she is envious;
Her vestal livery is but sick and green,
And none but fools do wear it; cast it off.
It is my lady; O! it is my love.
O! that she knew she were.
She speaks, yet she says nothing: what of that?
Her eye discourses; I will answer it.
I am too bold, 'tis not to me she speaks:
Two of the fairest stars in all the heaven,
Having some business, do entreat her eyes
To twinkle in their spheres till they return.
What if her eyes were there, they in her head?
The brightness of her cheek would shame those stars
As daylight doth a lamp; her eyes in heaven
Would through the airy region stream so bright
That birds would sing and think it were not night.
See! how she leans her cheek upon her hand:
O! that I were a glove upon that hand,
That I might touch that cheek.

Who can play?
Ages 9 and up.

What do we need?
Initiative, and maybe a glass of water. A good Shakespeare reference.

Running time?
However long it takes to memorize a soliloquy. You may take a few lines at a time to work on before dinner for a few nights one week. Or spend a concentrated two or three hours to get it done in one fell swoop. Some soliloquies are shorter than others.

Budget?
Free.

Part of the fun of soliloquy is just memorizing a fancy and dramatic speech. And the other part of the fun is in letting words roll off the tongue in ways they don't normally turn round in everyday conversation. Romeo's soliloquy is a good one because you may be familiar with the character of Romeo, and even if you are not, you can figure out what's going on by what he's saying.

The speech itself gives you a chance to express a range of moods and feelings. There's exaggeration (*The brightness of her cheek*), excitement (*It is the east and Juliet is the sun*), surprise (*But soft!*), brief, rapid-fire sen-

Shakespearean Soliloquies to Consider

The Taming of the Shrew, act V, scene 2; Katherina's "Fie, fie!"

Romeo and Juliet, act IV, scene 3; Juliet's "Farewell. God knows when we shall meet again."

Richard III, act I, scene 1; Richard's "Now is the winter of our discontent."

Twelfth Night, act V, scene 1; Feste's "When that I was and a little tiny boy . . . "

A Midsummer Night's Dream, act V, scene 1; Puck's "If we shadows have offended. . ."

Two Gentlemen of Verona, act II, scene 3; Launce and his Dog, "Nay, 'twill be this hour ere I have done weeping."

Much Ado About Nothing, act II, scene 3; Benedick's, "Love may transform me to an oyster . . . "

The Taming of the Shrew, act IV, scene 1; Petruchio's, "He that knows better how to tame a shrew."

A Midsummer Night's Dream, act II, scene 2; Helena's, "O, I am out of breath."

King Lear, act I, scene 2; Edmund's, "Thou, nature, art my goddess."

Macbeth, act II, scene 1; Macbeth's, "Is this a dagger which I see before me?"

tences (*She speaks, yet she says nothing*), questions (*What if her eyes*), yearning (*O! that I were a glove*). Think about these emotions and how best to modulate voice and diction when expressing them. Talk about the idea of the speech building to a crescendo and then tapering off in the end to express a more quiet longing.

You don't need to know everything there is to know about *Romeo and Juliet* to learn and enjoy reciting the soliloquy. But if you're curious, find out about the play and this scene. What time of day is it? Where is Romeo looking? What is he feeling? What movements or actions of the body would help him express himself and enhance the scene?

Once the soliloquy is memorized, practice reciting it in front of a mirror. Enunciate. Articulate. Exaggerate. Add gestures. Move about the room. Recite the soliloquy often and with vim. Astonish friends and family with the dramatic narration. Or, in true Shakespearean fashion, the soliloquy may be performed for no one's pleasure but your own.

Extrapalooza

Oration and Monologue

Memorize a speech (or part of one) from history such as Abraham Lincoln's "Gettysburg Address" or Dr. Martin Luther King Jr.'s "I Have a Dream." Or work on a comedic monologue such as Lily Tomlin's toddler in a rocker, Edith Ann. See *Winning Monologs for Young Actors* by Peg Kehret for more ideas.

<aside>

Shakespeare for Kids

A terrific introduction for young readers to the storylines of Shakespeare's work is the *Shakespeare Can Be Fun* series. One of these titles, *Romeo and Juliet: For Kids* by Lois Burdette, is great for background on Romeo's soliloquy. There's also the beautifully illustrated *Shakespeare Stories* by Leon Garfield. And Charles and Mary Lamb's classic *Tales from Shakespeare*, first published in 1806 as a prose introduction for children to twenty of Shakespeare's plays, is wonderful to read in its own right.

</aside>

Mime

Actions speak louder than words. Silence is golden. This palooza takes the words right out of our mouths.

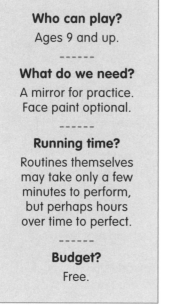

What's the Palooza?

Explore the highly physical art of mime by creating simple routines that use only gestures and body movements to tell a story, express an emotion, or communicate an idea.

Mime virtuoso Marcel Marceau, whose best-loved character is Bip, the little white-faced clown in a striped jersey and dilapidated opera hat, is said to have actually caused his audiences to lean forward in their seats as if to better *hear* his actions. This is a testament to Marceau's genius, certainly, but also to the magic of mime itself, which as a silent art form has a powerful magnetism all its own.

Some of Marceau's most famous mime routines find him tangling with a lion or flitting with a butterfly, skating, or being trapped inside a cage. Make a list of

situations you'd like to explore in mime. It might be something you do every day, like eating breakfast or making your bed. Or it might be something more extreme, like scuba diving or parachuting out of an airplane. Think about situations in which you react to things, animals, or people. A stalled car or a flat tire. A barking dog. A bag of potato chips that's difficult to open. What kinds of people might you encounter in a mime routine? A piano teacher? A dentist? A salesperson who keeps coming into your dressing room in a clothing store?

Props in mime are also established by movement and gesture alone, so say, for example, you choose to mime the breakfast routine. Props you would need to imagine and somehow "create" out of thin air in your routine might include a box of cereal, bowl, spoon, banana, refrigerator door, milk carton. Think about the size and weight of the objects. Where do you find them? How do you hold them?

Then think about the other movements that are required to perform the daily ritual of preparing the cereal breakfast and incorporate them into your act. Are you sleepy and rubbing your eyes when you enter the kitchen? (This would help to telegraph the time of day to your audience.) Is the milk carton heavy or practically empty when you pull it out of the refrigerator? Do you spill some milk over the rim of the bowl and slurp it up? Are you embarrassed that someone might catch you in the act of slurping your cereal bowl? Maybe there's a free prize inside the cereal box, and you can't get it out without digging your hand into the box and spilling mounds of cereal all over the floor. Do you make a big mess? How do you clean up the cereal? Do you find the prize? What is it?

Practice this cereal routine as a mime starter, or devise another routine of your own. Improvise as you go along. Be meticulous in your gestures. Keep them simple and resist too much exaggeration. The goal in mime is to simply and precisely communicate to your audience. The trick is to let them see what you see, as you see it—in your head!

Bip in a Book

Check out *Bip in a Book* by Marcel Marceau, Bruce Goldstone, and Steven Rothfeld, in which Marceau's lovable Bip gets trapped inside the book, mimicking in book form Marceau's actual performance of "The Cage." Two older books also worth searching out include *The Marcel Marceau Alphabet Book* and *The Marcel Marceau Counting Book* both by George Mendoza.

It's good to shut up sometimes.

—Marcel Marceau
(1923–)

Classic mime routines to try:

Pulling on a rope
Tying your shoes
The wall (in which you enact the flatness of a wall in front of you; practice first using a mirror as the wall)
Imaginary ball (in which you catch a ball that's either heavy or light, big or small)
Climbing a ladder
Riding in an elevator
Going fishing

Extrapaloozas

Imaginary Face Masks

"The Mask Maker" was yet another routine of Marceau's in which he flipped imaginary "comic" and "tragic" masks on and off his face, changing expressions with each one. When the comic mask gets stuck, his body contorts and demonstrates utter exasperation and sadness, all the while exhibiting a grin on his face. Practice facial expressions before a mirror. How many different ways can you convey happiness, sadness, fear, surprise, and anger?

Mime Game

Create flash cards for mime play. Write instructions on large index cards. Use emotion words such as *anger, sadness, happiness,* and so on. Add action words as well, or ideas that can be expressed in two or three words: *drinking hot tea, getting lost, finding a four-leaf clover.* When the game is played, guessers must guess the action or emotion exactly.

Signature Character

Marceau had Bip; Charlie Chaplin, the Little Tramp; Buster Keaton, the slapshoe buffoon. Create your own signature character or trademark moves for the performance of mime. What are the mannerisms that define your character? A twitch of the mouth? A habit of looking over your shoulder? Are you hard of hearing? Marceau taps his foot impatiently—tap, tap, tap, tap, tap. Practice *your* signature move and develop your signature character in front of a mirror.

Mime Makeup

Makeup isn't necessary for a mime (it's your performance that counts), but traditional mimes wear whiteface with a few distinct markings. To create a mime face, paint an oval outline around your face in kid-friendly white face paint. You don't have to worry about painting all the way to the edges of your hair. Fill in your face with white paint, starting at the nose and working outward to the edges of your oval. Go as close to your eyes and mouth as you can and cover your eyebrows with it, too. Outline the oval in black, if you like, when you're finished with all of your markings.

To create your markings, start with the eyebrows. Lift your eyebrows as high as they go, and you will see a wrinkle on your forehead; this is where your painted eyebrows will go. Paint nice arches in black as evenly as you can. Outline your eyes with black—don't overdo it!—extending the line slightly beyond the corners of your eyes. You can also paint little black upside-down triangles under your eyes. Paint your lips a bright cherry red. Fill them in completely, but be careful not to go beyond the edges of your lips, because it's tricky to correct. Now you're a classic mime!

Animal House

This palooza starts with a simple question: If you were an animal, what would you be? Ask everyone in the family the same question, and you may find yourself in a house full of roaring, squeaking, whinnying and oinking creatures.

What's the Palooza?

Put yourself in an animal's fur, feathers, or scaly skin. We think often of animals as having human characteristics—rabbits are nervous, owls possess wisdom, foxes are sly, and peacocks proud. Today's the day when we're the humans with the animal characteristics.

Pick an animal to "be" today. You may choose your animal either because it appeals to you—you would like to run like a gazelle, laugh like a hyena, or sleep like a bear in winter—or you may choose your animal persona because you want to be something that is not at all like you—a thing that slithers or hangs upside down or tramples bamboo under its huge feet while trumpeting loudly and waving a trunk.

Begin at breakfast with everyone choosing an animal and then explore the rest of your day as best you can as that animal. If you are a snake, you might slither and hiss; if you are a squirrel, maybe you'll be hoarding your cereal in your cheek pouches. Of course, you probably have go to school or work, walking on two legs and speaking English, but try to imagine how you can modify your experience with your animal in mind, for instance, eating for lunch something your animal might.

Try looking at the world through your animal's eyes. Maybe you're a lion, and you're used to growling and intimidating and bossing the other animals around. But maybe you're also used to watching out for hunters. Or for other lions who are hunting the same prey you are.

You may be the King of the Jungle, but that doesn't mean you don't have things to worry about.

Most animals have distinct behaviors and physical habits. Try to think of your animal's distinguishing feature. For instance, a rabbit has that twitchy nose, and a dog scratches himself so intently. How does a cat sprawl in a patch of sun? Study photographs or illustrations or videos of your animal and try to imitate what makes his signature gesture so distinctive. The actors and actresses in such plays as *Cats* and *The Lion King*, as well as the animators of the movie *The Lion King*, observed animals carefully to really capture their essence. Think about these animals and their distinctive traits. How would you try to behave like them?

> Haughty peacock
> Angry hen
> Nervous mouse
> Sleepy cat
> Hungry wolf
> Slow turtle
> Eager puppy

At the supper table at the end of the day, talk about what it felt like to be your animal. Describe chances you had to act or think like your animal. If you kept your animal identity a secret from each other all day, you can play a question-and-answer guessing game. What do you eat? Do you have fur? Do you come out at night? Eat meat? Are you a nocturnal flying creature who is blind and sleeps hanging upside down in a cave?

Extrapalooza

A Family Totem Pole

According to many Native American tribes, man and animals are bound together in intimate ways, and each of us has our animal spirit. For the Tlingits of the Northwest, people and animals are relatives who can cross back and forth into each other's worlds. Animals have

People are beginning to see that the first requisite to success in life is to be a good animal.

—Herbert Spencer
(1820–1903)

totem (to-tum), n.:
A natural object or
an animate being,
as an animal or
bird, assumed as
the emblem of a
clan, family, or
group.

the ability to appear before people in human form and to talk to people. The animal or bird associated with your family is known as your totem. If your family had a wolf totem, this would mean that one of your ancestors had once lived with supernatural wolves, and when he or she returned to the human world had been given permission to be represented by the wolf image.

A totem pole is a composite of images important to your clan and features your animal or animals, one image on top of another, usually carved out of wood. Take photos of each member of the family posing as their animal and create a photographic totem pole. You can draw a small version of each of your family's animals, decorating with sparkles or feathers. Then glue the animals one above the other onto an empty paper towel tube. Or create a small totem pole out of Sculpey.

Charades

Charades is a chronic condition in my family, I'm afraid. I played many, many hours of charades with my siblings—we still fall into our old habit at holiday gatherings. And it's a bug everyone was bound to catch in my own home.

What's the Palooza?

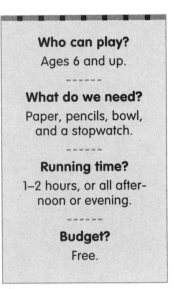

Act out short titles or phrases, without using any words or sounds, for others to guess. Charades is commonly competitive—the team who has taken the least amount of time to guess the charade wins—but beginners will probably do better without the time constraint and competitive angle. Younger children and beginners may find it easier to warm up to the game if you limit the first few games to a certain category, such as only movie titles.

Every player chooses a subject—movie title, book title, play title, TV show, song title, or a common phrase or quotation—and a charade to act out from that category. On a small piece of paper, each person writes his name, category, and charade. ("Mary, book, *Gone With the Wind*." "Mike, movie, *Buckeroo Bonzai*." "Ellen, song, 'I Only Have Eyes for You.'") All the pieces of paper are placed in a bowl and mixed up. Review the common charade gestures (see below) so all the players know what the gestures mean. You can even prepare a cheat sheet ahead of time so beginners can refer to the sheet for both pantomiming and for guessing.

The first player chooses a piece of paper, reads it to himself, and announces the author of that charade—the author can't participate in guessing that particular charade. The player gets a minute or two to review the charade and come up with a game plan. You begin acting out the charade by pantomiming the category of the charade—movie, song, or whatever. Once someone has guessed the category, you begin acting out the specific charade. You can either act out each word one at a time, or you can try to play out the whole phrase at once. Sometimes you might even need to break words into syllables. When the charade is guessed correctly, another player starts a round with a new charade from the bowl. The winner is either the team with the highest number of successful guesses or the team that has used the least time to get the correct guesses.

Extrapaloozas

Advanced Charades

Players are permitted to create charades of completely random words, phrases, or sentences, the more offbeat, the better. For example, "The parkway was flooded last night." Or "Gobbledygook."

Murder Mystery Charades

This charade is based loosely on that classic board game, Clue. Divide the group into two teams. Team A leaves the room, and Team B comes up with a person (the murderer), place (the murder scene), and thing (the murder weapon). For example, Spiderman, in a pet shop, with a hairbrush. Miss Piggy, at the airport, with a golf club.

Charades Gestures

To indicate a category:

Movie title—pretend to crank an old-fashioned movie camera.

Book title—put your hands together and open them as if you're opening a book.

Song title—open your mouth wide as if singing and spread arms in the air.

TV show—draw a square box in the air with your fingers.

Play title—pretend to pull the rope that opens the curtains on a stage.

Common phrase or quotation—make quotation marks in the air with your fingers.

To indicate other parts of a word or a phrase:

Number of words in the phrase or title—hold up as many fingers as the number of words.

Which word you're acting out—hold up number of fingers again for word position in the phrase.

Number of syllables in the word—lay that number of fingers on your arm.

Whole phrase—cross your arms over your chest.

Small word—hold index finger and thumb close together as if gesturing "itty bitty."

Long word—spread your hands out, palms facing each other.

Sounds like—cup your hand behind your ear.

Longer version of the word—pretend you're stretching an elastic band.

Shorter version of the word—chop your hand through the air.

Past tense—point behind you with your thumb.

Getting close, keep guessing—wave your arms toward you frantically.

On the nose (someone guessed correctly)— put your index finger on the tip of your nose while pointing to the person who made the correct guess. (This is my all-time favorite part of charades!)

Holiday Charades

Choose movies, book titles, TV shows, words, or songs relating to a holiday as your charade. Use titles of scary movies for Halloween charades or act out particular characters from scary movies. (*Frankenstein* or *Dracula* may be too easy; how about *Bride of Frankenstein* or the *Creature from the Black Lagoon*?) Act out carols or Christmas movies for Christmas charades. For Thanksgiving, act out a part of the Thanksgiving meal—a turkey, mashed potatoes, or a pumpkin pie. Or patriotic charades for Independence Day—Yankee Doodle Dandy or Lady Liberty.

Mask Theater

Masks have been used in theater since the Greek tragedies, giving performers a way to freely explore territory where they may never have dared go otherwise. This palooza lets you unmask by putting on a mask.

Who can play?
Ages 6 and up.

What do we need?
Paper plate, hole punch, twine or yarn. Also, character masks (animals, fairy-tale or cartoon characters, comedy and tragedy masks, superheros, and so on).

Running time?
At least an hour.

Budget?
$

What's the Palooza?

Discover the freedom a mask provides. The most shy or even the most extroverted among us can learn something from masked performance. Make a neutral mask, perform a few simple routines or skits wearing the mask, and become whomever or whatever you want to be.

Wear a faceless mask and tell a story or invent a character using only body language and gesture—no voice allowed. Legendary French mime Jacques Lecoq was a proponent of an acting technique known today as the neutral mask. In a neutral mask, actors concentrate on using their bodies—arms, legs, elbows, necks, and so on—to communicate rather than their faces. Lecoq's neutral mask is essentially a blank face created by a black or white mask with holes made only for the eyes and perhaps the nose. With the mask on, you needn't be concerned with who you are or with anyone's preconceptions about you. You're a blank slate, a tabula rasa, free to explore without giving clues about your character (or yourself) in your facial expression. In a neutral mask, anything is possible.

To make a simple neutral mask, take a paper plate and punch holes in it for your eyes and nose. Attach twine or yarn to the sides of the plate and tie it around your face. Lecoq believed that actors should get to an essential or "neutral" place before trying to get into character, and that's partly what the neutral mask requires. It also asks you to think of your body as your most important tool of expression. Without speaking or making a sound, and without touching your mask with your hands, perform a few simple routines, concentrating on physical gesture alone. Watch yourself in the mirror or perform for someone else.

Walk about the room wearing the mask. Without touching anything, walk about as if you are:

Frantic
Tired
Looking for something
Calm
In a hurry
Taking your time
Happy
Angry
Shy
Friendly and eager to chat
Lost

Find a book in the room and pick it up. How would you express the following about the book while wearing your neutral mask? The book is:

Hard to understand
Suspenseful
Long and boring
A quick read
Funny
Sad
One you've read a hundred times and still love

Still wearing your neutral mask, invent a distinctive character. Concentrate on your actions. How does your character:

Walk
Sit down
Stand up
Hail a cab
Meet a long-lost friend
Pick a flower
Push a grocery cart

Mask, n.: A covering for all or part of the face, usually worn to conceal one's identity; a piece of cloth covering the face of an actor to symbolize the character he represents, used in Greek and Roman drama and in some modern plays; a representation of a face or head, generally grotesque, used as an ornament.

> *Put a mask on a hypocrite and he can no longer lie.*
>
> —George Bernard Shaw
> (1856–1950)

When you are able to tell a story thoroughly in the mask, remove it and perform the same routine once again, adding facial expression to the mix. If you're working with a partner, take turns being observer and masked performer.

Extrapalooza

Character Mask

Japanese *Noh* theater, Balinese *Topeng*, and Italian Commedia dell'arte are rich theatrical traditions employing character masks. Actors don a mask and within the form of the mask develop the interior and exteriors of that character, capturing all the attributes of the mask itself and then some. Choose several inexpensive masks from a costume store (or make simple masks out of paper plates, with character faces or facial expressions, such as sad, happy, angry, surprised, drawn on them) and spend an afternoon or morning exploring the characters underneath those masks. The idea in character mask theater is to learn to work with whatever mask is presented to you. For example, if you're wearing a Snow White mask, how does Snow White walk? What kinds of movements suit her mask? Does she lilt about or tromp around? What about Bugs Bunny? Does he tilt his head forward and angled to the right? Put on a mask of the Hulk and strike bodybuilding poses. Wear a tiger mask and slink around the room, stalking imaginary prey. Choose a mask that bears only an anonymous but expression-laden face. What kinds of broad gestures can you make to further define the character and go beyond the expression on the mask?

Puppets

Puppets can charm and delight, entrance and amaze. And because you can make a puppet out of most anything (or almost nothing), a sweet puppet show is no farther than your kitchen cupboard or the sock drawer.

What's the Palooza?

Think of a story, make a few simple puppets, construct a puppet theater, and perform your play.

Create a play. Take a favorite story and break it down into simple parts. Your play doesn't have to be written down; you can make up the dialogue as you go, but move the story along by concentrating on just four or five main parts that you've worked out in advance. For instance, the story of Hansel and Gretel can be broken down into these scenes: Hansel and Gretel going through the forest dropping bread crumbs; Hansel and Gretel meeting up with the witch at the gingerbread house; Hansel and Gretel escaping the witch; and Hansel and Gretel's father finding them in the woods.

Make your puppets. Now that you know the story you're going to tell in your play, you know your characters. In our example, they are Hansel, Gretel, the witch, and Hansel and Gretel's father. Take a wooden spoon and draw a face on the back of the bowl part with markers or paint. Color the eyes or glue on small buttons for a more 3-D effect. Mark eyebrows, nose, and mouth that suit each character. Cut yarn for the hair (horrible hair for the witch, little pigtails for Gretel, and so on) and glue it to the top of the spoon. To make the body, take a Popsicle stick and glue or tape it onto the spoon handle crosswise, about 2 inches from the base of

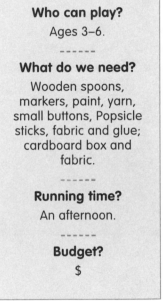

Who can play?
Ages 3–6.

What do we need?
Wooden spoons, markers, paint, yarn, small buttons, Popsicle sticks, fabric and glue; cardboard box and fabric.

Running time?
An afternoon.

Budget?
$

Come children, let us shut up the box and the puppets, for our play is played out.

—William Makepeace
Thackeray
(1811–1863)

the bowl. Make clothing (a swath of black around the witch, a hunter's vest on the father) from scrap fabric or felt, fit it to the spoon handle/Popsicle stick body, and glue to secure.

Make a stage. Take an empty cardboard box and turn it into your puppet stage. Lay the box on its side on a table. The open top of the box should be facing the audience, and the bottom of the box should face the puppeteers. Fold the flaps of the box out to the sides to help hide what's going on behind the box. Affix a piece of fabric to the back opening of the box to create backstage curtains in front of which your puppets will perform.

Fold the top flap of the box up and paint or color it like a marquee. Paint or color the outside of the box to look like a theater, and the inside to look like the set for your story. Paint or color the inside of the box in this case, perhaps, with trees. Cut two pieces of fabric to make the front stage curtains and staple them to the box so they hang down the front of the box. Tie them back with bits of yarn when the puppet show is about to begin.

When you're ready to stage your puppet play, stand behind the box flaps on either side of the stage. This way, you are hidden from the audience yet are able to move the puppets across the stage.

Pleased as Punch

Punch and Judy became a puppetry phenomenon in England in the mid-1800s, though the characters originated in Italy and France centuries before. The silly antics and lively dialogue of the bombastic, hook-nosed Punch and his long-suffering wife, Judy, enthralled children, while the undercurrent of social commentary, which the children ignored, delighted the adult audience.

Punch and Judy shows are traditionally performed by one puppeteer (who is always known as "The Professor"), so only two characters can appear on the stage at one time. Despite Punch's notoriously violent behavior (he carries a big stick and thinks nothing of pounding mercilessly on his stagemate), the shows always had a happy ending, with Punch summarily defeating his enemies. The phrase "pleased as punch" has its origins in the Punch and Judy shows, referring to Punch's extreme pleasure at having triumphed over his foes. A transcript of a typical Punch and Judy show from the 1840s can be found in Henry Mayhew's *London Labour and the London Poor*.

Perform the play. Hold the bottom of the spoons and move the puppets around the stage in front of the curtain. Give each of the characters a different voice. Give them brief but juicy lines of dialogue ("Into the oven, you old witch!" says a triumphant Gretel). Think of ways to show action and emotion. Use props. For example, if you want to include a gingerbread-house prop, cut a house shape out of paper and color it to resemble a gingerbread house. Glue it onto a Popsicle stick and pop the house into the play at the right time. Same goes for the witch's oven. You can make the bird who eats the bread crumbs the same way, moving them across the stage on Popsicle sticks, pecking at the ground. Have someone help you close the curtains between scenes to give you time to rearrange the set with the props you need. You can also have someone help with the puppeteering, but it's kind of fun to do it by yourself if you've got enough hands!

> ## Puppet Stars
> - - - - - -
> Bun-Bun
> Charlie McCarthy
> Howdy Doody
> Kermit and Miss Piggy
> Kukla and Ollie
> Lambchop
> Pinocchio
> Punch and Judy

Extrapalooza

Chopstick Puppets

Draw the front and back of a character, cut it out, and glue it onto a wooden chopstick. Or glue a paper doll onto a chopstick and turn it into a character in a puppet play. Or glue bits of Styrofoam balls, pom-poms, cotton balls, and shredded paper to chopsticks to create alien or monster puppets. Put the alien puppets together with the other chopstick characters, and you've got a story!

word
paloozas

Author, Author

Kids are constantly making up stories, whether it's about a trip to the beach or a favorite stuffed animal's fantastic adventures. And when two people alternate telling one story, with multiple doses of creativity at work, you never know quite how the story will end. Collaborative stories, part creative endeavor, part keepsake, can be kept on the bookshelf with the other books you read at bedtime.

Who can play?
All ages, at least two people at a time.

What do we need?
Blank book or sturdy individual sheets of paper; markers, crayons, colored pencils, collage materials, tissue, sparkles, glue, etc.; disposable camera for photos; mailing envelopes and postage for long-distance partners.

Running time?
One afternoon, a summer, or a lifetime.

Budget?
$

What's the Palooza?

Write an ongoing story with an adult or another child. You can work on the book side by side or mail it back and forth—especially fun to do with grandparents, aunts, or uncles. Start with a blank book—a small scrapbook or a blank journal. If you prefer, you can bind together a book yourself.

This project is all about collaboration. Each author takes turns adding to the story, following up on what has already been written. The work can be split sentence by sentence or page by page. It's more fun not to plan out or discuss the plot in advance. Instead, be as random and freewheeling as you want.

The book can be about anything. Dream up an imaginary character or cast of characters, or base them on friends, pets, or toys. More ambitious writers might choose to write several chapters, each one a different adventure. Create a sequel or a prequel to a children's book you love. Or tell a real-life adventure that you have had together. Then again, it can be an ongoing daily log, like a two-sisters-reporting-from-the-front-lines-of-camp journal.

Experiment with embellishing the format of the text. Different emotions can be written about in different colors, and perhaps different characters talk in different fonts. You'll probably want to illustrate what you write.

You can also create a comic book together, complete with frames and speech bubbles, telling a story more with pictures than with words.

Extrapaloozas

Play Write

If you really want to see your story come alive when it's finished, write a play. Come up with a cast of characters, a list of props, and a setting. Then take turns writing a line or scene of the script. Once the play is done, of course, you can perform it!

Circle Stories

Write a collaborative story without knowing the plot until it's finished. You will need several sheets of lined paper, pens, and three or more participants. Sit in a circle. The first person should start the story any way he or she likes. Then pass the paper around the circle. Everyone takes turns adding to the story, writing as much or as little as he or she wants. Here's the twist: every time it's passed from one person to the next, the paper must be folded so that only the most recent addition is visible—no cheating! The next writer must continue logically from what they see, but they will not know what came before it. With very large groups, you can keep more than one story going at a time. Continue to circulate the story until a page or two is written. No one knows exactly what the story is about until it's finished and read aloud. The result is a hilarious and entertaining story full of unexpected twists and turns.

Good First Lines

While "Once upon a time" has its charm, there are many other ways to give the start of your story a special kick and get the creative juices flowing. Some suggestions for intriguing opening lines:

It was a dark and stormy night, and someone was knocking loudly at the front door. . . .

She found a mysterious old box in her attic. . . .

He had the feeling that the old stone statue was watching him. . . .

The mad scientist thought his newest contraption might just work this time . . . .

With an enormous CRAAASH!!!! they landed on planet Earth. . . .

She noticed a door she had never seen before. . . .

Bibliomancy

The ancients tried to foretell future events and uncover hidden meanings by consulting randomly selected passages from sacred texts. Essentially, these wise owls would bring their Big Questions to a Big Book as if it were one of those Magic Eight Balls. "Will there be peace?" "Will the crops be bountiful?" This palooza is about bringing the little questions—"Will I pass that spelling quiz tomorrow?" "Can I have a dog?"—to a big book like the dictionary and seeing all the funny, clever ways your kids get the answer they're looking for.

Who can play?
Ages 6 and up.

What do we need?
A big, juicy dictionary.

Running time?
Anywhere from five minutes to an hour.

Budget?
Free.

What's the Palooza?

A fun, funky way to use the dictionary for your own devices. Take a dictionary—the bigger and fatter and more authoritative the better—and lay it on the table in front of you. Think of it as a kind of crystal ball—you will ask it a question, and it will present you with an answer. Now carefully formulate your question. The way you pose your question is important, in the same way it is important, say, not to ask for everything in the world when you close your eyes and blow out your birthday candles but rather be selective and precise, in order to increase your chances of seeing your dreams come true.

Close your eyes and think of your simple, careful question. It can be about anything—your family, your friends, school, sports, or other hobbies. You probably know what you want the answer to be. Ask your question three times out loud, then open the dictionary to a random page and drop your finger anywhere on that page. Open your eyes and find the dictionary entry closest to where your finger has landed. If you land in the middle of a definition, refer to the word being defined. Then start working the angles of the word and definition, being as creative and clever as you have to be to get the answer you're looking for.

For example, here's my question: "Will I do well in my script reading on Saturday?" I open the dictionary at random, drop my finger, and find I've landed on the word *eyehole*, which is defined as "a hole to look through, as in a mask or a curtain." Did someone say "mask"? Actors are often described as wearing the masks of the characters they play. Also, everyone knows the masks of tragedy and comedy. And "a curtain" must have something to do with a stage curtain. Now I'm feeling very certain I'm looking through an eyehole in a stage curtain and seeing myself do very well indeed on my script reading!

Other random samplings illustrate the power of bibliomancy:

"Will I do well on my spelling test?" gets *inclined*. I think that means you are inclined toward spelling and are likely to do well.

"Can I have more dessert?" gets *prayerful*, which suggests if you ask prayerfully, sincerely or earnestly, you just might get two scoops.

"What activities should I do in the fall?" gets *fusion*, which means a merging of distinct or separate elements into a whole. Hmm. Sign up for wrestling and tap dancing?

Now try it yourself with questions of your own. Use a dictionary or specialty references such as dictionaries of slang, clichés, or allusions.

divination (div-i-na-tion), n.: The art or practice of foretelling the future or discovering the unknown through omens, oracles, or supernatural powers.

Those Greeks Have a Word for Everything

Even though bibliomancy was practiced for hundreds of years before the Greeks got a hold of it, as usual, they were the ones who gave it an exotic, evocative name. *Biblio* is the Greek word for *book*, and *mancy* derives from the Greek *manteia*, which means the power of divination, or divination by means of. They also referred to this practice as *sortes Homericae* or *sortes Virgilianae*, as the books they often consulted were those of Homer or Virgil.

Poetry Slam

Poetry slams are a great way to bring poetry into your real world, where it belongs. In this form, poetry ricochets between people and is at its vivid best.

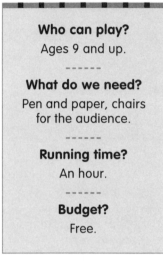

Who can play?
Ages 9 and up.

What do we need?
Pen and paper, chairs for the audience.

Running time?
An hour.

Budget?
Free.

What's the Palooza?

A poetry slam! Slam is the competitive art of performance poetry. It puts a double emphasis on writing and performance, encouraging poets to focus both on what they're saying and how they're saying it. It's usually an event in which poets perform their work and are judged by members of the audience. Typically, there is a host who emcees the performance. She also selects the judges, who are instructed to give numerical scores (on a 1 to 10 scale) based on the poet's content and delivery.

Though rules vary from slam to slam, the basic guidelines are:

Each poem must be of the poet's own creation.

Each poet gets three minutes to read one poem; if the poet goes over time, points will be deducted from the total score.

The poet may not use props, costumes, or musical instruments.

Slam is designed for the audience to react openly to the poet's performance, the judges' scores, and the host's banter. Audiences boo or cheer at the conclusion of a poem, or even during a poem. If they don't like a poet's performance, audiences can express their discontent with finger snapping and foot stomping. If the audience expresses a certain level of dissatisfaction, the poet gives himself the hook and leaves the stage. Though not every slam is so rough-and-tumble as to boo a poet off the stage, the vast majority of slams give the audience full freedom to express itself.

For a friends-and-family slam, you may want to make it more poet-friendly—no booing or cheering, for instance—at least until everyone gets used to the experience. Let the entire audience be the judge, handing out programs listing the names of each poet, with a space next to the name for a score, 1 to 10. The host tabulates the scores to determine the winner. Or just recite poems for the sake of reciting, no judges, no winners, no losers. Then you can work on developing a style of delivery that's all your own, without the performance anxiety!

What kind of poetry is read at slams? It depends on the venue, depends on the poets, depends on the slam. One of the best things about poetry slam is the diverse range of work at a slam, including heartfelt love poetry, searing social commentary, uproarious comic routines, and bittersweet personal confessional pieces. Poets are free to do work in any style on any subject.

For your slam, choose an emcee to host and pick poems to perform, either your own, each other's, or a published poet's. See the next page for ideas on writing poems. One of the best things about poetry slam is the range of poetry and poets it attracts. The Beats read poetry in smoky coffeehouses in the late 1950s and 1960s. You can wear a black beret and grab a copy of Allen Ginsberg's *Howl*, read some of his fantastically wild poems, and bend back time. Or you could model your

Great Poems for Young Poetry Slams

Carl Sandburg, "Horse Fiddle," *Smoke and Steel*

e. e. cummings, "maggie and milly and molly and may," *The Complete Poems: 1904–1962*

Edward Lear, *The Owl and the Pussycat*

Langston Hughes, "Dreams," *The Collected Poems of Langston Hughes*

Shel Silverstein, "Dancing Pants," *Where the Sidewalk Ends*

slam after *Def Poetry Jam* (see sidebar below), where poets are often influenced by hip hop and almost rap their pieces.

Have fun with inflections, stylizing the sound of your voice to emphasize certain words. Slams often involve a sort of singsong diction with the voice going up and down from syllable to syllable. Or invent your own distinctive style of delivery.

Extrapaloozas

Word List

If you don't know where to begin writing something original, make a random list of words and write a poem either inspired by or using those words. Go around in a circle if you have a group and toss out your favorite words. Anything goes: *magnolia, cream, Lamborghini, haystack, surge, starlight, velvet, mint.* Make up your own words, jumble sounds together. Now that you're lost in words, make word signs to stick around your room for random inspiration. Write words on paint chip samples and ticket stubs, or label objects around you: *ballerina* on a girly lampshade, *steel* on a jug of milk. Play with your perceptions and loosen up word meanings.

Start with a Familiar Phrase

You can also borrow phrases from other poets or writers.

Def Poetry Jam

In 2002, rap impresario Russell Simmons staged *Def Poetry Jam* on Broadway to expose a larger audience to slam poetry-performance. He enlisted nine young, inventive but experienced poet-performers, showcasing their strengths and differences as poets. The result is a blend of poetry and theater, stagecraft and self-expression. The only thing missing from this big but understated Broadway production is the slam itself—no competition or judges or audience approval. Still, slam or no slam, Simmons did his part to bring contemporary poetry back into fashion.

Pick up a volume of Shakespeare or Fitzgerald, Judy Blume or Dr. Seuss. Choose a favorite sentence for your first or last line and build the poem from there. You can play off the author's style or spin off in your own unique voice.

Place Poems

Grab a notebook and go on a Poem Walk. Find a place that catches your fancy and describe every detail that you notice. Write about the blades of grass tickling you, the cloud that looks like your dog, the smell of jalapeño jelly from your neighbor's kitchen.

You can also describe a place you haven't visited. Look at an atlas or spin a globe and randomly point to a place. Write a poem about Fiji in May or Prague in November. Or imagine a place that doesn't exist. Create it with words, describe the sky and the plants, the flowers and the buildings. Is the grass fuchsia? Are the cars made of soap bubbles?

Good Books

Check out *Writing Down the Bones* by Natalie Goldberg or *poemcrazy* by Susan G. Wooldridge for inspiration as you write. Or look at *Poetry Speaks,* a compilation of great poems by Alfred Lord Tennyson, T. S. Eliot, Langston Hughes, and many others, with CD recordings of the poets reading their work.

Newsstand

This palooza will bring out the ink-stained wretch in any kid.

What's the Palooza?

Publish your own newspaper. It can be a one-page news roundup or a twelve-page extravaganza, and you brainstorm, investigate, interview, write, edit, and illustrate the whole thing yourself. First, think about the theme or purpose of your newspaper: it might be family news, what's happening on your street or in your building; it might be a newspaper about a subject you're interested in (sports or Legos or animals, for example); or it might be classroom news.

Next comes an especially fun part: coming up with a name for your newspaper. Check out existing newspapers, magazines, and other publications for inspiration and then try a few on for size. Do you want your publication to sound serious? Some variation on the *News* or the *Times* might fit. Maybe you want it to sound a little more happy-go-lucky; the *Radboard Press* (for skateboarders) or *Neigh!-borhood News* (for horses and their people). For a school newspaper whose mascot is a bulldog, *Bulldogs Bark!* has some bite. For a neighborhood rag published on Maple Street, something simple like the *Maple Street Neighborhood News*.

If you're the publisher, editor, reporter, photographer, typesetter, and printer, well, you better get to work! If you are creating a newspaper with friends or siblings, here are some of the jobs that might need doing, depending on the focus of your paper and how long it will be.

Publisher
Editor
Photographer
Feature reporter

Sports reporter
Arts reviewer
Book reviewer
Opinion or editorial writer
Comics illustrator
Crossword puzzle/quiz creator
Layout/designer

Your paper may feature "hard news," serious, up-to-the minute stories, or "soft news," which includes human interest stories, reviews, opinion pieces, and sports. If you have the room and the human resources, you can also feature comics or cartoons, puzzles, games or contests, and advertisements.

If you're working with other people, sit down and brainstorm good story ideas. Or the editor can make story assignments and give reporters and photographers their deadlines. If you're working alone, write about anything you like! The questions and guidelines below will help you gather information for your story and write it.

1. This story is about _____
2. This story is important because...
     it is about something that is happening now;
     it is about something unusual;
     it is about an important person;
     other.

yellow journalism, n.: Journalism that exploits, distorts, or exaggerates the news to create sensations and attract readers. Derived from the use of yellow ink in printing *Yellow Kid*, a cartoon strip in the *New York World*, a newspaper noted for sensationalism.

Naming Names

The following newspaper monikers might come in handy when you're trying to name your own newspaper:

Bee	Free Press	Mail	Reporter
Chronicle	Gazette	Monitor	Review
Constitution	Globe	News	Sentinel
Courier	Herald	Observer	Star
Daily	Inquirer	Pilot	Sun
Dispatch	Journal	Post	Times
Express	Ledger	Register	Tribune

3. Who is the story about? What happened? When did this happen? Where did this happen? Why is this important? How did this happen?
4. Write some details about the story.
5. Write the lead or opening sentence, answering who is involved, what happened, when it happened, and where it happened.
6. Finish opening paragraph by answering why and how it happened.
7. Create a headline for story.

Once the stories are all written, you may need help typing them into a computer and printing them out. Arrange the stories and accompanying photos on a single page or organize them over two or more pages. Fill empty spaces with photos, cartoons, ads, or write short "filler" stories to fill the space (fun facts are good fillers).

Design a title logo to run across the top of your newspaper. Use a serious typeface to be sure readers understand this is a serious newspaper. Or use fun or zany type to suggest this is a lighthearted newspaper. If you've typed and arranged your newspaper on your computer, print it out, and read it over, and look for errors. Make your corrections, then print out the number of copies you'd like to distribute. Now the "Circulation Department" can staple, fold, and deliver the papers!

If you're pasting up your stories by hand (printing out the individual stories, and arranging and gluing them on a master page), read the stories for errors before you paste them. When you have your master copy all prepared, make as many copies as you'll distribute, collating the copies either automatically when you copy, or by hand after copying. Staple, fold, and deliver!

If you find that you've got a lot of news to report and you're getting an enthusiastic response from your readers, you might want to make it a monthly or even a weekly and start "selling" ad space to friends and family. Rupert Murdoch, watch out!

Extrapaloozas

Pulp Fiction

Make up newspapers based on fairy tales, tall tales, short stories, chapters from novels, and acts of drama. Choose a piece of literature and write a journalistic account of the literature, from the perspective of a reporter during that time period: "Little Women Save the Day." "Paul Bunyan Chops Down Trees." "Hansel Follows Gretel into the Woods."

Holiday News

Instead of a Christmas letter or card, create a newspaper to send to the whole family, complete with photographs, reports on travels, accomplishments, sports events, illnesses, milestones, and predictions for the upcoming year. Besides the news from your immediate family, collect photos and stories from Grandma and Grandpa, aunts and uncles, cousins, and close family friends. This is a great way to catch up on family news, and your readers will look forward to your annual edition!

It's amazing that the amount of news that happens in the world every day always just exactly fits the newspaper.

—Jerry Seinfeld
(1954–)

Secret Language

An estimated 6,800 spoken languages exist in the world today. Why not make it 6,801 by inventing your own?

Who can play?
Ages 9 and up.

What do I need?
Imagination.

Running time?
Forever.

Budget?
Free.

What's the Palooza?

Invent your own secret language. Secret languages are universal: some Russian kids speak a "ku" language to sneak past their parents, while English costermongers used to speak Cockney to disguise their illegal trading activities. The real science to keeping your secret language a secret is fluency: practice until you can rattle off double Dutch so that no one but a fellow speaker can catch on!

Some secret languages rely on changing vowels or consonants. To speak "-op," for instance, spell each word you want to say out, saying each vowel and adding –op after each consonant. So the phrase "word play" becomes:

wop-o-rop-dop pop-lop-a-yop

Inserting random sounds into the middle of words is also a simple language: Try adding "-ag" after the first consonant of every word, and you get *wagord plagay* (if the word is only one syllable, add "ag" after the first consonant).

One way to make a secret language completely your own is by adapting an already existing type of language. Pig latin is probably the most widely used secret language in America. It is spoken by taking the first letter of a word, putting it at the end of that word, and adding an "ay" sound. To use the same example, "word

What Hath God Wrought

- - - - - - -

Morse code isn't a secret language, but it might be your little secret, as fewer and fewer people know or use it these days. Samuel Morse introduced the electric telegraph to the United States Congress by transmitting the famous message "What hath God wrought" over a wire from Washington to Baltimore. He typed this message in a special code he created for each letter of the alphabet, numbers, and punctuation.

You can write your name or a message using this code of dots and dashes.

International Morse Code Characters

- - - - - - - - - - - -

A	. −	N	− .	0	− − − −
B	− . . .	O	− − −	1	. − − − −
C	− . − .	P	. − − .	2	. . − − −
D	− . .	Q	− − . −	3	. . . − −
E	.	R	. − .	4	. . . . −
F	. . − .	S	. . .	5	. . . . .
G	− − .	T	−	6	− . . . .
H	. . . .	U	. . −	7	− − . . .
I	. .	V	. . . −	8	− − − . .
J	. − − −	W	. − −	9	− − − − .
K	− . −	X	− . . −		
L	. − . .	Y	− . − −	Period	. − . − . −
M	− −	Z	− − . .	Comma	− − . . − −
				Question mark	. . − − . .

Short signals are known as *dits*, represented by dots. Long signals are known as *dahs*, represented by dashes. Morse code relies on very precise intervals of time between dits and dahs, between letters, and between words. The chart below outlines the relationships.

Dit	1 unit of time	Pause between letters	3 units of time
Dah	3 units of time	Pause between words	7 units of time

The speed of transmitting Morse code is measured in WPM (words per minute). The word *Paris* is used as the standard length of a word. To transmit the word *Paris* requires 50 units of time. If you transmitted the word *Paris* 5 times, you would be transmitting at 5 WPM. An experienced Morse code operator can transmit and translate information at 20 to 30 WPM.

There's a great Web site with a Morse code translator. You type in a word, and it translates your word into dots and dashes. You can also hear your word translated into Morse code! Go to www.lcss.net/morsecode.htm.

play" becomes "ord-way lay-pay." Create an alternative to pig latin—maybe it's cat latin, with "-eow" embedded in or ending every word or every third word.

Cockney involves coding words by replacing them with rhyming ones. Make your own version by thinking of new rhyming words. Here's an example of a real Cockney to get you started:

'Ullo, mate. Come in awf (out) of de frog an' toad (road) an' 'ave a cuppa Rosie (cup of tea). It's on de Cain an' Abel (table). But wipe yer plates o' meat (feet) 'cos de ol' trouble an' strife (wife)'s just scrubbed de Rory O'More (floor). She's up de apples an' pears (upstairs) 'avin' a bo-peep (sleep). Get into that lion's lair (chair) and let's chew the fat (have a chat).

Extrapalooza

Cipher Wheel

Some languages rely on keys to crack codes, so they can only be written, not spoken. The cipher wheel turns the English language upside down by randomly matching letters of the alphabet. To make your own cipher wheel, cut two circles out of paper. The first should be about 3 inches in diameter, the second, about 2¾ inches. On the larger of the circles, write the alphabet from A to Z along the edge. On the second circle, write the twenty-six letters of the alphabet in random order. Glue the smaller circle onto the larger one, so that the letters of the two line up. In order to write your code, find each letter on the outer circle, check its corresponding letter on the smaller one, and write that letter on the message. To hide your message even more, take out all spaces between words. In order for the recipient to be able to decode the message, he or she has to have the same decoder as the sender.

Read-Aloud Marathon

All the action in James Joyce's novel *Ulysses* takes place on a single day, June 16. Every year Joyce fans celebrate this date, known as Bloomsday. Marathon readings of the entire hefty novel take place, and people flock to Dublin, the setting of the story, to retrace the steps of the characters through the streets of the city. There is even a James Joyce lookalike contest. In the spirit of Bloomsday, this palooza is about loving a book or author so much you just have to celebrate it.

What's the Palooza?

Celebrate a favorite book by organizing a day or a week around a lively reading of it. This palooza can be done in a variety of ways. Your starting point is the book you choose. Family favorites are a good place to start, from Mom's beloved *Anne of Green Gables* to Dad's boyhood favorite *Black Beauty* to any number of your child's all-time or current favorites. You might choose a contemporary favorite such as *Holes* or a classic like *The Lion, the Witch, and the Wardrobe*. Or you may lean toward the books about favorite characters, like Madeline or Babar. Whose favorite book or books you choose to read is a family challenge you need to solve for yourself! Maybe you have several read-aloud marathons a year, and each member of the family gets a turn choosing the reading.

You might also use the read-aloud marathon to dis-

Who can play?
Readers should be about 8 and up, but kids of any age can participate.

What do we need?
One big book or a selection of shorter books, a comfy place to read, plus whatever relevant props you can think of.

Running time?
A single afternoon, an hour a day for a week, or as long as it takes to finish the book.

Budget?
Free.

Read-aloud Marathon Book Ideas

- - - - - - -

For Younger Children
Babar series, Jean de Brunhoff
Blueberries for Sal, Robert McCloskey
The Giving Tree, Shel Silverstein
Madeline series, Ludwig Bemelman
Paddington Bear series, Michael Bond
Where the Wild Things Are, Maurice Sendak

For Older Children
The B.F.G., Roald Dahl
Charlie and the Chocolate Factory,
    Roald Dahl
Charlotte's Web, E. B. White
The Chronicles of Narnia, C. S. Lewis
Gulliver's Travels, Jonathan Swift
The Jungle Book, Rudyard Kipling

The Merry Adventures of Robin Hood,
    Howard Pyle
The Odyssey, Homer
The Old Man and the Sea, Ernest Hemingway
The Phantom Tollbooth, Norman Juster
Tales of the Arabian Nights
Tom Sawyer, Mark Twain
Treasure Island, Robert Louis Stevenson
A Wrinkle in Time, Madeleine L'Engle

For Children of All Ages
Aesop's Fables
Alice in Wonderland, Lewis Carroll
Grimm's Fairy Tales
The Tales of Uncle Remus
Where the Sidewalk Ends, Shel Silverstein

cover books or authors you might not read on your own—or at least not until you have to in college!—like *Moby-Dick* or some of Mark Twain's lesser known works or short stories by Edgar Allan Poe. Or read something no one in the family has ever read before. Read a classic Mom never got around to reading. Or a brand-new novel by a brand-new author. Or a suspenseful mystery to keep everyone on the edge of their seat and begging for more. Or choose from a compendium of short stories or poetry. My family always read from a short-story collection called *Tellers of Tales*, edited by W. Somerset Maugham. It's almost as much fun figuring out what you want to read as it is actually reading it.

Once the difficult task of choosing the perfect book or books is completed, set your schedule for reading. Maybe it's a single Saturday night. Or a Saturday and Sunday night. Or a snowy Sunday afternoon. Or every night for a week (instead of TV!) Or a modest hour a night before bedtime, for however long it takes until the book is done.

Next choose your setting and format. You may all pile up like puppies on the living room couch. Or sprawl all over the room with pillows and blankets. Or it may be just you and your mom or dad, just the way it always is. Who reads? Anyone who can read. Everyone comfortable with the reading level of the book can take turns reading, chapter by chapter or in smaller sections if necessary. Or Mom or Dad can read longer stretches, while others read smaller bites. The point is for the reading to be as pleasurable for the reader as it certainly will be for those being read to. Get in the spirit by using body language, different voices for different characters, and pauses that create suspense.

Sometimes creating just the right setting makes your read-aloud marathon all the more memorable. If your book is *The Old Man and the Sea*, put Goldie's fish bowl in the center of your reading circle to create a nautical atmosphere. If you're reading a story full of mystery and suspense, dim the lights and use candles instead. If you're reading something wild like Rudyard Kipling's *Jungle Book*, play a CD of jungle sounds in the background.

Think of ways to keep the book you're reading in mind during the course of the day. If you're reading *Treasure Island*, wear eye patches and pirate hats to breakfast. Anyone who's chosen to read the adventures of Ludwig Bemelman's *Madeline* will surely need to have Madeline's scar drawn on their tummies.

Every time you make a point of staging a family read-aloud marathon, you celebrate the books and authors you love, as well as the act of reading itself.

And the more memorable you make the experience, by your enthusiasm for the books and your commitment to the time it takes, the more often it will happen by popular demand!

Extrapaloozas

Holiday Read-aloud Marathons

Instead of the book dictating the activities of the day, perhaps a day on the calendar can inspire you to hold a read-aloud marathon. Ghost stories for Halloween are obvious; so are stories of love for Valentine's Day, and any number of possibilities around the December holidays. But what books would be appropriate to read on January 20, National Cheese Day; October 15, National Grouch Day; or May 14, Dance Like a Chicken Day? You figure it out!

Thespian Marathon

To make this palooza extra interactive, organize a play reading. No costumes or staging required; simply choose a play and assign a character to each participant. Then sit in a circle and read aloud. But just because there's no stage and no audience doesn't mean that acting doesn't count—readers should use their voices to express everything that's going on. Many familiar books and plays have been adapted for performance by children.

Word Collage

We get so used to reading words—quickly translating them into meaning in our heads— that we don't actually see them as objects. We don't notice how some words are pointy and others full and round. We don't always appreciate the inherent beauty or humor or emotion in a word. In this palooza, the word itself takes center stage.

What's the Palooza?

Explore letters and words as graphic forms. Before the invention of the printing press, writing was a labor of love. Every book that was published was written by hand, usually by monks in their cells who devoted years to creating illuminated manuscripts where every letter was a work of art. It was hard not to appreciate the art and beauty inherent in every letter and word.

Start by taking a newspaper or magazine and scan the headlines or captions or articles for words that are unusual or distinctive. Try *not* to read all the words in relation to each other; instead look at each word or phrase as an individual object. For example, from today's newspaper I see words that interest me like *fox hole* and *closing bell* and *proxy*. In a magazine I find *blackbird substitute* in a cartoon caption. And an ad featuring the word *volumatic*. And an article entitled, simply, "Bark." I like that.

Cut out words from newspapers or magazines or even packaging on products that you use that you find interesting or funny or crazy or cool. If you're collecting words over time, save them in a folder or envelope until you have enough to create a collage. You can create a collage of random words you've collected. Or you can think about the kinds of words you might use to create

Who can play?
Ages 6 and up.

What do we need?
Newspapers, magazines, cardboard or posterboard, scissors, gluestick, letter stencils.

Running time?
An hour, though endless time can be spent collecting words.

Budget?
Free.

collage (col-ahj), n.: A work created by affixing various materials (paper, wood, newspaper, cloth) to a picture surface. From the French word *colle,* which means "glue."

a theme in your collage. Maybe they're all great words that have double o's—*school, maroon, noon, cartoon.* Or maybe they're all words that have to do with the sea—*wave, tide, shore, anemone.* Or you can arrange the words you've collected in a nutty kind of ransom note style.

Maybe the best kind of word collage is one you create over time, featuring words you love, in typefaces that make you see the words and experience them in different ways. This is the ultimate word collector's collage! You end up with a kind of a poem.

Word Art

Conceptual artist Barbara Kruger is famous for her photograph-based work, which incorporates simple words into an image to make a statement. Her piece called *Untitled (Seen)* features a photo of a rather grim looking man pointing to his own eye, with the work seen spelled out in the four corners of the piece. And *Untitled (Heard)* is a photo of a man with his hand cupped to his ear, with the word heard seeming to be funneled into the ear. Check out Kruger's witty work at www.art cyclopedia.com/artists/kruger_barbara.html.

Librarian

My daughter was a real book lover, hopelessly devoted to her books as if they were flowers in a garden. One day she decided to give her collection the respect it was due and organized her books into a library. I'm not sure she was using the Dewey Decimal System to categorize them, but she did make me a library card, encouraged me to "take out" one of her books, and then charged me a late fine of about $1.50 when I returned the book several weeks later. This palooza is for little book lovers—or little Virgos, who can't help organizing everything anyway.

What's the Palooza?

Create a personal library of all your books and magazines. Get out all your books; remove them from shelves or other places they live in your house and set them in stacks in the middle of the floor. Look at the kinds of books you have and think about ways to organize them. By category—picture books, storybooks, poetry, chapter books, true stories, biographies, reference, and so on. Or alphabetically by title or author. Or by your own method of organization—by size (big to little), by subject (animals or ballerinas or sports), in order of how much you like them, books with just pictures, books with words and pictures, books with just words. You find the organization that makes sense to you—whether it helps you find a book you're looking for or just showcases the books you really like.

When you've chosen your organization method, separate the books into piles according to your categories. If you have six different categories, assign each category a different color round sticker and apply one to the binding just where a library's call tag would appear. You can leave the sticker blank and let the color tell you

Who can play?
Ages 3–6, 6–9.

What do we need?
Whatever books and magazines your child owns, no matter how few or how many; sturdy paper, scissors, markers or crayons, 3-by-3-inch Post-it notes, small round multicolored blank stickers, small notebook.

Running time?
An hour or two or three.

Budget?
$

Good Book Words

About the Author
Acknowledgments
Appendix
Binding
Chapter title
Copyright page
Dedication
Dust jacket
Endpapers
Epigraph
Flaps
Frontispiece
Glossary
Half-title page
Index
Recto
Spine
Subtitle
Table of contents
Title
Title page
Typeface
Verso

what kind of book it is—yellow for all chapter books, blue for all biographies, and so on—or you can organize further within each category and mark the sticker with the first letter of the last name of the author, or with a star if the book is a particular favorite of yours.

Next apply a blank Post-it note inside each book. This will be the place where you record when the book should be returned to you if someone borrows it. You can also keep a record in a notebook when someone borrows a book: "Stacy B, *Little Women*, borrowed 9/1, to be returned 9/15."

Next reshelve your books in groups by the categories (and other orders) you've assigned: All the blues together, all the reds together, and so on. If you're not able to shelve all your books in one place, try to keep your categories together so you can keep track of what's where.

Do you collect *Highlights* or *Spider*, *Sports Illustrated for Kids* or *Nickelodeon* magazines? Do the same sorting, organizing, and Post-it applying to your magazines.

First Editions

Real bibliophiles get positively giddy over owning first editions of their favorite books. What's a first edition? It's a copy of a book that is from the very first printing of the book. Look at the copyright page on the inside of your book. If it's a first edition, somewhere toward the bottom of the copy on that page, it will say "First Edition." If it doesn't spell out "First Edition," it will show a bunch of numbers across the bottom, usually numbers 1 through 10, either in consecutive order, reverse order, or scrambled something like this: 10 8 6 4 2 1 3 5 7 9. If you see the number 1 somewhere in that string of numbers, you're holding a first edition. If the number 1 is missing, but numbers 2 and beyond are there, it's a second edition, or a copy from the second printing of the book. If the numbers 1 and 2 are missing, but numbers 3 and beyond are there, it's a third edition. And so on. The numbers 30 29 28 27 26 on the copyright page mean the book is in its twenty-fifth printing.

You can shelve them in a stack faceup on their backs so they won't flop over and you can see which magazines are where.

Extrapaloozas

Can I See Your ID?

If you're a real stickler, make library cards out of sturdy paper and markers for any members of your family or friends who might want to borrow your books. Assign each person an identification number that you write on their card and record in your notebook. Mark their name, address, and telephone number on the card. Draw a picture of them on it to make it a "photo" ID.

Shirts and Shoes Required

Clearly post rules for borrowing books on a sign near your library: Do not bend back pages! Do not draw or color in books! Do not eat while reading! Keep away from dogs and baby brothers! Please return on time!

Find It!

Go to your local library and search for something in particular, just for the fun of the hunt. A novel set in Timbuktu perhaps, or a picture book of jellyfish?

Cool Tools for Librarians

Even the youngest practitioner of library science will appreciate these state-of-the-art personal library accoutrements:

Ex Libris stickers, to glue on the inside cover of your books

Cardboard magazine boxes, to stow your mags together, upright and spine out on your shelf

Date stamp, for marking due date on Post-its

Cool homemade bookmarks, to give out to patrons each time they borrow

What's Your Story?

Everyone has a story to tell and this palooza gets your kids to tell yours.

What's the Palooza?

Investigate and tell the life story of someone you know. Think of a grown-up whose story you'd like to discover and tell—like your mom or dad, Grandpa or Grandma, your kooky uncle, a family friend, or your favorite aunt. You may think you know all there is to know about this person—you might even sit across from each other at the dinner table every night—but do you know where he lived as a child? Or what his dog's name was? What was his favorite subject in school? When you're writing someone's biography, you build it out of bits of pieces of information like this, as well as descriptions of things that happened to the person. You build a time line of their lives, and fill it in with details about who they are, what they have done, and their relationships with other people.

You gather these bits of information about your subject from a whole bunch of interesting sources, including:

Your subject. He will be your best source of information about his own life, of course, and if you interview him well and gather interesting details from other sources to add color and depth to your story, you will end up with a nice, juicy biography.

Interviews. Besides your subject, you can interview all

kinds of people who have known your subject, like relatives, old friends and neighbors, teammates or teachers. The more people you interview, the more layers of detail about your subject and his story you will get.

Historical documentation. Look for old yearbooks, scrapbooks, newspaper clippings, diplomas, report cards, letters, and so forth to help give you more information about your subject and his accomplishments.

Diaries. Diaries and journals are, of course, the mother lode of information about a person because the whole point of keeping them is to record what happened or what they were thinking or how they felt about someone or something. Juicy!

Photographs. Look at as many old photos of your subject as you can. You will learn a lot about his interests and the people he knew and the things he did, but you will also get quirky, colorful snips of information about him that you could never get just by asking him questions. Use the pictures to think of more questions to ask!

How to get started?

Make a timeline. Make a basic timeline of things you think you know of this person's life. Birth, grade school, broken arm falling out of a tree, high school, first car, college, first job, etc. Now begin to fill in gaps.

Look at photos. Ask your subject for several favorite photographs, starting from earliest childhood all the way through the present, to help you begin to think of questions to ask.

Prepare for your interview. Make a list of questions to ask your subject when you interview. Try to have a list of at least twenty major questions prepared, as well as possible follow-up questions. Other questions are likely to occur to you during your interview. Schedule some uninterrupted time alone with your subject to conduct your interview. Car rides, short or long, are great times for interviews.

biography (bi-aw-graf-ee), n.: An account of a person's life written, composed, or produced by another.

> *Biographies are but the clothes and buttons of the man. The biography of the man himself cannot be written.*
>
> —Mark Twain
> (1835–1910)

Good Books

Look at these few biographies to compare the techniques the authors used:

Love to Langston written by Tony Medina and illustrated by Gregory Christie. This is an illustrated biography of the great American poet, Langston Hughes, told in the form of fourteen poems that explore the themes and events of his life.

This Land Was Made for You and Me: The Life and Songs of Woody Guthrie, by Elizabeth Partridge. This biography uses some of Woody Guthrie's own writings and correspondence, interviews with his children and friends, song lyrics, and photographs to tell the gritty, sometimes tragic story of Guthrie's life.

Through My Eyes, written by Ruby Bridges and edited by Margo Lundell. Technically, this is a memoir by Ruby Bridges herself, but it is rich with original source material, including photographs, newspaper articles, quotes from family members and teachers—even a painting of Ruby by Norman Rockwell.

Ask away. With a notebook and pen or a tape recorder in hand, begin asking your questions. A good biography is built on good anecdotes—an anecdote is a small story that reveals a lot. A really sharp interviewer also listens for clues to experiences that might make lively anecdotes. Look for opportunities to direct your subject to "give me an example" or "tell me about a time when that actually happened" in order to tease anecdotes out of him. And at the end of your interview(s), do what lots or writers and reporters do: Ask "What should I have asked, but didn't?"

Write it. The best way to go about organizing information in a biography is to simply start at the begin-

ning and work your way to the end. Piece together the story in chronological order, mixing your subject's stories with other people's stories, as well as details and information from other sources. Remember to consider who, what, where, when, why, when telling stories so you don't leave out important facts. You don't need to use every single piece of information you gathered along the way in your biography; there are lots of tiny details that just aren't important. Edit down to the best, most interesting facts and stories to create a compelling overall picture.

Other fun facts to include in your biography might be based on general research: Make a list of the songs or

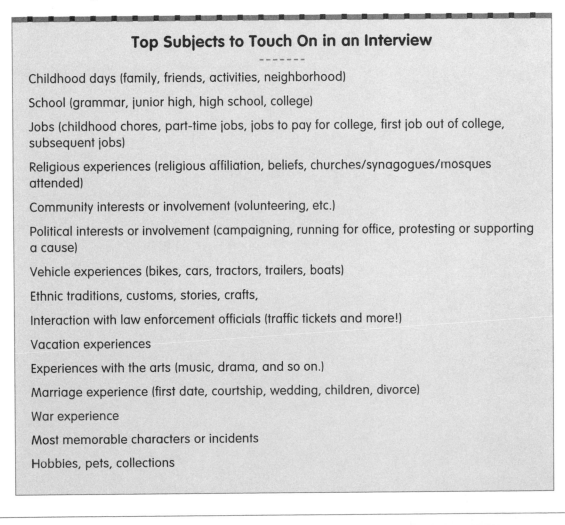

Top Subjects to Touch On in an Interview

- - - - - - -

Childhood days (family, friends, activities, neighborhood)

School (grammar, junior high, high school, college)

Jobs (childhood chores, part-time jobs, jobs to pay for college, first job out of college, subsequent jobs)

Religious experiences (religious affiliation, beliefs, churches/synagogues/mosques attended)

Community interests or involvement (volunteering, etc.)

Political interests or involvement (campaigning, running for office, protesting or supporting a cause)

Vehicle experiences (bikes, cars, tractors, trailers, boats)

Ethnic traditions, customs, stories, crafts,

Interaction with law enforcement officials (traffic tickets and more!)

Vacation experiences

Experiences with the arts (music, drama, and so on.)

Marriage experience (first date, courtship, wedding, children, divorce)

War experience

Most memorable characters or incidents

Hobbies, pets, collections

movies or television shows that were popular when he was in high school. Create a family tree that shows at a glance who's related to whom. Make mini-historical time capsules for various points in your subject's life (who was president at the time, who was the most popular movie star, what major events were happening). Illustrate the biography with photos or drawings, or other meaningful scrapbooky snips.

Create a cover for your biography, with a title and perhaps an illustration.

Extrapalooza

Lifemaps

Instead of a written narrative biography, tell the story visually by illustrating important events and facts about your subject. Start with a baby picture, a picture of a childhood home or a family pet, a postcard from a favorite vacation, a high school mascot logo, a picture of a stack of books (college), and so on. Be creative with your illustrations and your captions. Arrange the images on an elaborate map you've created with winding roads, hills and valleys, cities and oceans. It doesn't need to look like a map of any real place because it's just a way to tell a story in the form of a map. Frame it and give it to your subject as a gift.

Journaling

Technically, a diary is a daily account of the details of daily life and a journal a more free-form reflection on personal experience. Truth be told, it can be hard to tell one form from the other—Virginia Woolf's diaries are rich with personal revelations and seem like journals, while Henry David Thoreau's journal, belaboring a bit of daily minutiae like how much money he spent on nails, has the air of a diary, until he dissolves into a brilliant reflection on philosophy. This palooza is about nudging open the door to thoughts and feelings by keeping a journal.

What's the Palooza?

Keep a simple journal. Sometimes the best way to discover what you think and feel about something is to write about it. A journal is a perfect, private place to try to put words on what you're thinking. No one's going to read it or grade it or have opinions about what you write. It's for you and you alone—hey, no one's looking, so you don't even have to use your best grammar if you don't want to!

How to get started keeping a journal? First you need something to write in; an inexpensive spiral-bound notebook or composition book is fine. You need a writing utensil, a favorite pen or pencil you keep together with your journal. You also need a little privacy—that is, a place to keep your journal where no one will find it and read it.

Finally, you need time to write. Even just a few minutes a day is enough to get the journaling juices going. You can close the door to your bedroom and gather your thoughts in solitude. Or you can keep your journal with you and write in it during the day as thoughts or impressions occur to you.

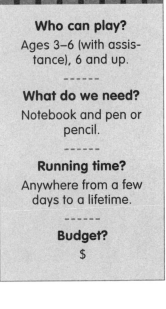

Who can play?
Ages 3–6 (with assistance), 6 and up.

- - - - - -

What do we need?
Notebook and pen or pencil.

- - - - - -

Running time?
Anywhere from a few days to a lifetime.

- - - - - -

Budget?
$

Special Journals

People keep all kinds of special journals, like travel journals, for instance. In food journals, people write about great meals and restaurants and keep recipes. There are nature journals about the natural world. Gardeners keep garden journals, recording garden ideas, lists, sketches of what they've planted, and descriptions of plants they've seen. Some people keep journals that are full of sketches or ideas for stories or projects.

Oh, and you need something to write about! That's the best part; you can write about anything and nothing. Big serious thoughts, silly little thoughts, questions, answers, dreams, disappointments, lists, crazy ideas, descriptions of people or places that interest you, snips of interesting conversations you hear, sayings, words you think are cool, poems, song lyrics—you name it.

Bottom line is, it doesn't matter how you write or what you write—or even if you can write at all! Younger kids can dictate a journal to a parent or older sibling, or try to keep a visual journal made up of drawings or pictures cut out of magazines. The idea is to make a habit of noticing what you see and think and feel and getting it down on paper. You won't know what kinds of things you like to write about until you get writing. So giddyup!

Writing Prompts

Sometimes you'd like to write in your journal, but your mind is blank, and so is the page in front of you. Here are a few ways to get started when your pen is stuck.

Make a list about anything—favorite books, movies, television stars. Or even pet peeves. Give yourself a number to aim for—20, 30, or even 100.

Engage in a back-and-forth dialogue with yourself about something. Look at the pros and cons of a subject— piano lessons, homework, having a bath.

Cluster. Put a single word in the middle of a page and let other words and thoughts literally branch off from there. You don't need to write in complete sentences or phrases, and you don't need to write on the lines of the page. Just write whatever other words pop in your head. This is what some people call free association.

Think about the last dream you can remember having. Try to note any details you can recall images, colors, people in the dream. See if you can make any sense of the dream once you're looking at all the details together.

Adaptation

We've all played the game, "If this book were a movie, who would play the lead?" How about going a little further and asking questions like, "If this book were a movie, where would it begin?" Or "If this poem were a song, what would it sound like?" Adapting a story in one form to another—that's a palooza of a different color!

What's the Palooza?

Take a story told in one form and retell it in another. Sometimes a great big epic story can be retold in the few carefully chosen words of a song. Or in no words at all, but in the form of a dance. You can transform a fairy tale into a play, a play into a poem, a poem into a painting—the possibilities of adaptation are endless.

Think of a piece you know well and try to imagine all the ways you might explore the characters. For example, we all know that poem "There Was an Old Lady Who Swallowed a Fly." What if it was a story, with dialogue and characters interacting? If you wrote it as a story, whose point of view would you use? What if you told the story from the fly's perspective? He's bound to be annoyed at his predicament. And what if the Old Lady was telling her own story? She probably has a bit of explaining to do about why, exactly, she swallowed the fly, don't you think? Imagine the Old Lady at her therapist's office trying to get to the heart of her fly-eating problem. What if the fly is recounting his traumatic experience to his therapist?

Start by looking carefully at your original story form to figure out your new form. Do you want to write a tell-all tabloid newspaper exposé (headline: "Old Lady on Fly-Eating Rampage!")? If you were the reporter covering the incident, you'd have to spell out all the important things—who, what where, when, how—right up

---

Who can play?
Ages 6 and up.

What do we need?
The book, movie, song, or poem you want to adapt.

Running time?
From an hour or two to a week or more.

Budget?
Free.

adaptation (ad-ap-ta-shun), n.: 1. Something that is changed to become suitable to a new or special application or situation. 2. A composition that has been recast into a new form: *The play is an adaptation of a short novel.*

front. How would that telling be different from the original poem?

Perhaps you want to make up a modern dance that works itself into an escalating frenzy as each animal is swallowed? How would you choreograph the move-

There Was an Old Lady Who Swallowed a Fly

There was an old lady who swallowed a fly.
I don't know why she swallowed a fly. Perhaps she'll die!
There was an old lady who swallowed a spider,
That wriggled and wiggled and jiggled inside her.
She swallowed the spider to catch the fly;
I don't know why she swallowed a fly. Perhaps she'll die!
There was an old lady who swallowed a bird.
How absurd to swallow a bird!
She swallowed the bird to catch the spider;
She swallowed the spider to catch the fly;
I don't know why she swallowed a fly. Perhaps she'll die!
There was an old lady who swallowed a cat;
Fancy that, to swallow a cat!
She swallowed the cat to catch the bird;
She swallowed the bird to catch the spider;
She swallowed the spider to catch the fly;
I don't know why she swallowed a fly. Perhaps she'll die!
There was an old lady that swallowed a dog;
What a hog, to swallow a dog!
She swallowed the dog to catch the cat;
She swallowed the cat to catch the bird;
She swallowed the bird to catch the spider;
She swallowed the spider to catch the fly;
I don't know why she swallowed a fly. Perhaps she'll die!
There was an old lady who swallowed a cow.
I don't know how she swallowed a cow.
She swallowed the cow to catch the dog;
She swallowed the dog to catch the cat;
She swallowed the cat to catch the bird;
She swallowed the bird to catch the spider;
She swallowed the spider to catch the fly;
I don't know why she swallowed a fly. Perhaps she'll die!
There was an old lady who swallowed a horse ...
She's dead, of course!

ments of the Old Lady? What about the fly, the spider, the bird, the cat, the dog, the goat, and the horse? And how would you choreograph the dramatic ending?

How might you turn this story into a mystery? Or a play? Or a comic book? Or a rap song? What if you dispense with the fly entirely and have the old lady swallow something else, as she does in the *I Know an Old Lady Who Swallowed a Pie* by Alison Jackson and *There Was an Old Lady Who Swallowed a Trout!* by Terri Sloat?

With a little bit of creativity you can have a great time making something familiar into something new and exciting—and *yours*.

Extrapalooza

Scholars estimate that there are more than 700 versions of the story of Cinderella, which has been adapted in Turkish, African, Egyptian, and Native American cultures, to name a few, and in forms ranging from the traditional written/illustrated fairy tale to paintings to opera (Rossini's *La Cenerentola*) to ballet (Prokofiev's *Cinderella*) to the Rodgers and Hammerstein television musical. There is a plethora of film versions, from the 1950 animated Disney film, to Leslie Caron in *The Glass Slipper*, to the nutty 1960 Jerry Lewis version called *Cinderfella*, to Drew Barrymore's you-go-girl *Ever After*.

Choose three or four versions and compare and contrast them.

Crossword

As writer Norman Mailer once said about his daily *New York Times* crossword puzzle habit, "You have to understand, this is how I comb my brain every morning." Exactly. A crossword puzzle is a wonderful, horrible compulsion that is as much about clearing your head as it is about immersing your head in the language. "Doing the puzzle" is a habit you wouldn't mind seeing your child develop . . . and this palooza lets him create one himself.

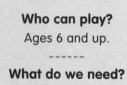

Who can play?
Ages 6 and up.

What do we need?
Graph paper, pencil, ruler, dictionary, thesaurus.

Running time?
An hour or two.

Budget?
$

What's the Palooza?

Build your own crossword puzzle for someone else to solve. The idea is to create a numbered set of word clues, the answers to which are written by the solver in corresponding numbered boxes on a crossword grid. When you're solving a puzzle, you start with the clues to get to the word answers. When you're constructing a puzzle, you start with the word answers, and then invent the clues. With something like three million words in the English language at our disposal, we have plenty of words to work with!

Start your puzzle constructing by keeping it simple, until you get used to the arrangement of theme words, black squares, and other words, as well as the revising you will often have to do when you find you've boxed yourself in with combinations that don't work. To get started:

Make a grid. Working with a pencil and eraser, start by taking a sheet of graph paper and marking off a square grid of at least 9 x 9 squares (12 x 12 squares would give you a little more room to work; most newspaper puzzles are 15 x 15 squares).

Choose a theme. Next decide on the theme of your puzzle, which determines the longer words or phrases that are the foundation of your puzzle. Themes can be anything from holidays, sports, movies, technology, history, science—you name it. After you choose a theme, come up with your theme words. Let's say your theme is the fourth of July. Your theme words could be *fireworks*, *flag*, *patriot*, and *picnic*. Rough out the location of the theme words in the grid, trying to balance your spacing to leave room for your other words.

Mark in the black squares. The black squares on a puzzle may look random, but they're actually supposed to be diagonally symmetrical, which means if you rotated the grid 180 degrees, the squares would be in exactly the same place they were before you rotated it. For example, if you have a vertical line of three black squares in the upper right corner of the grid, there must be a vertical line of three black squares in the lower left corner of the grid. Every pattern of black squares must be symmetrical in this way.

You may have to fiddle with your squares as you construct your puzzle—if you have created words and black square combinations that are impossible to fill (a four-letter word that begins with X and ends with Z), you'll need to erase and reconfigure. That is, of course, while maintaining the symmetry of your black squares! Don't go overboard on the black squares; most crossword puzzle publishers don't like more than about one-sixth of the grid to be black squares.

Fill in the words. Now to fill in the rest of the puzzle with the rest of your words. These can be ordinary words or abbreviations, phrases or proper names, and come from anywhere, from people or places, animals or astronomy, geography or geology, mythology or math. You can use a dictionary or thesaurus or any one of a number of terrific word books to help you choose great words for your puzzle. Here are a few important rules to keep in mind when choosing words:

Do not use two-letter words, and keep three-letter words to a minimum.

enigmatologist (e-nig-muh-tah-lo-jist), n.: Someone who makes or solves enigmas, or puzzles and riddles. *The New York Times* crossword puzzle editor Will Shortz is the only person in the world to have earned a university degree in enigmatology.

Symmetry (si-me-tree), n.: The exact correspondence of form on opposite sides of a dividing line or plane.

All words must be verifiable in standard references such as a dictionary, an encyclopedia, or an almanac. The exception to this rule is any wordplay or puns you may use for your theme words, which won't be found in references.

Avoid really crazy, old words that are no longer in common usage (like the ones people always try to get away with using when playing Scrabble!).

Write your clues. Here's the part that separates the easy puzzle from the harder one to solve. Create clues from things you know—books you're reading, cartoons or foods you like, sports, things you're studying at school. Challenging puzzles have a mix of clue styles, including:

Traditional—very straight, clear clues; for example, "Chevrolet" for CAR.

Tricky—Clever and a little mind-bending (but fun!); for example, "Between the streets" for BLOCK.

Proper names—For example, "George and George W." for BUSHES.

Fill-ins—Simple fill-in-the-blanks; for example, "The Cat _____ Hat" for INTHE.

Theme clues—For a Christmas-themed puzzle, "Santa wins the Series in 4!" for CHIMNEYSWEEP.

Number your grid and clues. When you've got all your words and squares in place, and all your clues written, working horizontally from the top of the puzzle, consecutively number the letter squares that begin any Across or Down word. Then create your Across list of clues by consecutively numbering each Across clue to correspond with each Across word on the grid. Create your Down list of clues by numbering each Down clue to correspond with each Down word.

Make the unsolved puzzle. Now take out a fresh sheet of

graph paper, mark off your grid, copy all your black squares from your solved puzzle, copy all your numbers onto the blank letter squares, and write your Across and Down clue lists below. Now you've got a crossword puzzle!

Extrapalooza

The Blue Period

Create a puzzle that is a 100 percent theme puzzle. Let's say your theme is Blue. First, create a word bank of things that are blue or other words for blue: *Ink, berries, sky, jeans, ocean, birds, Smurfs, lapis, azure, aqua, turquoise,* etc. Build your puzzle around these words, with perhaps one really tricky theme phrase and clue at the heart of it: "Miles Davis hit record" for KINDOF-BLUE. You can create a holiday theme puzzle this way (all Halloween words, for instance) or even a custom birthday puzzle, with all words and clues related to a certain someone (her favorite food, how old she is, birth month, her favorite book, and so on), then have everyone at her birthday party solve the puzzle. Professional crossword puzzle constructor Gayle Dean once created a puzzle that had no Es in any of the words *or* clues. Since E is the most common letter in the English language, this was no small feat!

Syzygy, inexorable, pancreatic, phantasmagoria—*anyone who can use those four words in one sentence will never have to do manual labor.*

—W. P. Kinsella

Stranger Stories

This palooza is all about wild imagining—inventing a character and his story, preferably with someone to help spin your yarn.

What's the Palooza?

Use the phone book as a starting point for creating characters and telling tales. Open it up to a random page and start looking for a name that strikes your fancy. I open to the Ks and find a name I like: Kovacs. Under "Kovacs" I find a bunch of interesting prospects for first names. There's Betty Kovacs. She sounds like she might be a quiet middle-aged bank teller with a secret penchant for Harley-Davidsons. Or there's Lubo Kovacs. He came to America from Slovakia in the 1980s to make his fortune as a hairdresser. There's also Magda Kovacs. She's probably Lubo's sister, who followed him to the States a year later to help him run his tiny beauty shop in Brooklyn.

Once you decide on the name of the character you want to invent, close the phone book and just start asking yourself questions about your character—and then answering with your imagination. What does he look like? Is he tall and dark or short and fair? Is he hearty and athletic or slight and bookish? What is his personality like? Is he good-natured or moody? Is he friendly and outgoing, or does he keep to himself? What does he do for a living? What's the name of his business? Where does he live? What is his house or apartment like? What is his neighborhood like? Who are his neighbors? Where does he come from? Does he have a family of his own? If so, who are they? Does he have friends? Who are they? What was his childhood like? Does he have any hobbies? Does he have any secrets?

You can write down your questions and answers, to keep track of the details that are emerging. Or you can just let them come to life inside your head. Or even more fun is inventing a character out loud with a friend, where you work together to come up with the details of your character's life. Before long, you will have sketched out a character portrait of a person you've created completely from your imagination.

Now what? You can write down his story, just for fun. You can invent things that he does or that happen to him and create an ongoing tale about your character. You can draw a picture of this person you've invented. You can introduce him to other characters you've invented (see Extrapalooza below) and see what happens.

All this palooza takes is a minute or two with a telephone book and your lively imagination. Once you've invented a character, you can take him with you in your head wherever you go, adding details and backstory and new events. He's not quite an imaginary friend; he's more like a very interesting imaginary acquaintance.

Extrapaloozas

Character Journal

A writer friend of mine who's particularly good at this keeps a Character Journal, where he files away all the great names and personality profiles and life stories he has invented. He's written pages and pages about some of these characters, and the very best, most interesting often turn up in the short stories he writes!

Your Character Journal can consist of anything you want: a running list of the great names you come across when thumbing through the phone book; full portraits (words and pictures) of the favorite characters you've invented. You can even make your Character Journal scrapbooky, including pictures snipped from magazines of products your character uses or clothes he might wear.

It's fun to go back and read what you wrote about a character long after you invented him. Because you spent so much time imagining him and in such great

detail, it's almost like looking at old photos of people you used to know.

Ivan, Meet Wendy

Choose two names from the telephone book, invent their personalities and stories, and then create a story about how they meet. On a bus. In line at the Post Office. Stuck on an elevator during a power outage. In the dairy aisle at the grocery store. What happens after they meet? Do they become friends? Do they dislike each other? Is there some coincidence of their meeting that changes either of their lives? If each of the characters you invent are interesting enough, the circumstances and outcome of their meeting can be a great story all by itself.

music
paloozas

Found Sound

I've often marveled over how one person's noise is another's music—and vice versa. Aren't our ears strange and wonderful accessories? This palooza is quite flexible because it can be done off and on over any period for as long as it seems fun

Who can play?
All ages.

What do we need?
Portable tape recorder, tape, conductor's baton (feather duster, ruler, pencil).

Running time?
As long as it takes.

Budget?
$

What's the Palooza?

Create a composition of interesting sounds you collect in your everyday life. John Cage's infamous 1952 composition, "4´33´´", called for four minutes and thirty-three seconds of silence to be filled by whatever random sounds were heard in the concert hall each night: coughs, rustling, sneezes. Considered rather radical at the time, the first performance was held in Woodstock, New York, at the Maverick Concert Hall.

Okay, silence as music might be hard to imagine. But Cage also used rubber mallets, metal hammers, toy pianos, and wooden objects. So point your tape recorder toward a toilet flushing, hanging pots and pans, a fan, or the washing machine—be a maestro and create a musical composition, à la John Cage. Set sound free!

Record various sounds, exploring all over the house, in nooks and crannies. Living room sounds. Kitchen sounds. Bathroom sounds (oops, excuse me!). Take the activity outside to record in the backyard, at the park, in train stations, at stores—as many places as you can.

Try to avoid the obvious "musical" objects. Instead of the telephone's ring, record the dial tone or a busy signal. Rather than a doorbell, try the click of the bolt lock.

Now listen to all the found sounds you've collected, picking and choosing favorites to use in a composition. Decide what order you want the sounds to be in, maybe jotting them down on a piece of paper: clanging pots, dripping faucet, whistle, vacuum cleaner. (A younger child can dictate a composition to an adult.) You might want to think about whether there's a scale of some kind, perhaps from lowest-pitch to highest-pitch sounds. Go back and rerecord them in the particular order that you like best.

Arrange a concert hall with the tape recorder positioned on a pedestal, a podium perhaps in front, and chairs for the "live" audience—whether it's the family, the family pet, or a collection of action figures. Make a sign with the name of the auditorium and a program listing the composer (that's you!), the "instruments," and the date. Naming the composition is half the fun: Concerto for Blender and Bathtub? Sonata in Six Spoons Sharp? Of course, you must "conduct" as the tape plays, and then take a modest bow!

My favorite music is the music I haven't yet heard. I don't hear the music I write. I write in order to hear the music I haven't yet heard.

—John Cage
(1912–1992)

Name Your Score

Use this delicious list of musical terms for found sound opuses (or is that opi?).

Adagio	Etude	Minuet	Presto
Allegro	Forte	Musette	Quadrille
Andante	Fugue	Nocturne	Rigaudon
Canon	Galliard	Nonet	Rondo
Cantabile	Gavotte	Obbligato	Scherzo
Cantata	Glissando	Octet	Serenade
Capriccio	Grandioso	Oratorio	Sonata
Cavatina	Grave	Ostinato	Sonatina
Concerto	Grazioso	Partita	Staccato
Courante	Impromptu	Piano	Tessitura
Da capo	Intermezzo	Pizzicato	Tremolo
Energico	Legato	Portamento	Trill
Espressivo	Madrigal	Prelude	Vivace

Extrapaloozas

Radio Days

Create a radio play based on found sounds. Think of old-timey radio shows and how amusing they were. Or tune in to Garrison Keillor's NPR radio program for inspiration in how to use sound effects to great comic effect. Then brainstorm characters and a plot to connect to the sounds. For example, the sound of a rubber ball bouncing on pavement might inspire a story about a heavy-footed ballerina. A recording of rifling through a toolbox? Maybe that's the sound of a chain gang.

Guessing Game

Take turns recording found sounds and guessing what they are. The challenge is to find ten sounds within a time limit of five minutes. This of course will involve a lot of sneaking around so that the guessers don't see what the recorders are recording. It could even turn into a sort of found-sound hide-and-seek.

A Sound Library

If you're not up to composing, you can create a set of sounds just for listening and dreaming. They could be grouped according to feelings they evoke: happy sounds, angry sounds, funny sounds. Or maybe sounds equal colors: blue sounds, orange sounds, purple sounds.

You can even collect sounds just for the fun of collecting, as cool as any collection of baseball cards or bugs. Dad, I found the best sound today!

Air Guitar Star

Roll over, Jimi Hendrix. Anyone can play "Rock Me, Baby" with an air guitar. It's all about improvisation. Give yourself over to the music and let your imagination take you where you want to go. There, on stage, in front of a hundred thousand screaming fans.

What's the Palooza?

Turn up the volume, crank up your imaginary amp, and step onto the stage with your air guitar. As any experienced air guitarist will tell you, if you're really hearing the music the way it is meant to be heard, letting loose with an air guitar is practically an involuntary reflex The idea is to let go of your inhibitions and get into the groove. Be the rock star you were meant to be, if for no other audience than yourself.

Old-school air guitarists say the art is best approached holistically: it's a way to experience the music physically and emotionally, and not with your ears alone. When dancing without a partner became acceptable (thank heaven for rock and roll!) air guitar evolved naturally as a way to dance solo. It's a thoroughly gratifying way to express yourself by yourself. Think of Tom Cruise's virtuoso, career-making performance of "Old Time Rock & Roll" in *Risky Business*. The idea is to move in rhythm with the music. By imitating guitar playing, you pay homage to the guitar hero or guitar music you're grooving to. So who needs a dance partner when you've got an air guitar?

Dress like your favorite rock star, or invent your own fantasy rock-star look. Go extreme and spike your hair with gel. Paint it with a blue streak. Add hair extensions or wear a wig. Or opt for a more mellow look à la John Mayer or Eric Clapton. Put on worn and faded denim jeans and a T-shirt that has seen better days. Jerry Gar-

Who can play?
Ages 6 and up.

What do we need?
CD player and CDs. Jeans, T-shirt, temporary tattoos, arm bands, bracelets, other rock star–inspired jewelry, and whatever hair accoutrements complete the look (headbands, extensions, wigs, dreadlocks, braids, gel, temporary color, mousse, etc.). Full-length mirror. A little privacy.

Running time?
Fifteen minutes to choose a song and choreograph some good moves; years of practice to truly master the art.

Budget?
$

bottleneck (bot-tel-nek), n.: A style of guitar playing in which an object is passed across the strings to achieve a gliding sound.

cia always wore a black T-shirt, but any T-shirt will do. You could "rock up" an old T-shirt (with permission) by decorating it with a permanent marker or safety pins, or cutting out the neck ribbing or cutting off the sleeves and sewing them back on with lanyard. Whatever look you choose, make it suit your choice of music.

Listen to the songs of some of the all-time great rock guitarists for inspiration. Santana. Clapton. Van Halen. Ry Cooder. Ask family and friends who their favorite guitarists are and borrow CDs from their personal collections for an air guitar foray. Most artists' riffs can also be sampled for free on amazon.com. Or choose an artist or song you already know and love and just start working your magic. Your right hand (if you're a righty) picks at the strings fast or slow, depending on the riffs. Your left hand moves up and down the fret board. Go high on the fret board for low notes; low on the fret board for that high-pitched guitar bravado sound.

Things to keep in mind while playing air guitar include the complexity of the moves—chord changes, finger picking, speed and dexterity on your imaginary fret board but also your stage presence, artistic expression, and the audience's reaction to your performance. Imagine the stage. Is it a football stadium or Radio City? Or are you rocking it out in a small club? Have some signature moves and give the audience what they want. Chuck Berry always did the low hop-on-one-leg move when he played "Johnny B. Goode." Jimi Hendrix played "Foxy Lady" with his teeth. Don't hold back.

Air guitar postures and moves to try:

Air guitar in both hands, stand with feet apart. Lean forward slightly. Head rolls around and around or shakes from side to side.

Step over your air guitar, bending at the knees in a slight lunge. Play air guitar between your legs.

Stand on one foot with the other leg raised; play your air guitar under your raised leg.

Air guitar in hands, get on your knees with knees spread apart, toes curled under supporting part of your weight and your pelvis tipped slightly forward. Bite bottom lip, squint eyes, and play.

Bottleneck à la Duane Allman. Slide your left hand up and down the fret board. Look down at your guitar with intensity. Try this while listening to "Blue Sky" or "Whipping Post."

Boogie like Keith Richards. Gyrate hips, bop, shake head up and down while playing air guitar to "Satisfaction."

Rock and soul like Lenny Kravitz. Hold the fret board perpendicular to the front of your body and then play along your side.

If air guitar is feeling so right to you, maybe you should go out and get a real guitar and learn to play it.

Extrapalooza

Air Guitar Garage Band

When you know you're good—really top-of-the-bill, headliner good—get more than one air guitar aficionado in on the act and form an air guitar garage band. Choose a song and let everyone pick an instrument bass, rhythm and lead guitar, drums, keyboard, and so on. Somebody gets to be the front man and strut like Mick Jagger. Keep the improvisation going for at least one whole song. Videotape your act. Or photograph your air guitar band in concert and send it out with the family holiday card.

Great Air Guitar Jams

"Wipe Out," Surfaris

"Wild Thing," the Troggs

"Johnny B. Goode," Chuck Berry

"Taking Care of Business," Bachman-Turner Overdrive

"Layla," Derek and the Dominoes (Eric Clapton)

"Black Magic Woman," Santana

"Smoke on the Water," Deep Purple

"Soul Serenade," Derek Trucks

"Freebird," Lynyrd Skynyrd

"Pinball Wizard," The Who

"That'll Be the Day," Buddy Holly

One-Man Band

Who hasn't stopped on a city sidewalk in slack-jawed awe of a one-man band? This palooza lets you be your own band. And a one-man band is as much fun to make as it is to be.

Who can play?
All ages, with supervision.

What do we need?
All or some of the following, depending on the instrument: rubber bands, small noise-making items (buttons, corn kernels, beads, and so on), paper, scissors, fishing line, tissue boxes, oatmeal cartons, coffee and soup cans, balloons, pie tins, a hammer and nails (for use by parents and older children with supervision), string, a broomstick, small silver bells, shoe boxes.

Running time?
A couple of hours to create the one-man band; individual instruments can be made in less than an hour.

Budget?
$

What's the Palooza?

Create a one-man band à la Dick Van Dyke in *Mary Poppins*. Build instruments using objects that are guaranteed to make noise. Mix and match items to produce unusual-sounding instruments. Then put them all on and make a joyful noise.

Ankle and Wrist Bells

For this one you'll need: a few pieces of string and some small jangly bells (or anything that makes a comparable noise and can be threaded onto string).

Thread the string through the eye of each bell, securing it in place by tying a knot around each eye.

Place the string around your wrist and get someone to tie the two ends together.

Shake, rattle, and roll.

Knee Cymbals

For this one you'll need: two sauce pot covers (about 8 inches in diameter) and string.

Tie a string around or through the pot cover handles.

Place a cover on the inside of one knee, and tie the string snugly around your leg, like a cowboy's leathers. Do the same on the other knee.

Knock knees together. People from miles around will show up for dinner.

Cacophonic Broomstick

For this one you'll need: one broomstick, a hammer and very thin 2-inch nails, a rubber stop (the kind you put on the bottom of stool legs), metal bottle caps, bells, keys, metal spoons, string or tape.

Attach the rubber stop to the bottom of the broomstick. (This protects the floor.)

Using the hammer and nail, parents and older children with supervision make holes in the center of all the bottle caps. Make sure the holes are large enough to allow the caps to slide up and down the nail. Put three or four bottle caps on each nail, and then hammer the nails into various parts of the broomstick. Leave room on the top of the broomstick for your hand.

Attach the keys, spoons, and any other noisy objects to various parts of the broom using string or tape. Knock the stick against the floor, bandleader style.

Shoe Box Guitar

For this one you'll need: a shoe box, ruler, and 5 or 6 rubber bands.

Place the rubber bands around the width of the shoe box, making sure that they are fairly taut.

Insert a ruler between the rubber bands and the back of the shoe box, creating the "neck of the guitar."

Pluck and strum the bands to create different sounds.

Extrapalooza

Invent an Ear-Opening Instrument

Music for Homemade Instruments is an ensemble of classically trained musicians who invent, compose for, and perform on musical instruments made from found objects. The group plays mupejas (multiple peanut butter jars), legimbas (table leg marimbas), and fork wind chimes. Invent, build, and name your own instrument using tennis rackets, broiler pans, or whatever.

Figaro! Figaro!

This palooza celebrates opera singing, whether we know an aria from an arioso or not.

What's the Palooza?

Sing like a diva or basso profundo in the comfort of your own home or shower (shower acoustics are hard to beat!). People can go a whole lifetime without exploring opera because they think it's difficult or highfalutin. Actually, opera is just a marriage of words and music, telling what is usually a pretty simple story. Many of the great operas were written in Italian or German, so you might think, "Oh, well, I can't understand what they're saying or singing, so it's not for me." But it is! Just give yourself a chance to listen to a little bit of some of these operas. I guarantee that you will be helplessly attracted to the music.

Listen to some kid-friendly opera recordings for inspiration. Two worthy compilations to seek out are Pavarotti's *Opera Made Easy: My Favourite Opera for Children* (Polygram), which includes pieces from *Hansel and Gretel* and *Madame Butterfly*, among others, and *The Classical Child at the Opera* (Classical Child), which includes translations (happy day!) of works from *Carmen*, *The Magic Flute*, and others.

Both of these compilations include a personal favorite of mine, "Largo al factotum," Figaro's merry aria from act I, scene 1, of Rossini's *The Barber of Seville*. In fact, Figaro's cheerful lauding of his own many talents is a perennially appealing introduction to opera for anyone. Even if you think you don't know a thing about opera, chances are you've seen Bugs Bunny as maestro conducting a much-put-upon baritone in "Long-Haired Hare" or "The Rabbit of Seville." So you see, you actually know more than you think about opera. And now that you know the name of the tune you've probably heard a hundred times thanks to Cartoon Network, find a Rossini recording of it and sing along.

Familiarizing yourself with some of the actual operatic favorites is half the fun. But whether you adapt some famous opera tunes or compose variations all your own, this palooza wants you to sing out loud, and with brio.

Figaro!

Listen to a recording of "Largo al factotum," the aria from *The Barber of Seville*, as Figaro, the barber, sings one morning about how good life is for him, the best barber in the town. The libretto (the words to the opera) is available online at www.aria-database.com, so turn up the music and try to sing along with the good parts: "Figaro, Figaro, Figaro, Figaro, Figaro, Figaro, Figaro, Figaro, Figaro, Figaro!" Think of Figaro mimicking his clients as they call out to him for help with matchmaking or a really close shave. Once you know the tempo and tune, sing, "Figaro," or other familiar parts of the aria (La la la la la la la la!) in your best deep baritone. Once sung and listened to a few times, parts of *Barber* are quite memorable, so don't be surprised to be humming it to yourself and singing it when you least expect. Sing in Italian: *"Ah, che bel vivere, che bel piacere (che bel piacere) per un barbiere di qualita!"* Or sing in English. Listen to the translation recording available on *The Classical Child at the Opera* and give it your best shot.

Linguini!

Anything that can be said can be sung. Take an everyday occurrence or even a wonderful word, such as *linguini* or *lasagna,* and turn it into an opera you sing to yourself or along with someone else: Oh, mother! What is for dinner? Linguini! Linguini!

After school, perhaps a little something to the tune of "Summertime," from George Gershwin's opera *Porgy and Bess*:

Homework time!

And the math it ain't easy.

Opera Lingo

Aria: Italian for "air"; a melody sung solo or as a duet in an opera.

Arioso: With intense feeling; as a noun, a short aria.

Bravo: Italian word exclaimed by an audience at the end of a dazzling aria or performance.

Diva: A female opera star; sometimes suggests a temperamental or demanding female singer.

Libretto: Italian for "little book." The words of an opera or dramatic musical, including both sung and spoken parts.

Maestro: Italian for "master." A title given out of courtesy to a skilled musician, conductor, or music teacher.

Got my spelling, and my reading to do!

Oh, Mrs. [teacher's name here]'s all right.

But there's no extra credit.

So hush, little baby, don't you cry.

And remember to warm up. A young friend and a member of the Metropolitan Opera Children's Chorus works out his voice daily. He suggests the following breathing exercises to keep the pipes in good order:

While sitting, take your arms from your sides, raise them parallel above your head, and breathe in, filling your lungs. Then slowly lower your arms, deflating your lungs in a steady whistling release of air. As your arms move down, keep count with your foot or by snapping with one of your hands. This should improve your ability to stretch out breath evenly for a long period of time.

While standing, place your hands six inches away from your head, as though cupping your ears, but without actually touching them. Starting at a low note, perhaps

Operas in This Palooza

La Bohème. Composer, Giacomo Puccini. Libretto in Italian by Giuseppe Giacosa and Luigi Illica. First performed in 1896.

Carmen. Composer, Georges Bizet. Libretto in French by Henri Meilhac and Ludovic Halevy. First performed in 1875.

Hansel and Gretel. Composer, Engelbert Humperdinck. Libretto in German by Adelheid Wette. First performed in 1893.

Porgy and Bess. Composer, George Gershwin. Libretto in English by DuBose Heyward. First performed in 1935.

The Barber of Seville. Composer, Gioachino Rossini. Libretto in Italian by Cesare Sterbini. First performed in 1816.

The Magic Flute. Composer, Wolfgang Amadeus Mozart. Libretto in German by Emanuel Schikaneder. First performed in 1791.

Madame Butterfly. Composer, Giacomo Puccini. Libretto in Italian by Giuseppe Giacosa and Luigi Illica. First performed in 1904.

E, for example, sing an open vowel ("oooooooooooh") while swiveling your wrists forward and back; then move up the scale, continuing the rocking motion. This enhances your ability to project your voice.

And always, when singing, send a steady flow of breath. Then while sustaining the flow of breath, send the voice along with the breath. And finally, as his favorite instructor at the Metropolitan Opera Children's Chorus always says, "Smile when you sing, darn it!"

Extrapalooza

Sing the Stories

Retell a famous opera story (see sidebar) in your own words in song. Sing in third person a synopsis of the story. Or choose a particular scene to act out and sing from a particular character's point of view. Pretend you are Tamino, the young hero in *The Magic Flute*, rapt by the beauty of Pamina, and singing a love song to her though you've never even met. Or maybe you're the witch in *Hansel and Gretel*, tempting the children with song to get them into the candy house. Be *The Mikado's* Yum-Yum, admiring her own beauty ("Yes, I am indeed beautiful"), as she readies herself to marry Nanki-Poo. Listen to a recording of the opera you choose for inspiration. Use tunes you like from the original composition, or make up your own melody. Bravo!

Good Book

Check out *Sing Me a Story: The Metropolitan Opera's Book of Opera Stories for Children*, by Jane Rosenberg and with an Introduction by Luciano Pavarotti. This beautiful book retells the stories of fifteen popular operas, including *The Barber of Seville*, *La Bohème*, *Carmen*, *The Magic Flute*, and *Porgy and Bess*, among others.

Rounds

Singing in the round means the melody can go on and on and on. One of my favorites is "Great Tom Is Cast."

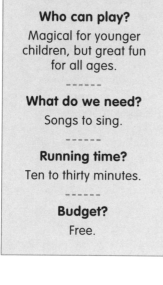
What's the Palooza?

Celebrate rounds. Sing them often and with flair just you and another person or in groups. It's an art that's been around since Shakespeare's day and has never lost its appeal.

To sing in a round, one singer or group begins to sing a song, such as "Are You Sleeping" ("Frère Jacques"). So a first singer begins, "Are you sleeping, are you sleeping," and then once a certain point in the melody is reached, in this case the second "Are you sleeping," the first singer is joined by a second singer or group, who starts at the beginning of the song. When this second group reaches the same point in the melody, a third group begins to sing, and so on until all the singing parts have come into the song. When the end of the song is reached, the first singer begins the song again without missing a beat and is followed by the second and third groups in the same manner as before. Usually, there's an agreed-upon number of repetitions to sing before the first singer stops, or the singing of rounds can go on and on and on. And that's the fun of it.

Before introducing a round, sing the song through once or twice so the singers all know the words and tune. But for three or more parts entering a round, the leader not only helps to get each part started on time, he also signals when the singers should stop singing.

Learning how to hold your part (not be distracted or overwhelmed by the other singers) can be tricky. Lightly plug your ears for the first two or three times to help you not fall in with the others' words and tune. But once you get the hang of it, and especially once you get to hear the harmony that results in even the simplest of rounds, you'll be hooked. Singing in rounds is a great palooza for two or more individuals or groups, large or small. Vary nighttime lullaby singing with rounds. Sing holiday songs as rounds. Sing rounds in the car; backseaters are one group and frontseaters are the second group. For more information and resources related to singing rounds, see www.roundsing.org.

Some Favorite Rounds

I LOVE THE FLOWERS

I love the flowers, I love the daffodils.
I love the mountains, I love the rolling hills.
I love the fireside when all the lights are low.
Boom-de-ah-da, boom-de-ah-da, boom-de-ah-da, oh-oh.

KOOKABURRA

Kookaburra sits in the old gum tree,
Merry, merry king of the bush is he,
Laugh, koo-ka-bur-ra laugh, koo-ka-bur-ra,
Gay your life must be!

O HOW LOVELY IS THE EVENING

O how lovely is the evening, is the evening
When the bells are sweetly ringing, sweetly ringing,
Ding, dong, ding, dong, ding, dong.

DAY IS DONE (TAPS)

Day is done, gone the sun
From the lake, from the hills, from the sky.
All is well, safely rest,
God is nigh.

ARE YOU SLEEPING? (*FRÈRE JACQUES*)

Are you sleeping, are you sleeping,
Frè-re Jac-ques, Frè-re Jac-ques,
Brother John, Brother John?
Dor-mez vous, dor-mez vous?
Morning bells are ringing, morning bells are ringing,
Son-nez les ma-ti-nes, son-nez les ma-ti nes,
Ding, ding, dong, ding, ding, dong.
Din, din, don, din, din, don.

Extrapalooza

Your Turn

Write your own round to the tune of a round song you already know. How about something like this, to the tune of "Three Blind Mice":

There's no milk.
There's no milk.
No Pops, no Smacks, no Flakes.
No Pops, no Smacks, no Flakes.
Mom's asleep and there's nothing to eat.
Mom's asleep and there's nothing to eat.
And there's no milk.

Or take a song you know from the radio and try to turn it into a round. If it has a simple, even melody and a standard verse structure, it's begging to be a round.

Can You Kazoo?

I love the kazoo. You don't need to know how to read music or play a fancy instrument. All It requires is a little joy in your heart—and maybe a little ham on your bones.

What's the Palooza?

Become a virtuoso kazoomer—with little or no training! There's no instrument in the world that is more a reflection of the true you than the kazoo. That's because there are no notes to play; any sound you make is the result of your own particular brand of humming. Take careful note of these few basics and then begin experimenting with all kinds of music—pop, rock, jazz, even classical.

Hold it. There are three basic positions in which you can hold your kazoo. First, hold the kazoo horizontally in front of you, top end up (that's the side with the circular piece that causes the vibration), large open end in your mouth, small open end facing out. (These open ends are called "bells.") This position gives the loudest sound and the most buzz. You can also play the kazoo with the small bell in your mouth to achieve a quieter sound that is closest to your natural humming.

Finally, you can play through the vibrating hole, almost in the manner of a harmonica. This is a little known position that produces a mellow, sometimes haunting sound. Try it with both bells open, with the small bell covered tightly with the palm of your hand, or with the large bell covered with your hand.

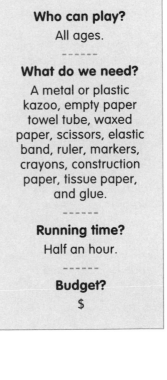

Who can play?
All ages.

What do we need?
A metal or plastic kazoo, empty paper towel tube, waxed paper, scissors, elastic band, ruler, markers, crayons, construction paper, tissue paper, and glue.

Running time?
Half an hour.

Budget?
$

Hum it. If you think about it, regular humming is like a song trapped inside your closed mouth—hum a little tune and feel the vibration of your throat while you hum. Kazoo humming comes from the same vibration of your throat, but requires your mouth to be open a little to let your breath vibrate against the membrane inside your kazoo. So your humming, combined with the little bit of air your open mouth emits, makes your kazoo do!

Hone it. Now try these little instrumental flourishes that'll make you kazoo like a pro. First, you can produce a muted sound by partially blocking the open bell with your hand. Cup your hand over the open bell and fiddle with more and less muted sounds, much like the "wah-wah" of a muted trumpet.

You can also totally block the bell with a swift motion of your hand to stop the music completely. And you can create a vibrato sound by jiggling the skin at your throat in front of your voicebox while you play the kazoo. This is a very distinctive sound, to be used very selectively.

Play. Now you're ready to play! Remember, anywhere your voice can take you, your kazoo can take you further. Any song at all, from "Twinkle, Twinkle Little Star" to an aria from *La Traviata*, is fair game for the kazoo. Practice on some simple songs and then move on to more challenging tunes. Experiment with the three different positions playing the same song. Look for ways to bring in your flourishes for dramatic effect. Develop a signature kazoo tune, one that is so uniquely interpreted and performed, no one will forget it. And keep your kazoo handy; it can be a pocket-sized bit of sunshine on a gloomy day.

Extrapalooza

Kitchen Kazoo

Make your own kazoo. Decorate an empty paper towel tube using markers or crayons or by gluing bits of colored construction paper and/or tissue paper to get a tubular collage effect. Make it look as spectacular as it's going to sound. Cut a five-inch circle of waxed paper, place it over one end of the tube, fold down the edges, and secure with an elastic band. Like any kazoo, all you have to do is hum into the open end of the tube to let the music fly.

What we play is life.

—Louis Armstrong
(1901–1971)

dance
paloozas

Body Parts

It doesn't matter who is a Balanchine and who has two left feet; this dance is all about freedom of movement and improvisation. By exploring rhythm and tempo through isolated body parts, anyone is a dancer and choreographer.

What's the Palooza?

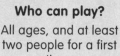

Who can play?
All ages, and at least two people for a first time.

- - - - - -

What do we need?
An open space, a CD or tape player, and music of your choice.

- - - - - -

Running time?
Play a quick round, or bop till you drop.

- - - - - -

Budget?
$

Get your whole body moving one glorious body part at a time. For first-time body-parts dancers, it's helpful to have a leader, perhaps an older sibling, who can call out the body-parts directions and demonstrate the movements for everyone else to follow. Once everyone gets into the groove, rotate leaders or let the dancers do their own thing. Keeping eyes closed during the dance allows everybody to move without inhibition.

First, set the scene. A clear and open space is necessary for body-parts dancing—really any room where there is nothing sharp to bump into and the furniture can be moved against the walls. Turn off the lights or use dim, colored bulbs for a more artistic atmosphere.

Next, pick some music. If you're bursting with energy, turn on oldies rock or contemporary pop. If everyone's mellow, Herbie Hancock is a favorite for body-parts dancing. Look for strong percussion recordings or, for a truly rousing and joyful experience, try body-parts dancing to Prince's "Rainbow Children."

Dancers need to stay more than an arm's length away from anyone or anything. Start in stillness, with everyone standing as tall and motionless as possible, listening to the music, and feeling relaxed. After a few moments, the leader calls the first body part (usually the head), and everyone follows by moving his or her head in any way and keeping all other body parts still. After a period of time, the leader calls the next body part, and dancers keep moving the head and add the second body part. This continues until the whole body is moving. Sequencing the body parts from top to bottom is a good way to make sure everything has been called: head, shoulders, elbows, hands, fingers, back, belly, hips, knees, ankles, feet, and finally toes.

When the leader shouts "Freeze," the dancers isolate and move two or three body parts at once. If everyone's eyes are open, the leader can instruct the group to mimic one person's movements. If the pace of the music changes, the leader can call a slow-motion or fast-paced dance.

To end, play some slow music and have the leader call various body parts to slow down and stop, one at a time, until the room is still.

Extrapaloozas

High-Low

For anyone who may be shy about moving, adapt the dance by calling out only "high," "middle," or "low." The leader calls and demonstrates either a high, middle, or low-level shape—from a high stretch to a low crouch and all points in between—and the other dancers respond by making their own shape at the designated

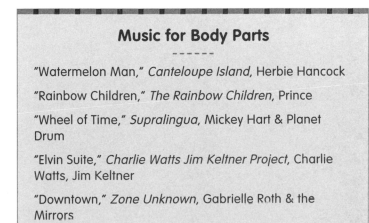

Music for Body Parts

"Watermelon Man," *Canteloupe Island*, Herbie Hancock

"Rainbow Children," *The Rainbow Children*, Prince

"Wheel of Time," *Supralingua*, Mickey Hart & Planet Drum

"Elvin Suite," *Charlie Watts Jim Keltner Project*, Charlie Watts, Jim Keltner

"Downtown," *Zone Unknown*, Gabrielle Roth & the Mirrors

level. High-low dancing can be an icebreaker/warmup, and as soon as everyone feels comfortable, begin the body-parts dance as described above.

Body Partners

When all body parts have been called, dancers continue to move around the room while using the whole body. The leader then tells everyone to find a partner. The partners do not necessarily have to dance together, as in a ballroom dance. They can mirror each other, dance back-to-back, or even find another couple to dance with. When the leader calls "Switch," everyone changes partners. Do this until everyone has partnered with every other person in the group.

Sounds

Encourage the body-parts dancers to make a circle and add sounds! Each person makes an audible contribution, until there is a singing, shouting, laughing, clapping, stomping, shaking, wiggling symphony.

Isadorables

Shoes and tutus are not allowed. This palooza is inspired by modern dance pioneer Isadora Duncan, and like her courageous and revolutionary work, it's all about self-expression, moving unfettered, and letting the body communicate thoughts and feelings.

What's the Palooza?

Kick off the shoes and socks, loosen up the pony-tails, and dance, Isadora Duncan–style, in the living room or backyard, imitating the natural, free-flowing movements of the mother of modern dance. Isadora Duncan shocked early-twentieth-century audiences when she rejected the rigidity of classical ballet and instead championed dance that harkened back to the classical Greek arts and folk dancing. She incorporated vigorous skipping, running, jumping, and leaping into her choreography, and is known for advocating movement that is continuous, natural, and free.

Wearing loose-fitting clothes and bare feet, choose music from any one of the composers Isadora Duncan preferred—Schubert, Strauss, Chopin, or Brahms, for example. Play the musical selection through once just for listening and to get the feel of the piece. Put the music on a second time and dance, taking into consideration the kinds of ideas Duncan promoted in her dancing. For first-time modern dancers, you may want to call out the following Isadora-inspired instructions:

Lift from your chest. Duncan's choreography emphasized the torso and solar plexus.

Breathe freely. Breathe like an ocean wave ebbs and flows.

Extend your arms to their fullest potential. Stretch. Reach.

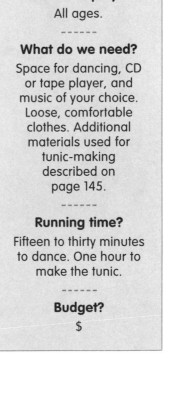

Who can play?
All ages.

What do we need?
Space for dancing, CD or tape player, and music of your choice. Loose, comfortable clothes. Additional materials used for tunic-making described on page 145.

Running time?
Fifteen to thirty minutes to dance. One hour to make the tunic.

Budget?
$

Look up at the stars.

Think about the natural force of gravity. Use the ground and floor.

Your body can express thoughts and feelings. How does the music make you feel? What does it make you think?

Incorporate any or all of the following in an Isadorable dance:

Skipping
Running
Kneeling
Reclining
Falling
Rising
Walking
Jumping

Add specific emotions or actions to your dance:

Passing an imaginary gift to someone
Accepting an imaginary gift from someone
Embracing the moon
Kicking off shackles
Lifting boulders
Tossing a ball
Catching a ball
Gazing at stars
Seeking shelter from a storm
Laughing in the rain

The Original Isadorables

Isadora Duncan established dance schools in Germany, Paris, and Russia, and was committed to teaching her philosophy of dance and life. Duncan adopted six of her most devoted students, giving them the Duncan name. They became known around the world as "The Isadorables," and through them the Duncan legacy was passed on to new generations.

Rolling down a hill
Crossing a stream by stepping stones
Feeling the breeze in the air
A tree swaying in the wind
An eagle soaring

Use these dance expressions you've created to choreograph your own Isadora-inspired dance. And then name your piece!

Extrapalooza

Make a Tunic

Isadora Duncan eschewed lavish scenery and costumes. For dancing, she made her own tunics, reminiscent of those seen in classical Greek sculptures. Children can make their own tunics out of large adult-sized white T-shirts, tying flowing scarves loosely about the waist.

The more ambitious Isadorable can make a simple tunic using inexpensive fabric, about three yards, thirty-six inches wide. Duncan dancers often wore silk tunics, but any light, gauzy material will do. Cut the fabric in half and tack the two pieces (one and a half yards each) together at the shoulders, leaving an open slit for the head. Cut the tunic from the bottom to the desired length for the dancer. Sew the two side seams, leaving plenty of room on the arms for movement and open slits at the bottom.

Wrap a generous length of elastic or gauzy ribbon around you, just under your chest, from front to back. Crisscross the chest, wrap around the back, around to the front again, and tie. (It's a kind of Helen of Troy look.) Sew bits of fabric or silk scarves at the shoulders for an even more ethereal effect. Frolic away.

Music for Duncan Dancing

"On the Beautiful Blue Danube," Johann Strauss

Mazurka Opus 68, No. 2, Frederic Chopin

"Ave Maria," Franz Schubert

Symphony No. 9 in C Major, "The Great C Major Symphony," Franz Schubert

Hungarian Dance No. 5 in G Major, Johannes Brahms, or any Brahms waltzes

---

Isadora Duncan's Signature Pieces

Blue Danube
Dance of the Furies
Mother
Revolutionary

---

solar plexus (so-lar plex-us), n.: A point on the upper abdomen just where the ribs separate.

Walk Like an Egyptian

This palooza looks at walking as something more than how you get from place to place. In fact, a walk can be a dance all its own. So taking a cue from Groucho Marx, via Marty Feldman and Aerosmith, "Walk this way. . . . "

What's the Palooza?

Make up an original way of walking. People's walks are almost as distinctive as their fingerprints. Think about how much memorable detail there is in the way some folks walk: A lumbering Frankenstein. A cheerfully ambling Bugs Bunny. A swaggering Ace Ventura, Pet Detective. The way to begin to choreograph a new walk is to choose something or someone to imitate. A robot. A rooster. Your nutty, nervous Aunt Susie.

This isn't mimicking; it's isolating distinct features of a walk and copying them with just the slightest exaggeration. Think of it as a physical, live-action caricature. Start with something obvious. For instance, walk like someone teetering on a high wire. Your steps are very tentative, and the rest of your body is shifting back and forth to help you keep your balance. Walk all the way down to the (imaginary) end of the tightrope and walk back and forth until you're so convincing you could probably get a job with the circus.

Can you weave this tightrope walk together with your regular movements? Take a few normal steps, then break into your tightrope walk for several steps, then fall back into your regular gait. Now you've got yourself a walk!

Explore a variety of physical states or conditions—walk as if you are a person with a long torso or a large behind, with a cane, in high heels on a subway grate, barefoot on hot coals, with gum on the bottom of your shoes, carrying a heavy sack of potatoes, on stilts, up stairs, down stairs, through mud up to your knees. Once you get started doing funny walks you might have to add another—walk like a person who can't stop laughing.

Introduce music, and your walks become even more dancelike. Look for recordings that inspire ways to walk "The Baby Elephant Walk" or "The Pink Panther." Do secret-agent walks to the theme from *Mission Impossible* or *Johnny English*. Brazilian music for salsa walks or "Girl from Ipanema" walks. Cowboy walk to Roy Rogers singing "Don't Fence Me In." Saunter like a model on a catwalk to a current pop tune. Walk like an Egyptian to (what else?) "Walk Like an Egyptian" by the Bangles—or to "King Tut" by Steve Martin. You get the idea. Make a party mix of your favorite make-a-walk tunes for your next big bash. And see how quickly a distinctive walk can become a dance step.

Few people know how to take a walk. The qualifications are endurance, plain clothes, old shoes, an eye for nature, good humor, vast curiosity, good speech, good silence and nothing too much.

—Ralph Waldo Emerson
(1803–1882)

The Ministry of Silly Walks

The Monty Python comedy team worked to come up with new ideas for sketches in Graham Chapman's house, which looked out over a very steep hill. During a conversation about how many different government departments seemed to be springing up, John Cleese noticed a man walking up the hill. From where Cleese sat, this man appeared to be leaning backward with his body at a 90-degree angle to the ground. The conversation about the government and the fascination with the odd walk merged into the sketch known as "The Ministry of Silly Walks," which was first seen in episode 14 of *Monty Python's Flying Circus*. The skit featured John Cleese (the minister) interviewing a candidate for government funding to further develop his silly walk. This sketch is one for which Cleese became famous and led to years of people asking him to "do the silly walk." Check out his silly walks at http://guardian.curtin.edu.au/cga/art/tv.html.

gait (gait), n.: A particular way or manner of moving on foot.

Extrapalooza

Cakewalk

Popular among slaves on southern plantations in the 1850s, chalk-line walks involved walking a straight line made of chalk while balancing a bucket of water on your head. Over time, the chalk-line walk evolved into a dance called the cakewalk, where the "walkers" would prance around, poking fun at white high society by exaggerating their dignified walks and low bows, with their canes and high hats and their elegant ballroom dances. On Sundays there might be a contest among the slaves for the best walk; the prize for the winner would be a piece of cake. (Hence the expression, "That takes the cake!" as well as "It's a cakewalk," meaning very easy.) By the 1890s, the cakewalk was a wildly popular dance of high-stepping and kicking, with many variations, but always at its heart a joyous mimicking of high society. Do your own version of a cakewalk. Walk tall with a book or a pillow on your head, like a king or queen at a royal affair. Add some high steps. Take a grand turn. What if the queen were to break into a leap?

AKA the Cakewalk (and Other Dances That Followed in Its Footsteps)

Bunny Hug	Horse Trot
Buzzard Lope	The Itch
Camel Walk	Kangaroo Dip
Crab Step	Lame Duck
Eagle Rock	The Squat
Fanny Bump	The Tangle
Fish Walk	Texas Rag
Funky Butt	Turkey Trot
Grizzly Bear	

Tango Fandango

Find a partner and step to the beat—no rose between the teeth required! The family that dances together has a lot of fun.

What's the Palooza?

Teach yourself to tango! There are many different versions of tango—the Argentine tango, Ballroom tango, International tango, and Show tango. Learn an American tango step in this palooza. Once you have the basics down, you may want to continue your tango foray—adding *adornos* (embellishments) as you become more skilled. Even if you only learn enough to toss the basic tango walk into a regular dance sequence, you'll be the life of the dance party wherever you go.

The essence of any tango is in the rhythm, so practice hearing the rhythm before you start in on the actual steps. Choose music with a slow, steady beat. The slow beat allows dancers to concentrate on the corresponding steps more easily.

Start by counting out a rhythm without music ONE two THREE four, ONE two THREE four. The ONE and THREE beats are the upbeats, and where you place the most emphasis. Now sit and listen to the music and count off the beats. This gives you the rhythm that goes with the steps. Once everybody's got the beat, move on to the first step.

The basic tango step is simply a walk. Begin by standing and listening to the music, counting the beats, and stressing the first and third beats. Now, starting

Who can play?
Ages 6 and up.

- - - - - -

What do we need?
Space and music.

- - - - - -

Running time?
An afternoon or an evening.

- - - - - -

Budget?
$

The tango is a direct expression of something that poets have often tried to state in words: that a fight may be a celebration.

—Jorge Luis Borges (1899–1986)

with either foot, step in place and in time to the music on the first upbeat. Once you're comfortable with this and you're stepping to the beat, start moving forward with each step. Continue walking around the room, stepping only on the upbeats. Practice backward and forward until you are comfortable with the movement.

As the saying goes, "It takes two to tango." So choose a partner and stand face-to-face. The leader (usually the man, but whoever wants to lead should!) puts his right arm around the small of his partner's back. The partner's left arm is placed on the leader's right arm, at about the bicep. Clasp your other hands together and lean in close to your partner. Beginners may want to stand about a foot apart so as to be able to watch their own feet and not step on the feet of their partner. But once the steps are down, tango pros like a close embrace.

In the basic five-step American, the leader walks starting with the left foot, while his partner mirrors his movements and travels backward. The leader's steps are: step 1 (left foot), step 2 (right foot), step 3 (left foot), step 4 to the side while still moving forward (right foot), and step 5 bring feet together. The partner begins with her right foot and moves backward. The partner steps are: step 1 (right foot), step 2 (left foot), step 3 (right foot), step 4 side and still moving backward (left foot), and step 5 feet together. When you've finished the movement, repeat the whole sequence.

Ready for the tricky part? In the tango, you do these five steps in four counts of music. So the breakdown of the rhythm and steps is slow step, slow step, quick step, quick step, slow step bringing feet together. Practice the move first without any music. You can say "slow-slow-quick-quick-slow" as you do the steps to help you remember how the rhythm works as you move your feet. As dance teachers always say, anything you can say, you can do.

Now turn on the music and listen for the upbeats. They're easy to hear in tango music. Start your first step on an upbeat. If you don't get on the beat right away, don't worry. Keep dancing. There's always a next measure in the song and another opportunity to get onto the beat. Once you're comfortable with this, improvise by

Tango Lingo

You don't have to know Spanish to dance the tango, but knowing some of these terms will make you sound more like a *tanguero*.

Adornos: Embellishments.

Arrastre: To drag, i.e., to drag your partner's foot with your own.

Barrida: A sweeping motion, i.e., sweeping your partner's foot with your own.

Boleo: A quick flick of the lower leg on a turn or figure eight.

Cadena: Chain.

Caminar: To walk.

Cruzada: Crossing one foot in front or in back of the other.

Enganche: Hooking or wrapping your leg around your partner's leg.

Enrosque: Corkscrew.

Gancho: Hook; i.e., to hook your leg up and around the inside of your partner's.

Giro: a turn.

Lapiz: Pencil; a circular figure executed with a nearly upright foot drawing on the floor.

Media vuelta: Half-turn.

Milonga: An event where people go to dance tango.

Mordida: To bite; one person's foot is sandwiched between the other partner's feet.

Ochos: Eights; figure eights.

Parada: A stop.

Pasos: Steps.

Patada: A kick.

Resolucion: An ending to a basic pattern.

Salida: First steps of dancing tango; the beginning of a pattern.

Sentada: A sitting move; the woman sits on her partner's bent leg.

changing the length of your steps (the longer the step, the more dramatic) and circling around the edge of the room with your partner.

Finally, add a bit of flourish. The real cha-cha of the tango is in the *adornos*, the embellishments and gestures that make every tango dancer's expression unique. Watch tango in the movies, and you see the *adornos* in an instant—*golpes*, little toe taps that can come at the end of a step sequence, or *rondes*, little circles drawn on the floor with the toe of your shoe. In *gancho*, literally translated "the hook," the partner quickly hooks her leg up and around the inside of the

Learn the basics as well as more elaborate tango moves with books like *Quickstart to Tango*, by Jeff Allen, or *Tango Argentino* by Paul Bottomer. See also *Tango: The Dance, the Song, the Story*, edited by Simon Collier, to get a full-flavor introduction to the history, beauty, and mystery of the tango. Videos worth seeing include Cal Pozo's *Learn to Dance in Minutes—Tango Passion* (Parade) or *The Tango Fundamentals Volume 1: Basic Elements*, starring and directed by tango impresario Fabián Salas.

leader's leg. And lastly, try the *sentada*—which you've surely seen in a movie or cartoon—where the partner ends up sitting on the leader's bent leg.

Extrapalooza

Make a Night of It

Have Argentina Night, now that you've got the tango down. Women typically wear dresses that flow, adding a dramatic flair to the movements. Take a large, fringed scarf, fold it in half into a triangle, and wrap it around your waist so the point of the triangle hangs down one side of your body. Rich, deep colors add to the mood of the dance. Make paella for dinner and serve kid-friendly sangria. When dinner is over, turn on the stereo, put a rose (sans thorns!) between your teeth, and start to tango.

Tango at the Movies

There are tastes of tango in movies ranging from *True Lies* (Twentieth-Century Fox), Evita (Disney), *Scent of a Woman* (Universal), *Frida* (Buena Vista Home Video), and *Murder on the Orient Express* (Paramount) to the amazing and inimitable Rudolph Valentino in *Blood and Sand* (Kino Video), a silent black-and-white film that is worth the watch. Actor Robert Duvall is a passionate tango dancer whose love of the form led him to produce and star in *Assassination Tango*, a suspense story loaded with tango.

Warning! When you rent these movies, cue up to the tango scenes in advance for family viewing—all are R-rated except for *Evita* and *Murder on the Orient Express*, which are rated PG.

Hulapalooza

Inspired by the grace and beauty of Hawaiian hula, this palooza is about storytelling through gestures and facial expression.

What's the Palooza?

Use your face, hands, and body to tell a story the hula way. Ancient Polynesians used hula as a way to communicate long before it became the dance we associate with ukulele-style Hawaiian luaus. In ancient times, in fact, there was no real musical accompaniment to hula; it was originally performed with chanting to communicate prayers, love songs, and praise for the land. The hula itself was a language. And because the aim of hula was to tell a story, not dance to a beat, the eye movements, facial expressions, and gestures are more elaborate and more important to the dance than any of the other elements of hula.

The basic foot movement in hula is simply to take a small step to the right and slide your left foot over to meet your right foot. Then take a small step to the left and slide your right foot over. With each step, lean gently in the direction you are moving, sort of like a palm tree swaying in the breeze. Keep your knees soft and bent. Rather than lifting each foot to move it to the side, you can also slide your feet together on this swaying step. Try stepping from side to side now while also gently rotating your hips around in a circle. Try stepping around in a very small circle, at the same time gently rotating your hips. Then point one foot forward and bring it back. Point the other foot forward and bring it back. Dance in your bare feet, smoothly, without any jumping or jerky movements.

The basic arm movement should also be done smoothly and without any jerks and jumps. Hold your right arm out to the side, palms facing down. Your left

Who can play?
All ages.

What do we need?
Hawaiian music, green drawstring garbage bag, scissors, colored tissue paper, needle, thread.

Running time?
An hour.

Budget?
$

hand is held to your left hip with fingers facing down. Bend your arm slightly, keeping your wrists and hands somewhat loose. Dip your fingers in a downward motion, followed by your wrists and then your arms, so that, in effect, you are emulating the motion of a wave. Then draw your elbow in closer to your body and repeat the flowing movements of fingers, wrists, and arms. Draw your arms in even closer to your chest and repeat the waving motions. Repeat the same movements with your left arm, placing your right hand on your right hip, fingers down. Practice these swaying, undulating arm movements until there's a relaxed, easy feeling to the motions.

The more interesting moves in hula are the pictorial gestures you make with your fingers, hands, arms, head, and face to communicate a message or story. Here are some simple movements to include in your hula dance:

Meaning	Movement or Gesture
Love	Cross your arms gently in front of your chest as if in an embrace; tilt your head slightly to the right and close your eyes.
Sun	Raise your arms and hold them in a circle over your head; big smile.
House	Put your fingertips together, elbows somewhat lowered; your arms suggest the two sides of a roof at a slight angle.
Sing	Hold your mouth open in a circle and, with your palms facing you, gesture charmingly with your hands to suggest that song is pouring forth out of your mouth. Close your eyes.
Rainbow	Place your palms together on your left side. Lift your right hand and, making an arching rainbow shape with it, move it back to your right side.
Tides	Roll your hands over each other repeatedly to suggest a rolling sea.

Hula Tunes

Even though music was not authentic to ancient hula traditions, it is an important part of modern Hawaiian customs and hula practice. Much of contemporary Hawaiian popular music is suitable for hula dancing, with lyrics that just beg for interpretation. Look for Don Ho's classic *Tiny Bubbles* (Collector's Choice) or *Hawaiian Favorites* (Brentwood). Nearly all of the songs on Elvis Presley's *Blue Hawaii* (RCA), from "Rock-a-Hula Baby," to "Hawaiian Sunsets," to "Aloha Oe" are crying out to be hula-ed to.

Luau

When you've got your hula moves down, have a little luau. Serve small skewers of pineapple chunks and cubes of ham, macadamia nuts, decorated sugar cookies made using tropical-shaped cookie cutters (palm tree, dolphin, hula dancer, and so on), and fruity beverages in colorful plastic cups with those little paper umbrellas you can get at a party store. Wear Hawaiian shirts and flip-flops. Have a hula contest. Play hula charades or island-themed Pictionary or Pass the Coconut (a variation on Wonder Ball).

Meaning	Movement or Gesture
Remember	Your right hand with first finger gently pointing up rests on your right cheek; meet your right elbow with the fingertips of your left hand.
Island	Make a circle with both arms lowered, fingertips gently touching, and raise the circle slightly to the right side. A proud look on your face, as this is your home.
Me	Use both hands to gesture toward yourself. Eyes open.
Wind	Hold your left arm forward, hand outstretched, and circle your right arm twice around your head.
Palm trees	Use your left arm as the land. Make swaying movements with your right hand and fingers to suggest swaying palms.

Make up an easy story that incorporates these movements. Add new movements that you make up yourself. Make up gestures for words like *baby, mother, father, you, ocean, sky, earth, running, walking, talking*. Pretend you are an elder telling a story to the village children about

hula (hoo-la), n.: A flowing Hawaiian native dance with intricate arm movements that tell a story in pantomime, usually danced to rhythmic drumming and chanting.

luau (lu-au), n.: A Hawaiian feast, usually with music and entertainment.

ukulele (u-ku-le-le), n.: An instrument similar to a small guitar with four strings, associated with Hawaiian music.

fishing on the island. Or pretend you are describing a volcanic eruption to your neighbors. How would you depict emotions in hula, such as fear, anger, happiness, sadness, or surprise? Keep the moves smooth, and let one flow into the next gracefully.

Extrapalooza

Lei and Grass Skirt

Make a grass skirt and a lei, or flower necklace, to enhance your hula-dancing pleasure. Use a green plastic garbage bag with drawstring closure for the skirt. Trim the bottom seam off of the bag and cut the body of the bag into thin vertical strips to create the strands of the grass skirt. Tighten the drawstring around your waist to fit. Make a lei using colored tissue paper. Crumple small sheets of tissue paper to form balls or "flowers," then sew the flowers together with a needle and thread to form a necklace.

Once Upon a Ballet

A great story or fantastic piece of music almost always turns into a performance in my head. I was thrilled by the opportunity Christopher Wheeldon presented to bring Camille Saint-Saëns's *Carnival of the Animals* to the stage. What better way to express its fairy-tale quality than in a ballet? A ballet tells a story without words, and that's just one of the things we get at in this palooza.

What's the Palooza?

Create a ballet. Use a familiar story or fairy tale or make up a story of your own to perform. And don't worry about not being a Baryshnikov if you happen to be cast in a principal role—I put on ballet slippers for the first time in my life for *Carnival*, at age fifty-seven.

If you don't already know which story or poem you want to adapt, look for one that doesn't have too many characters, unless you're up for a pretty big directing job. Most often, simple familiar stories are the best choices, as they can be easily expressed without words. Consider fairy tales like "Goldilocks and the Three Bears," "Hansel and Gretel," or "The Three Billy Goats Gruff." Or a picture-book classic such as Maurice Sendak's *Where the Wild Things Are* or any of Eric Carle's wonderful books.

Or stage a portion of a larger story. Harry Potter fans might choreograph a Quidditch match to Tchaikovsky. You might also make a scary ballet out of a witch scene

---

Who can play?

All ages to perform; 6 and up to write, choreograph, and direct.

What do we need?

Homemade props, costumes, and sets. Basic materials might include old fabric scraps and bedsheets, cardboard (its uses are endless), glue and scissors, paint and paintbrushes, hair and stage makeup, accessories, paper and markers, and Post-its for tickets.

Running time?

Four or five hours from start to finish.

Budget?

$

Visual Dictionary of Ballet Steps

The American Ballet Theatre has an online dictionary with videos of its dancers executing various ballet movements. Find it at www.abt.org/education /dictionary/index.html. Use this site to prepare for your ballet class.

Good Books

For visual instruction on basic ballet steps, see Liese Friedman's *First Lessons in Ballet* and The Royal Academy of Dancing's *Step by Step Ballet*.

from *Macbeth* or *The Wizard of Oz*. The idea is to choose a story you want to tell or a scene you want to play out and set it to music in the form of a ballet.

Choosing a cast is easy: enlist anyone and everyone who wants to join, including younger kids and adults. You can assign the parts, but ask all cast members for their ideas, and maybe even let them choreograph their own solos. Sometimes the best ideas for a piece come from the dancers simply playing together during "rehearsal." Ask friends who suffer from stage fright to be prop masters, costume designers, and set builders. Including everyone in the set and costume-making process is a great way to get things done easily and quickly.

Once the story and cast are set, write an outline or short script for your piece. How do you envision the opening scene? Goldilocks frolics solo on the stage? Is the beginning an elaborate wild rumpus, such as a scene in the jungle, or does it start out quiet and mysterious—a scowling Max putting on his pajamas and going to bed without his supper? What does the denouement or final resolution scene look like? If there are only three or four dancers, everyone gets to be a principal and a member of the corps de ballet. Stage a "Dance of the Trees" for your "Goldilocks and the Three Bears" ballet. Stage a "Dance of the Birds" scene for when the bread crumbs get gobbled up on the forest path in "Hansel and Gretel."

Once you have your plan, find music to go along with the story. It certainly doesn't have to be classical, though this type of music does lend itself to the ballet.

Mix it up by surprising the audience with a quick rock and roll interlude in the middle of your "Cinderella," for instance. Choreographer Twyla Tharp is known for mixing musical styles this way to clever effect.

Incorporate traditional ballet moves if you dare, or better yet, break with convention and invent your own steps. A great part of the fun of this palooza might be in learning a smidgeon of ballet's distinctive vocabulary, whether anyone in the house has ever attended a ballet class or performance or not. Goldilock's three bears or Macbeth's three witches should, of course, perform a *pas de trois*, or dance for three. Max, in *Where the Wild Things Are*, performs *pas seul*, or a solo dance, before the wild things enter the stage to wreak havoc. A *pas de chat,* or "step of the cat," is hard to resist trying, whether you really know how to do the step or not. Modify choreography and steps to everyone's abilities. Ballet is an art form anyone can *pretend* to execute, especially in the privacy of their own living room. Participants will enjoy the creation of the ballet almost as much as the performance of it.

Once the ballet is nearly ready for performance, set a date and time to put on your ballet, and advertise. Have everyone make flyers and hand them out to friends and family. Bring a table outside and set up a mini box office on the lawn or sidewalk, encouraging passing neighbors to come experience your tour de force. Ask a family member to videotape the performance so you have a record of your new masterpiece—it might become a classic in your repertoire.

Music for Ballet

Eine Kleine Nachtmusik, Mozart

The Four Seasons, Vivaldi

Brandenburg Concerto No. 3 in G Major, Bach

Water Music Suite, Handel

The Sleeping Beauty, Tchaikovsky

"Chit-chat Polka," Strauss

"Stars and Stripes Forever," Sousa

Favorite Classics of Ballet for Ballet Class, Dmitri Roudnev (Vox)

Famous Ballet Music, Berliner Philharmoniker (Polygram)

The Language of Ballet

Ballerina: Female dancer who performs a company's leading classical roles.

Balletomane: A ballet lover.

Corps de ballet: Members of a company who usually dance as a group. Like the chorus in musical theater.

Danseur noble: Male dancer with a noble style.

Glissade: A sliding step in any direction.

Jeté: A jump from one foot to the other.

Port de bras: Carriage of the arms.

Terre à terre: Ground to ground; a dance with few jumps.

Tour en l'air: A turn in the air.

Tutu: Ballet skirt.

Extrapalooza

Teach Each Other Ballet

Have everyone in the cast go out on their own and learn one step from a parent, friend, a book, or online. Gather for a class where you teach each other the steps you learned. Play music for your class (Dmitri Roudnev's *Favorite Classics of Ballet for Ballet Class* has some wonderful selections.) After you've mastered all the steps, try to invent combinations to use in your ballet.

Ballet Mime

Dancers in classical ballets use mime to express the story to the audience. The vocabulary of standard gestures used by ballet dancers throughout the world dates back a few hundred years. Incorporate as many of the following traditional gestures in your own ballet as the story allows. Then invent some gestures of your own!

Love: Cross your hands over your heart.

Anger: Shake your fists in the air.

Beauty: Make a circle around your face with your hand.

Death/dying: With clenched fists, cross your arms in front of your body.

Hear: Hold your hand behind your ear as if trying to hear.

Seeing: Place one hand by your eye, pointing to it.

Thinking/remembering: Touch your temple with your index finger.

You, he, or she: Gesture toward the other person with your palm up.

Crying: Trace tears down your face with your index finger.

Stop: Hold up your hand with the palm facing out toward the other person (à la "Stop, in the Name of Love").

Yes: Nod your head up and down.

Hoofin' It

Legendary hoofer Bill "Bojangles" Robinson choreographed routines for some of America's best dancers. He even taught Shirley Temple how to dance up and down a staircase in *The Little Colonel*. But he was also known for being very proprietary about his tap steps. You didn't want to try one of his trademark moves while he was looking. This palooza doesn't undertake anything so flashy as a Bojangles buck-and-wing, but we do take a tip (or tap) or two and learn to love the rhythm of this great American art form.

What's the Palooza?

Tap dance! Discover the countless variations in rhythm you can create with your feet. Tap has always been more about the beat than the melody. Its origins go back to the days when slaves, who were prohibited from drumming on plantations, improvised by tapping out a beat with their feet on wooden floors. Nowadays, dancers like Savion Glover are like rock stars, giving tap dance an astounding and hip new virtuosity all its own.

Number-one piece of advice about tap? Say the steps out loud to yourself as you dance: "Toe, step, toe, step." Any tap teacher will tell you that any step you can say out loud, you can do. It'll help you think clearly about what you're doing and give you a way to control your pace. Think about isolating parts of the feet as you dance and take note of the distinct sounds made by each of the following basic steps:

Toe tap (forward). Tap your right toe in front of you, working from ankle down. Holding your foot in front of

---

Who can play?
Ages 6 and up.

What do we need?
Tap or other shoes suitable for dancing. Sneakers don't work well, but a neighborhood shoe shop can fit simple taps on most any street shoe. Teletone taps are basic, come in a range of sizes for both toe and heel, and can be fitted onto your shoes with screws by a cobbler.

Running time?
A few minutes to try the most basic steps. Hours—even years!—to perfect combinations and speed.

Budget?
$

tempo (tem-po), n.:
The speed at which
a musical
composition or
passage is formed.

juba (ju.ba), n.: A
lively dance
characterized by
hand-clapping and
thigh-slapping,
developed by
plantation slaves in
the American
South.

you, lift and lower to tap your right toe repeatedly.
Bring your right foot back to center and repeat toe taps
on the left.

Toe tap (backward). Lift your right foot and tap your
toe behind you, again working your ankle. Repeat with
the left foot.

Step. Step your foot down in an easy rhythm. Say, for
example, you do a toe tap with your right foot. To make
this a "toe, step," bring your right foot back to center
after completing the toe tap. Steps can be done lighter
and faster if only the ball of the foot is used. Beginners
and very young tappers may be more comfortable using
the whole foot to step a foot back into place.

Try a simple combination. Begin with the right foot
and, alternating right and left, do four toe steps: toe,
step, toe, step, toe, step, toe, step. Add four counts to the
back, doing back toe steps, beginning with the right
foot: toe, step, toe, step, toe, step, toe, step. Keep repeat-
ing the step names as you do them. Note the distinct
sounds of the forward and backward taps. Which is the
softer sound? Do this next time you're waiting in a
checkout line. Smiles all around.

Other steps to try:

Shuffle step. Brush the ball of your foot out in front of
you and then back in, and then step down. Repeat with
your left foot.

Shuffle step, step, step. Shuffle step as above, adding
two steps with alternating feet in between shuffles. This
step is really fun to do when you get up some speed and
can do the "step" on the balls of your feet. Or try "shuffle step, shuffle step, shuffle step, step, step."

Dig. This can be done with either the heel or toe. Stand
with weight on your left foot and "dig" your right toe in
close to your left ankle. Step your right foot back in
place. Repeat with the left foot. A heel dig is the same

idea, only you use your heels to "dig" in close to your standing foot.

Stamp. Make a heavy downbeat on the flat of the foot. You may change weight on a stamp or not. Practice first without changing weight. Stand on your left foot and "stamp" the right foot down hard—like you're stomping a bug—lifting it up immediately.

Music is optional with tap because you make your own music with your feet. But if you want to tap with accompaniment, put on a soundtrack like *Singin' in the Rain* or *42nd Street*. (Steps known as "time steps" in tap are actually called this because vaudeville dancers, unaccustomed to rehearsing with musicians, used to

Tap in the Movies

- - - - - -

These are irresistible dance pairs in irresistible movies where tap is as much a star of the show as the biggest name on the marquee.

An American in Paris, Gene Kelly and Leslie Caron

Carefree, Fred Astaire and Ginger Rogers

The Cotton Club, Maurice and Gregory Hines.

The Little Colonel, Shirley Temple and Bill "Bojangles" Robinson

Royal Wedding, Fred Astaire and Jane Powell

Shall We Dance, Fred Astaire and Ginger Rogers

Singin' in the Rain, Gene Kelly and Debbie Reynolds

Stormy Weather, Bill "Bojangles" Robinson and Lena Horne

Tap, Gregory Hines, Savion Glover, and Sammy Davis, Jr.

Top Hat, Fred Astaire and Ginger Rogers

White Nights, Gregory Hines and Mikhail Baryshnikov

Bojangles, Gregory Hines and Savion Glover

Selected Tap Step Names

Clap step
Comic slide
Cramp roll
Flap
Hoofer steps
Paddle roll
Pull backs
Riff
Roll
Shuffle
Slide
Stamp
Time step
Trill
Wings

. . . and these moves, which probably ought to come with a "Warning" sign!:

Buck-and-Wing
Cincinnati
Maxi Ford
Paddle and Roll
Shim Sham Shimmy
Shuffle Off to Buffalo

begin tapping without accompaniment to signal the tempo for a performance.)

One-upmanship has always been a big part of tap culture. One dancer does a step and another dancer repeats it, but adds his own twist or syncopation to the move. Try a chair tap challenge at the family dinner table. You tap out a rhythm, and the person next to you adds to it. No dessert until you've tapped a beat from your seat.

Extrapalooza

Hat and Cane

Tap using a bowler hat and cane. Even the simplest steps look elegant and refined when you dance with a hat and cane. Hold the cane horizontally in front of you with hands at either end and swing the cane in a big circle (without ever letting go of either hand) and end up in a lunge to one side with the cane in outstretched arms pointing to that same side. Or, hold the cane perpendicular in front of you with one end on the floor. Walk around the cane while holding it in place on the floor without ever showing your back to your audience. Next, hold the cane horizontally in front of you, with hands at either end. Do four forward toe taps while pushing the cane away from your body and back with each step. Do four backward toe taps while lowering the cane to your knees and back up with each step. Now, try to get your hat off your head with your cane without dropping it. Then take an elegant bow.

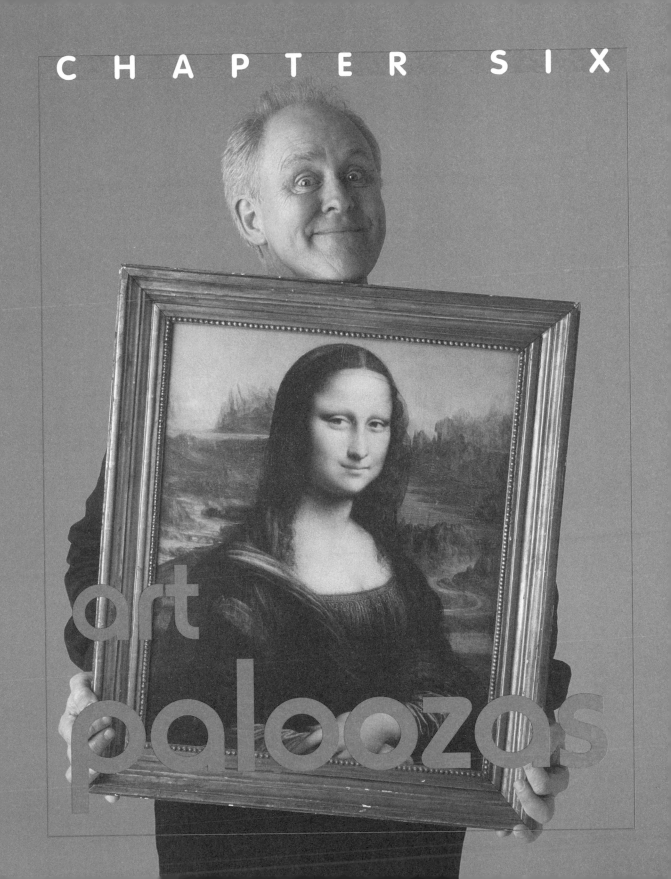

art
paloozas

Pulpture

What I love about this palooza is that it's a sneaky combination of brainstorming, problem-solving, and making art.

What's the Palooza?

Use the news to create an unusual work of art. A work in the Solomon R. Guggenheim Museum in New York City called *Bedspring* is a mixed-media assemblage on wire bedspring created in 1960 by artist Jim Dine. Dine's work is composed of old clothing, bedsprings, crumpled paper, and other trash taken from the city streets. Have a look at *Bedspring* (www.guggenheim collection.org) and try not to want to create an assemblage or sculpture just like it. That's the idea behind Pulpture: create a spontaneous work of art made from newspaper, twine, and tape.

Forget about recycling for a week and save stacks of newspapers for Pulpture. Gather a good-sized stack of papers, several day's or a week's worth if possible, along with masking tape and twine. Clear a workspace in the family room or kitchen, or set up outdoors in the yard or on a patio or driveway in nice weather. Parents give yourselves over to this one, and don't worry about containing the mess, at least initially.

The goal is to create a Pulpture, aka newspaper sculpture, using the paper, twine, and tape in any way you can imagine. Think crumpled paper. Think folded paper. Think paper taped to the twine. Think about how it's possible to tape one piece of crumpled paper to another to create a figure. Or how a Pulpture can hang from twine that is taped or tied to the ceiling or to other household objects. Pulptures can also be mounted with tape onto everyday items such as a garbage can lid, a sled, or a tricycle. Or Pulptures can stand on their own. How might a Pulpture stand up—perhaps folded paper bases and tripod constructions—figuring it out is the most satisfying part of this process.

You can work for hours (or days, if the spirit moves). Have at it for as long as it takes. Make Pulpture animals or human figures. Pulpture buildings. Pulpture forts. Alternatively, use a timer and start a frenzy of Pulpture design and construction. Who can make the tallest Pulpture in five minutes or less?

Name the pulptures (*Reclining Math Teacher, Uncle Jack Walking, All The News That's Fit to Crumple*) and—here's the best part—display the sculptures prominently in your home for a week. Out of respect for the art and artist, of course. Take pictures. Invite the neighbors in for the Pulpture Gallery opening.

Pulp, n.: A magazine, newspaper tabloid or book printed on coarse, low-quality paper made of wood pulp, usually containing shocking stories.

Extrapaloozas

Kitchen Junk Drawer Sculpture

Old keys, batteries, rubber bands, wine corks, and so on are all fair game. Tape the items together to create an

---

Marcel Duchamp

- - - - - - -

Marcel Duchamp is credited with coining the idea of found or "readymade" objects as art when he created *Fountain* in 1917, a piece that consists of a porcelain urinal turned upside down and signed with the pseudonym, "R. Mutt." Duchamp boldly and anonymously entered the urinal in an open art exhibition in New York City sponsored by the Society of Independent Artists, of which he was a member. Duchamp said of the piece at the time, "Whether Mr. Mutt with his own hands made the fountain or not has no importance, he chose it." The society rejected the work for the exhibition, not knowing it had been submitted by Duchamp, and the original piece was subsequently lost. In 1999 a fifth-edition replica of *Fountain*, one of eight made under the supervision of Duchamp himself in 1964, was sold at auction at Sotheby's for $1,762,500. Sotheby's press release quotes the buyer saying he regards *Fountain* to be "the origin of contemporary art."

unusual sculpture. Or, à la Marcel Duchamp (see sidebar) find one item and immortalize it by pronouncing it "art" in and of itself. Mount a key on Styrofoam for posterity. Tape a broccoli band onto an index card and give the piece a highfalutin name. The artist can take a pseudonym, especially if the piece is controversial.

Fridge Sculpture

Zucchinis, carrots, apples, onions, bananas. And what about pineapples? Use toothpicks to stick strawberries or grapes or raisins onto oranges or apples. *Banana Man. Marshmallow Fellow.* Fruiture!

Basement Sculpture

Sweeping Beauty is a broom! Give her duct-tape eyebrows and gardening gloves for hands. Mops, brooms, rubber boots, sleds, and ski poles are all found objects worthy of a work of art or basement sculpture. Use extra twine and tape to tie larger items together. Make a whole family—the Mops, the Yardsticks—out of basement sculptures. Make scary basement sculptures for your lawn on Halloween.

Carton Architecture

An impressive city skyline is within the grasp of even the littlest architect or city planner. With an eye toward architectural form, some artful wrapping, gluing, and drawing, a discarded pasta box becomes the Empire State Building, an egg carton an original and unmistakable new addition to a child's imaginary city vista. Construct cardboard buildings for a city block and see a new skyline take shape on a child's bedroom rug.

What's the Palooza?

Rescue empty cartons of all shapes and sizes from landfill fate to create a funky 3-D metropolis. Look at a photograph of a famous skyline for inspiration. Together, browse through coffee-table books on the world's grandest cities or spread postcards you've saved over the years and choose an image for a model complete with structures of all sizes, shapes, and textures. Or dream up your own distinctive skyline with pointy skyscrapers and majestic towers.

Construct buildings one at a time, or collect eight or nine different empty containers for an all-afternoon architecture extravaganza. No building is impossible to replicate with wrapping paper, tinfoil, and imagination. Wrap a tall spaghetti box in shiny wrapping paper and

Life is chaotic, dangerous, and surprising. Buildings should reflect it.

—Frank Gehry
(1929–)

voilà! a sleek skyscraper. Reproduce the columns on the Coliseum by decorating long paper towel rolls with markers. Secure a tube to your cardboard base at an angle, and there's no mistaking the Leaning Tower of Pisa. Use cartons of different heights and shapes to create unique pieces. Think about what you would build in the World Trade Center site and make a model of it.

A strip of cardboard from a big, sturdy box, decorated to look like a city street or a grassy knoll, can serve as a foundation for the skyline. Before decorating each carton, seal a small rock or weight inside to ensure that each building stands tall and steady in the finished skyline. For tall, narrow cartons such as spaghetti boxes, leave the flaps open on one end so that they can later be securely attached to the foundation. Attach each piece to the cardboard with heavy-duty glue, stand back, and imagine what's going on inside all those buildings.

Extrapaloozas

Home Sweet Home

Look no further than the familiar streets that make your neighborhood a home. A tall, cylinder-shaped oatmeal carton bearing the name of your town or city at the top is an eye-catching miniature version of the local water tower (skip the water). Sketch a brick pattern and windows onto red construction paper and glue to a stout pasta box to create a residential building.

Interior Design

The construction doesn't have to stop outside the boxes. A decorated egg carton can host Broadway's next runaway hit or the summer's biggest blockbuster film—just decorate the "seats" with some fun fabric and sketch a dramatic scene onto a stage or screen to create a theatrical atmosphere. Furnish the inside of an empty shoe box with dollhouse beds, couches, and even carpet samples. Cut out windows in a variety of sizes and shapes and glue "curtains" cut from old clothing.

Thinking Outside the Pasta Box

Look around the house for household objects that inspire great building design. The landmark Chiat/Day Building in Venice, California, designed in 1991 by Frank Gehry, is easily spotted by the larger-than-life binoculars sculpture by Claes Oldenburg flanking the entrance. View the Chiat/Day headquarters and other Gehry projects at www.guggenheim.org/exhibitions/past_exhibitions/gehry/chiatday_07.html. Sketch designs for buildings using household objects—toasters, doorknobs, lamp-shades— as part of the building's facade, form, or design.

Great Skylines to Model Carton-Style

San Francisco
New York
Chicago
Tokyo
Rome
Saint Petersburg
Moscow
Jerusalem
London
Paris
Istanbul

One-of-a-Kind Structures

Flatiron Building (New York): triangular, shaped like an old flatiron

Leaning Tower of Pisa

Lipstick Building (New York): elliptical, like a tube of lipstick

Boat Building (Hartford, Connecticut): two-sided ("elliptic lenticular cylinder," in architect-speak)

Swedish Ice Hotel (Jukkasjaervi, a village a mere 120 miles above the Arctic Circle): a sixty-room (and growing) ice hotel built from scratch each year in December. Book early, rooms melt by May!

Chiat/Day Building (Venice, California): huge binocular sculpture at entrance

Waipio Treehouse (Honakaa, Hawaii): $250-per-night luxury treehouse, twenty-five feet above ground!

The Big Ones

Eiffel Tower (Paris, France): 985 feet tall

Chrysler Building (New York): 77 stories

John Hancock Center (Chicago): 100 stories

Empire State Building (New York): 102 stories

Pyongyang Hotel (Pyongyang, North Korea): 105 stories

Taipei 101 (Taipei, Taiwan): 106 stories

Sears Tower (Chicago): 110 stories

Still Life

The still life, or *nature morte* in French, is part of the great tradition of painting and a genre that almost all artists experiment with at some point. Artists from the great masters to the Impressionist innovators to the Cubists of the early twentieth century were attracted to this form because of its inherent challenge, not just to present beauty in a still life, but to present intelligence or emotion or conflict. That's no easy bowl of apples!

Who can play?
Ages 6 and up.

What do we need?
Paper, crayons, markers, colored pencils or paint, construction paper, pictures of food, flowers, or other interesting objects cut from magazines, newspaper, scissors, glue stick.

Running time?
Half an hour or more.

Budget?
$

What's the Palooza?

Try your hand at the fine art of composing and creating a still life—Cubist style! The term *still life* was coined by the Dutch in the seventeenth century (*stilleven*, meaning motionless aspects of nature). Artists had depicted motionless objects in their work for centuries before, but mostly as decorative features of a larger work, not as the focal point of the work itself. The art of still life flourished in the Netherlands, especially on the subject of flowers. The emphasis in these years and beyond was on realism, where one could almost smell the fruit or flower, it was painted so true to life.

Fast forward two hundred years or so, when early-twentieth century modern artists like Pablo Picasso, Georges Braque, and Juan Gris looked at still life through Cubists' eyes. A Cubist isn't from Cuba (!), he's an artist who steps back from a realistic observation of what he sees and reinterprets it in terms of broad shapes and exaggerated or simplified forms. Where a realistic still life is rich with depth and true color, a Cubist still life is composed of flat shapes that slide into each other. A Cubist looks at a subject, breaks it up, and reassembles it in an abstracted form. The Cubists also sometimes pulled fragments of words, newsprint, musical notes, and other materials into their work, to further challenge and explore the notion of still life. Go to http://www.artlex.com/ArtLex/s/stilllife/1851-1900.html to look at still lifes by the Cubists Picasso, Braque, and Gris.

How to create a Cubist still life? As with all still life, it starts with composition. This means you need to compose or orchestrate the elements of the still life you want to create. Start by thinking about what object or combination of objects you'd like to depict. Classic components include fruit, flowers, bowls, pitchers, and musical instruments. You can think along those lines, or you can think outside of the still-life box. How about pencils, keys, a sneaker, an eggbeater, barbecue tongs, a baseball, or your lucky rock? Look for things with interesting or unlikely shapes or purposes, or that work in unusual combination with each other.

Now think about color. A bright green Granny Smith apple might be more fun than a serious dark red McIntosh, at least to start with. How about that golden orange #2 pencil or a pale pink ballet slipper? And these objects and colors against what background will you place them? A subtle, distinct color or a bold, purposeful textured color? And will your objects be on a table or a box or some other platform?

Arrange your objects. Try arranging them grouped close together, perhaps one leaning into the other. Or try placing the objects a distance from each other and see if this creates an interesting scene. Put your hands up in front of you (like to "L"s facing each other) to create an imaginary frame around your objects, to get an idea of how the objects will look in relation to each other in your piece. Look for an arrangement that challenges your eye somehow. And remember, this is Cubism, not realism, so you can bend and reinvent your objects any way you like.

Now get started! On a sturdy piece of art paper, use markers, crayons, or pencils to begin sketching broad shapes that your still-life objects suggest to you. For instance, the pencil in your group of objects is long and thin, with a tiny gray point at the end. Think of how to play with the shape, exaggerate or minimize or simplify it. Maybe it becomes the biggest form in your still life, a

Ontbijt (ont-beeszt), n.: Dutch for "breakfast piece," describing still lifes that feature an arrangement of foods and objects that might appear on a breakfast table.

Good Books

Great family library references on the subject of still lifes include *Still Life* by Norbert Schneider and *Objects of Desire: The Modern Still Life*. And a wonderful introduction for kids to cubism is *Cubism*, from the Art Revolutions series by Linda Bolton.

chunky rectangle with a lopsided triangle of a tip. The bright red coffee mug in your composition? It doesn't have to be shaped like a real mug. What can you do with the shape or position of that mug to make us think of it in a new way? Think of your objects as seen in a funhouse mirror—they can be bigger, smaller, distorted in shape, tipped upside down.

Your finished product will be your singular vision of a still life, a *nature morte* of the unique and most lively, Picassoesque variety!

abstract (ab-strakt), n.: A concept or idea in art not representing or imitating a specific external reality.

Extrapalooza

Scrap Still Life

Create a still life using collage materials, from pictures and colors cut out of magazines to snips of fabric or string or pieces of newspaper. The red book in your still life might be depicted with a swatch of bumpy red wallpaper. The seeds of your cut apple might be real seeds glued to the shape representing the apple. Play with cut-up materials, arranging them at odd angles, and mixing the types of materials you use. And whether you create your still life with paint or colors directly on paper or with collage materials or a mix of both, you can add finishing details like shadows and outlines with markers or pencils.

Great Artists

The Michael Jordan of still life was probably Jean-Baptiste-Siméon Chardin, an eighteenth-century French artist. He was the master of the sensitive use of light and shade and color, and he used a delicate hand to create memorable paintings. Although there are very few, if any, artists known exclusively as still-life artists, Chardin inspired many artists known for their work in other genres to experiment with the form. In that way that artists have of influencing each other, Chardin inspired Edouard Manet to paint still lifes. Manet, in turn, influenced great artists such as Claude Monet, Paul Gaugin, Edgar Degas, and Vincent van Gogh, among many others. Paul Cézanne caught the still-life bug in a big way, with some 20 percent of his life's work devoted to the form. And later in life, Cézanne experimented with short, overlapping, almost architectural brushstrokes that inspired Picasso and company in their work.

Museum Hunt

When my youngest kids were four and five, I took them on their first museum hunt at the National Gallery in Washington, which was also the first museum I had ever visited as a child. I would go into a gallery and find five things for them to locate in the paintings (a butterfly, a dog eating a bone, and so on) and then send them in to find them. While they were looking, I'd go into the next gallery and find the next set of five things to look for. This palooza is great fun for you to plan and for them to play . . . and you may end up with a kid who knows a Rembrandt from a Rothko.

What's the Palooza?

Make a visit to the museum into a visual scavenger hunt. The simplest way to make clues is to come up with a list of common objects for everyone to find. You don't have to actually know anything about art or much about the holdings of the museum you are visiting in order to do this. Give each seeker a list of things to hunt for in paintings or other works of art, which might include items like this:

Basket
Baby
Bird
Boat
Bowl of fruit
Bug
Child
Claws
Fire
Flowers in a
  vase

Glasses
Horse
House
Jug
Lion
Mirror
Moon
Mustache
Ocean
Piano

Picture within a
  picture
Snake
Skull
Umbrella
Wedding
Woman's hat
Ship

Who can play?
Ages 6 and up.

What do we need?
A museum or a computer with Internet access, art and art history books, a notebook, and a pen.

Running time?
An hour to plan, an hour or more to play.

Budget?
$

Words to Use When You Talk about Art

Background
Balance
Color
Contrast
Depth
Foreground
Medium
Perspective
Rhythm
Shape and form
Space
Texture
Value

As each child checks off an item, they must note the artist and the title of the painting, as "proof" they found the item.

There are many more objects you might include on your museum-hunt list. Dip into your Janson's *History of Art* or Phaidon's *The Art Book* for loads of ideas. Obviously, the fun is in talking about what you find—quirky things like the mirror in Jan van Eyck's *The Arnolfini Marriage*, who's sitting where in any version of the Last Supper, what a skull almost always symbolizes in a painting, and so on. While this palooza isn't meant to teach about art, no one will walk away without having learned a whole bunch.

For older kids, a hunt can focus on types or periods of art or individual artists or any one of the "isms." If the museum you are visiting has a particularly strong emphasis on one of these categories, research its collection in advance and craft a hunt around it. Most museums have Web sites that can give you a good idea of what you can see there. The same idea is at work—a list of items to look for, but meant to be found in a specific area of the museum. And your list is more keyed to the particular art you will be seeing.

Extrapaloozas

Postcard

This is great because it requires no advance planning and is appealing even to the youngest kids. When you arrive at your museum, go straight to the gift shop and pick out some postcards of art in the museum's collection. Now the game is simply finding the real version of the postcard art. Once you return home, you can set up your own miniature exhibition with the postcards or keep an album of all your museum-hunt expeditions.

I Spy

When you walk into a room of a museum, take a moment to identify a particular detail in a piece and

Good Books

I Spy: An Alphabet in Art, by Lucy Micklethwait

Dan's Angel: A Detective's Guide to the Language of Paintings, by Alexander Sturgis and Lauren Child

Art Fraud Detective, by Anna Nilsen

From the Mixed-up Files of Mrs. Basil E. Frankweiler, by E. L. Konigsburg

Discover Great Paintings, by Lucy Micklethwait

History of Art for Young People, by H. W. and Anthony F. Janson

The Annotated Mona Lisa: A Crash Course in Art History from Prehistoric to Post-Modern, by Carol Strickland and John Boswell

get your seekers to find it: "I spy a woman who isn't really smiling or frowning," or "I spy something that flies in the air."

All in One

Another way to hunt is to look for as much as you can within a single painting or piece. In Pieter Brueghel the Elder's *Children's Games* there are at least eighty games being played. How many can you find? What are the names of the games the children are playing? Choose your favorite game in the painting and make a list of the rules for playing. You can play this hunt at home by looking at this painting online at http://breughel.8m.net.

Pieter Brueghel the Younger (son of the Elder) painted *The Village Fair*, which is filled with commotion. In a picture book based on this painting called *The Fair* by Ruth Craft, the little vignettes that comprise the larger canvas are made into short poems. Try making up stories or poems about different scenes you see in a single painting.

Be a Pollock

They say that imitation is the sincerest form of flattery. It's also one of the best ways to understand an artist and an art form. This palooza is a way of teaching children a bit about contemporary art through a truly exuberant hour or two of pure play.

What's the Palooza?

Imitating notable twentieth-century artists with very distinctive styles. The place to begin is looking through art books, exhibit catalogs, or if you can, a modern art museum—or a great art-and-artist-finding Web site like www.artcyclopedia.com. Pick an artist whose work you think you will be able to make a reasonably close facsimile of: Jackson Pollock, Piet Mondrian, Mark Rothko, Andy Warhol, Keith Haring, or Morris Louis are standouts.

Pollock's drip or action-painting technique is a good first choice. After looking at reproductions of Pollock's work, think about what you both saw and how he painted. Pollock would spread his canvas out on the floor and pour paint from a paintbrush or even a stick straight onto the canvas in thick layers. He would move around to splash the paint all over the canvas.

Don't be surprised to say to yourself, "I could do that!" Spread out an old white sheet on the floor and place your large paper canvas in the middle of it. Use your brush or sticks like Pollock did, pouring, dripping, splattering across the canvas.

If Pollock doesn't inspire you, look at the opposite extreme in the work of Piet Mondrian (1872–1944). His paintings are made up of squares and rectangles in bright primary colors divided by geometric black grids. You might even use a ruler to paint the lines straight enough.

Anyone can imitate Abstract Expressionists such as Rothko or Barnett Newman, who painted asymmetrical blocks of color. After studying Andy Warhol, perhaps you might paint a still life of a common household object—a soup can or a box of Brillo pads, like he did—or copy a photographic portrait of a famous person, the way Warhol silk-screened Marilyn Monroe and Jacqueline Kennedy. Or do a photographic portrait of someone in your family—or even of yourself.

It's much more fun to imitate the way artists made art than to try to make an exact replica of a specific painting.

My painting does not come from the easel. . . . On the floor I am more at ease. I can walk around it, work from the four sides . . . be in the painting.

—Jackson Pollock
(1912–1956)

Extrapaloozas

Black Is Black

Robert Motherwell was an Abstract Expressionist whose signature color was black. He experimented with broad forms of black against a background of white, as well as on a variety of other colors, most notably in his series *Elegy to the Spanish Republic*. He also created huge canvases of black on black, with one shade and shape of black turning imperceptibly into another. Franz Kline is also best known for his black-on-white paintings. Mark Rothko painted entire canvases as a study in a single color. Make an abstract painting using only different

If you want to know all about me, just look at the surface of my paintings, it's all there, there's nothing more.

—Andy Warhol
(1928–1987)

Good Books

Two children's books on artists share an insider's perspective. An informative, beautifully written and illustrated children's book on Jackson Pollock is *Action Jackson,* by Jan Greenberg and Sandra Jordan. Its illustrator, Robert Andrew Parker, knew Pollock as young man.

Uncle Andy's: A Faabbulous Visit with Andy Warhol is by Warhol's nephew, James Warhola. (Andy dropped the final "a" from the family surname.) James Warhola's father, who was Andy's brother, was a junkman. The family lived in a house filled with an abundance of random items, which may explain Warhol's fascination with odd but common objects.

shades and shapes of a single color. Paint to the very edges of your canvas. Paint to somewhat near the edges of your canvas. Or just paint one small portion of your large canvas in your single color.

Mixing Media

Once you've tried painting like a specific artist, experiment with other media. Make a Mondrian by cutting and pasting squares and rectangles of construction paper. Tape pieces of colored yarn on paper for a woolly Pollock. Use a camera to capture the photo-realism of Warhol.

Strawing

You can make wonderfully original paintings using ordinary drinking straws. Simply pour a glop of paint on a piece of paper placed on a table and, without touching the paint, blow through the straw. The power of your breath will move the paint around the paper, creating interesting patterns that will look impressively *moderne.*

Self-Portrait

There's no higher compliment to a young self-portraitist than "That really looks like you!" This palooza invites the artist to really see himself—and find a way to express what he sees.

What's the Palooza?

Make a picture of yourself. Start by looking in a mirror. Don't look at the person you barely glance at every day when you brush your teeth. Instead, look at yourself carefully, as if you are seeing this person for the first time. What do you notice about yourself? What's interesting about your face? Does your face tell you anything about how you feel?

Let's say you're going to draw your head and shoulders on a large sheet of paper. What shapes are involved with your head and shoulders? Will you think of these shapes when you do your self-portrait? What about the placement of the head in the portrait? On a big piece of paper, where will it be (and how big will it be) in relation to the shoulders and the bottom of the page?

Now think about where your features are in relation to each other. Where are your ears in relation to your eyes? What about your ears and your mouth? Where are your eyes in relation to your hairline? Not at the top of your head but somewhere below your forehead, right? Can I see my ponytail? How big is my mouth? How many teeth can you see when you smile? Will you be smiling in your self-portrait?

You can see now that there are lots of good thinking questions to ask yourself before you make a single mark on your paper. When artists do self-portraits, they paint what they see, but they also paint what they want other people to see. What is it about yourself you'd like people to see in your self-portrait?

Get your paper and a pencil and begin to sketch out

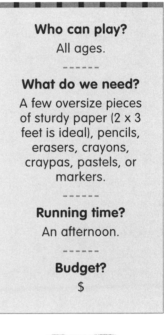

Serial Self-Portraitists

Certain artists spent a lot of time exploring self-portraiture. Van Gogh said he often painted himself because he had no money to pay a model. Rembrandt's collection of self-portraits shows how he's aged throughout the years, reflecting a kind of comfort with the fact of his growing older. Check out some of Picasso's self-portraits, and you'll see how his style—and his message—changed over time. Frida Kahlo often painted herself in unusual backgrounds, sometimes blending her image into nature. Her self-portrait titled *Diego on My Mind* is an amusing depiction of what was "on her mind" at the time she painted that picture. Max Beckmann liked to paint himself in different costumes and disguises. Find examples of self-portraits of these artists at:

Rembrandt—www.ibiblio.org/wm/paint/auth/rembrandt/self/

Vincent van Gogh—www.vangoghgallery.com/painting/main_se.htm

Pablo Picasso—www.artchive.com/artchive/P/picasso_selfportraits.html

Frida Kahlo—www.artchive.com/artchive/K/kahlo.html

Max Beckmann—www.artcyclopedia.com/artists/beckmann_max.html

I paint self-portraits because I am so often alone, because I am the person I know best.

—Frida Kahlo
(1907–1954)

the bigger shapes of your head and shoulders. Think about proportion and how you want to fill the page. Begin to gently sketch in the details—ears, eyes, nose, mouth. Keep looking at yourself in the mirror as you work, especially to check where different features are in relation to each other. Feel free to erase and adjust features. Then begin to fill in your portrait with your final material, whether it's charcoal, colored pencils, crayons, or craypas. Don't forget your freckles, eyeglasses, that little cowlick of hair, the logo on your favorite T-shirt— these are the little details that make you you!

Extrapalooza

Photo Self-Portraits

Photography is a wonderful way to create a self-portrait. Artist Chuck Close is famous for his self-portraits, especially his use of many small photolike images of himself pieced together to create a larger portrait. How would you create a photo self-portrait? You could just hold the camera out in front of yourself and take a picture or set the timer on your camera to take your picture for you. But what about a photographic self-portrait over time?

I have a friend who created a self-portrait collection using photos he took of himself every day for a year. He took the pictures at different times of the day; sometimes he'd stage the photo with objects and a background, sometimes it was just a simple straight shot. The result was this wonderful collection of 365 photos that chronicled all different aspects of his life. You could see the change in his image over time, but you also could pick out certain photos from the group and see something special or different in his face that day.

Take a bunch of different photos of yourself, especially when you're feeling different emotions—happy, sad, bored, nervous. See how much of your feeling is reflected in the photograph. Take one first thing in the morning and last thing at night. Play with light and shadows. Do profiles and face front photos, or a photo of you looking over your shoulder. Explore all the ways a camera can pick up on your expression.

Self-realization is the urge of all objective spirits. It is this Self which I am searching for in my life and in my art.

—Max Beckmann
(1884–1950)

Mirror, Mirror

Check out Norman Rockwell's Triple Self-Portrait at www.nrm.org/eyeopener/eye/self.html. Here Norman Rockwell paints a self-portrait of himself looking in a mirror, painting his self-portrait in the picture. This self-portrait inside a self-portrait is difficult to paint or draw, but you can try a version of this trick using a camera. Take a picture of yourself in the mirror. Take pictures of yourself in different reflective surfaces—windows, car mirrors, calm water, or mirrors in different sizes. Try taking your picture in a window where you can see what's on the other side of the window a person, your cat, a winter storm. You'll see yourself in the reflection, but you'll also see the other subject in the picture.

Kolam

America has its pot of flowers on a porch, India has kolam. Early in the morning, before the bustle of the day, the women of India take time to make kolam, the beautiful patterns drawn daily in front of the doorways of their homes.

What's the Palooza?

Express yourself through the ancient art of kolam. Women in India create their designs on the ground in front of their houses, setting up a large grid of dots around which they create a design using lines, curves, and curlicues made of white and colored flour, or colored sugars. We'll just start with a paper and a pencil.

To create a kolam design, first draw a grid of dots. An easy one begins by drawing five dots in a horizontal line. Above and below this line, draw another row, this time with four dots. Above and below the four dots, draw three. Above and below the three dots draw two. And at the top and bottom of the grid draw one dot. Now draw around the dots with continuous loops.

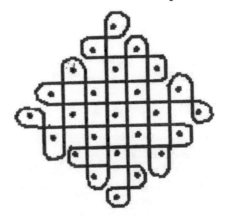

Another basic design begins with four dots on all sides of one dot. Connect the four outside dots with loops, creating a diamond shape. Practice using those two basic design grids and then expand on them. Have a first horizontal line of eleven dots instead of seven. This gives you a bigger canvas to work on, more space to play with your pattern. You can copy classic kolam or come up with your own.

Now that you've practiced on paper, move your kolam outside. Using chalk, draw your kolam on the sidewalk or driveway. Kolam, like Zen sand gardens, henna tattoos, snowmen, and sand sculptures, do not last forever. But half of their beauty is in the process of creating them. You will have fun seeing the design emerge. And it's a lovely ritual that leaves something beautiful for everyone to enjoy.

Extrapaloozas

Signature Kolam

Perfect a single kolam that really expresses your person-

Kolam in India

The ancient folk art of kolam was handed down from generation to generation of Tamil Nadu women. On any given day in India, somewhere between 35 to 40 million kolam are drawn twice a day, every day. The practice is passed down through the generations, so a toddler and teenager may gather with their grandmother to make kolam. Tamil Nadu women channel a lot of individuality into kolam. They take a simple design and add flourishes that tell of their passions, their favorite flower, their new baby, and the time of year. Kolam can tell of happy life events: marriage, birth, coming of age. Kolam are also supposed to bring good luck, good health, abundance, and fortune.

The artist may weave auspicious symbols like peacocks, stars, snakes, and birds into her kolam. Kolam communicate messages through these symbols. They speak from your home to your neighbors, your gods, your family, and your world. Even if the house is bare, and the inhabitants poor, there is almost always a lovely kolam outside the front door. Cluttered city streets may not leave rooms for gardens, but oleanders, cosmos, zinnias, chrysanthemums, mango, and green leaves in kolam are abundant. Kolam can be visual prayers. Lotus-flower kolam are for gods Lakshmi, Vishnu, and Brahma. They are also thought to ward off evil spirits. During competitions and festivals like Pongal, streets are crowded with bright, elaborate kolam.

The Sari and the Bindi

The sari is considered the most enduring of all items in the history of women's clothing. It has its roots in the story of a woman, the beautiful Draupadi, who was lost to an enemy clan in a gambling duel. Lord Krishna, a hero of the five-thousand-year-old Indian epic legend the Mahabharat, promised to protect the woman's virtue, and he draped her in an endless swath of beautiful material, which if pulled would unravel but never reach its end. Today, women wear saris in a variety of ways—draped between the legs to create flowing pants, arranged elaborately to look like a Western full-length gown, or in the classic style, with six yards of fabric draped around the body and over the shoulder. Like the kolam, a sari can be subtle or elaborate, made of shimmering silk or gauzy cotton, decorated with embroidery or tassels in a riot of color. The sari has endured since 3000 B.C. because it's simple yet luxurious, and above all comfortable. And cuter than sweatpants by a long shot!

The bindi is the mark many Hindus wear on their foreheads between their eyes. This point, also known as the Spiritual Eye or the Third Eye, is thought to be the major nerve center of the body, and the ancient bindi, made of sindhoor powder and sandalwood paste, was said to cool the nerve center and calm and quiet the mind. The bindi mark doesn't have a standard shape, size, or color; it is applied differently by members of different Hindu sects and subsects. Bindis are often worn by women as a sign that they are married, but today they are most commonly worn in worldwide popular culture as a fashion accessory.

ality. Use your own signature kolam design, like a monogram or your initials, to say, "This is me" or "I've been here." Make your own notepaper by drawing your kolam at the top of each sheet. Play with color: maybe use gold pen on red paper to make it exotic. Or scan your kolam design on the computer and create stationery that prints your kolam every time you write a letter on the computer. Make a kolam calendar, with different colored versions of your kolam design decorating each month. It's your kolam, you can draw it anywhere you like—on notebooks, with fabric paint on a T-shirt or sweatshirt, or decorating the hem of your jeans.

Indian Festival Celebration

Choose a traditional Indian festival date and then have your own. In the morning, throw a kolam on your doorstep. Wrap a bright piece of fabric or sheet about you like a sari. Wear a bindi and spangly silver bracelets. Cook a classic Indian menu of vegetable korma, fried new potatoes with coriander and curry, and almond and pistachio brittle. Write your menu on paper decorated with kolam. After dinner, draw temporary henna tattoos on your palms (you can buy an inexpensive henna kit at www.hippiegear.com). Draw an evening kolam, and watch *Bend It Like Beckham* or Satyajit Ray's lyrical Apu trilogy.

Indian Festivals

January 13	**Lohri**—the Punjabi Harvesting Season
January 14	**Makar Shankranti**—Return of the Sun to the North
January 18	**Pongal**—the Harvest Festival of the South
February 6	**Vasant Panchami**—Celebrating Spring
February 25	**Khajuraho Dance Festival**
March 18	**Holi**—the Festival of Color
April 14	**Naba Barsha**—the Bengali New Year
August 12	**Raksha Bhandan**—the Bond of Love
October 24	**Choti Diwali**—the Festival of Lights
November 8	**Gurpurab**—the Festival of the Gurus

Vegetable Korma

Basmati rice
1 onion, chopped
1 tbsp olive oil
½ cup green beans, sliced
½ cup peas
½ cup cauliflower florets
½ cup carrots, peeled and sliced
1 bottle creamy curry sauce (korma sauce)
½ cup cream
4 ripe tomatoes, chopped

Prepare rice as directed on the package. In a large skillet over medium high heat, cook onion in oil for 1 minute. Add green beans, peas, cauliflower, and carrots. Cook 3 minutes. Stir in korma cooking sauce. Cover and simmer 10 to 15 minutes or until vegetables are tender. Stir in cream and tomatoes. Heat to just boiling, then serve over hot, cooked basmati rice.

Art Gallery

When art really needs to be seen, a little panache can go into its presentation.

Who can play?

All ages, with supervision as necessary.

What do we need?

Art to be displayed, various materials of your choice for framing (wood, cardboard, poster board, construction paper, and so on), fixtures for hanging (nails or picture hangers, pushpins, string or fishing wire, small clothespins, temporary sticky wall tack), poster board for frames, index cards for exhibit labels, paper and markers or crayons for catalog.

Running time?

An afternoon.

Budget?

$

What's the Palooza?

To create a special showing space for a single piece of art or a collection. Every artist has loads of work he's created that never sees the light of day. But how to honor his best or breakthrough work? By making a gallery for it, of course.

First find the best available spot in your home that can be dedicated to showing your work. Is it a long hallway where several pieces can hang? Or a big blank wall somewhere else in the house? Perhaps it's on top of the bookshelf in your own room.

Next decide how you want to hang your work. A favorite display technique involves hanging a length of clothesline, string, or fishing wire along the length of a wall, affixed at either end with a small nail or picture hanger. Then hang your work with clothespins from the rope or string. This way the hanging technology is permanent, but the art can change as often as you like. A long hallway strung this way makes a great display for a collection with work grouped by theme or subject or season.

Obviously, you can hang a work on paper just the way it is, with a clothespin on your line or thumbtack in the wall. Or think about ways to frame the piece, perhaps mounting it on a piece of cardboard that is larger than the work, then decorating the visible edge of cardboard. Corrugated cardboard makes for a great mounting/framing surface. You can also cut appropriate-sized frames from colored poster board and reuse the frames when displaying new pieces. Create or decorate frames using all kinds of found materials, from branches and twigs to Popsicle sticks to balsa wood.

Now that you've established where your gallery will be and how you'll frame and hang your work, it's time to create exhibit cards for each piece. On index cards, note your name, age, maybe your grade, and certainly the title of your work. Have fun titling your art—be as creative when you name it as you were when you made it! Your drawing of your mom in a red dress? Red Song. That collage you made of the human eye? Eye See You. Other gallery theme ideas might be illustrations for a favorite book or story, family portraits, a child's Picasso exhibit, or paintings honoring a holiday or some other special event or day (see "Celebrate This!" page 208).

Stage an opening of your show—send out invitations, serve punch and hors d'oeuvres, turn it into a party. Take photos of your fabulous guests. Make it an annual

Home Is Where the Art Is

Writer Gertrude Stein may have had the most interesting home gallery, at 27 rue de Fleurus in Paris in the early decades of the twentieth century. Of Miss Stein's home, loaded with the early works of avant-garde artists like Picasso and Matisse, Ernest Hemingway said, "[I] loved the big studio with the great paintings. It was like one of the best rooms in the finest museum except there was a big fireplace and it was warm and comfortable and they gave you good things to eat and tea. . . . [I] had taken to stopping in at the studio . . . and I looked at the pictures and we talked. The pictures were exciting and the talk was very good. She talked, mostly, and she told me about modern pictures and about painters." She advised him to collect the art of young people like himself, "good new serious painters" whose work he could afford. She also told him, "You can either buy clothes or buy pictures, it's that simple. . . . Pay no attention to your clothes and no attention to the mode . . . and you will have the clothes money to buy pictures."

event, a show of your favorite work from throughout the year. It could even be a family art festival, combined with a get-together or reunion. Whether it's a show for friends and family or a little spot on the wall in your bedroom that's just for you, the idea is to give your best or favorite work a moment in the spotlight, a respectful acknowledgment of the effort it took to create and an appreciation of the work itself.

Extrapaloozas

Old Masters

Look for a couple of big, ornate empty picture frames in secondhand shops. Hang or arrange them in a permanent spot and just tape your latest pieces inside the empty frame, rotating the works on display. This elegant, old-style presentation makes a place of honor for even the humblest of family art.

A Movable Feast

Another unusual way to present your art is affixed to a folding screen. And another great secondhand-shop find is a shoji-style screen, which folds in thirds. Attach your work to each of the three panels, front and back, and you have a portable gallery of six or more pieces. Change your artwork frequently; create theme installations (all still lifes, all holiday art, all portraits, and so on); move the screen to different places in your home.

Gallery Electronica

The technologically exceptional are making the most of today's digital capabilities by scanning their art and saving the best of it on a CD. This electronic gallery may be the most thorough way to catalog and preserve your work. It also enables you to use your art for other purposes, say, turning a favorite drawing into greeting cards. You can organize the work, write exhibit notes for each, even (virtually) frame it.

Georgia O'Keeffe

Inspiring things are all around you, but it sometimes requires focus to see them. Georgia O'Keeffe, perhaps America's best-known female artist, looked at the parts and not the wholes in her work. She believed she could get a better feel for what something was, if she only looked at it close up and in pieces.

What's the Palooza?

Finding the intimate details of a larger object can be an exercise in observation as well as creation. Georgia O'Keeffe's flowers are enormous and fill up the entire canvas, blossoming in paint in dramatic ways that they never did in gardens. If you look at her most famous works such as her poppies, calla lilies and her jack-in-the-pulpit series, you can see how she used the organic, free-flowing lines of nature to create close-ups that made flowers not simply delicate, pretty things, but powerful images. By looking closely at small things and rendering them huge, she makes us know what it might feel like to be a tiny creature hovering over a plant or to inhabit a world where all proportions have changed. It's like *Honey, I Shrunk the Kids*, but in art.

To gather inspiration for creations like O'Keeffe's, all you need to do is look in the veggie drawer of your refrigerator or go outdoors. Leaves, fruits and vegetables, flowers, can all provide you the opportunity to look at the flow of organic lines. If it's not obvious at first glance, take a knife and cut your still life in half. You need to look with sharp eyes and a sense of discov-

---

Who can play?
Ages 6 and up.

What do we need?
Good eyes and interesting things—flowers, plants, fruits, or anything that can be fascinating close up. Paper, crayons, markers or pastels, and scissors. Kitchen knife (with supervision).

Running time?
One hour.

Budget?
$

I often painted fragments of things because it seemed to make my statement as well as or better than the whole could. . . . I had to create an equivalent for what I felt about what I was looking at . . . not copy it.

—Georgia O'Keeffe
(1887–1986)

ery at that apple cut in half, where you can see the star formed by the seeds, or trace the veins inside that pepper, the hairs on the stalk of the daisy, or the jewel-like insides of a pomegranate.

Draw what you see. (Crayons are fine, but pastels, because of their smudginess can be even better.) Fill the page with it. Magnify the details. Make a game of it by looking at something up close, drawing what you see, and letting everyone else play detective to figure out what they're looking at. You don't need to limit your subjects to nature; the man-made can work just as well—have you ever really looked closely at the fabric of the curtains?

Extrapalooza

Playing with Scale

Find some photos of plants and cut them into squares. Make each small square into the inspiration for a big painting or drawing. Or play with the scale of objects in a collage, making big things little and little things big. For instance, juxtapose cutouts of an elephant and an insect, a house and an egg carton. When you paste these things next to each other, the world becomes disproportionate. Think about how it felt to be Gulliver enormous among the Lilliputians or Tom Thumb living in a thimble. There's something wonderfully appealing and puzzling about a world where all your sense of size is thrown aside and you find yourself, like Alice in Wonderland, suddenly small, or vastly oversize.

Memento

This palooza lets you take those treasured symbols and mementos and turn them into an artful, multidimensional time capsule.

What's the Palooza?

Make a shadow box to preserve and display special mementos of your life, a period of your life, or a moment of your life. Shadow boxes are kind of like a 3-D scrapbook created out of all those little items that are dear to you and remind you of something special. Your memento shadow box can contain an odd mixed bag of items—all your little treats and memories from third grade—or it can contain a collection of similar things that mean a lot to you—all the seashells and sea glass you have collected on your summer vacations to the beach.

Think of all the nooks and crannies in your room where you stow all the little stuff you just can't bear to part with. How much of it might you use in your shadow box? That special birthday card from Grandpa, bits of play jewelry, stamps, dried flowers, newspaper clippings, buttons, those tiny plastic toy charms. Choose items that say something about what you enjoy doing, your sense of humor, things you love, like your dog or your skateboard—things that will tell the story of you!

If you're using a cigar box, decide if you want to keep the lid or remove it. To remove, cut carefully with strong sharp scissors or a cardboard cutter (with assistance!) to keep the cut clean. Or keep the lid so you can close and open your shadow box like a book. Decorate the outside of the box before you begin assembling the items in the box (so you won't disturb the items with movement or paint or markers) with paint or lace or ribbon or buttons or beads or acorns and pebbles. Remember that everything you glue to the outside or the inside of your box has to dry before you can move on to the next step.

Who can play?
Ages 6 and up.

What do we need?
A box (a cigar box is best because it's durable and it's the perfect size, shape, and depth; you can also use a very sturdy shoe box), assorted acrylic paints, scissors and paintbrushes, glue or a glue gun, little treasured trinkets and mementos (photos, ticket stubs, fortune-cookie or bubble-gum fortunes, party favors, trading cards, post-cards, seashells or small stones, ribbons, beads, paper or cloth flowers, stickers, and so on).

Running time?
Up to three hours (or more).

Budget?
$

So fast-drying glue is a good idea!

Line the walls of the box (at least the bottom of the box, which will be the back wall of your shadow box) with paper or fabric or felt. Now set your box upright, so you're looking into it head-on. Think about which bigger items will be best in the background, or which flat items, like photos or postcards, might look good peeking out from the back. Remember, you can also glue pieces on to the side walls of the box, so there's plenty of room for photos and other paper mementos.

If you're using photos, you can use the photos as is, or cut out figures from the photos and glue the cutouts to the wall of the box—or glue the cutouts to a traced shape of shirt cardboard (like a paper doll) so the figure can be glued to the bottom of the box and really appear in 3-D!

Your box can have a specific theme—memories from every show you've performed in your acting group or things you've collected on Boy Scout nature outings. Or it can be more general, and contain a broad mix of items that are more of a crazy-quilt picture of you—a baby picture, a baby tooth, a favorite action figure, a piece of the plaster cast from your broken arm in second grade. Or it can be about a single moment or experience in your life—when you won first place in the swim meet or caught your first fish. After you make one memento shadow box, you'll have a hard time thinking of a better way to display and save the things you love.

Top Box Artist

Joseph Cornell was an artist famous for his shadow-box-style creations. Going on pilgrimages to thrift shops and old book-stores, he collected all sorts of oddments to use in his art. Most of his boxes are simple and glass-fronted, but inside, he very carefully arranged surprising collections of photographs and commonplace objects he had discovered in his travels. Check out his work at www.ibiblio.org/wm/paint/auth/cornell/

Memento
(mu.men.to), n.: A reminder of the past, a keepsake.

Shadow Boxers

- -

The best shadow boxes come from the creator yearning to preserve a strong feeling from childhood. One young boy made a shadow box of cutout photos of every pet his animal-loving family had ever had—every beloved cat and dog, a chick, a box turtle, and a bunny. In the background of his box, he put photos of the houses his family had lived in and assembled the animals in the "yard," as if they were they were all there at a family reunion.

Color
Concentration

This palooza is a colorful reincarnation of the classic memory game also known as Concentration, which requires a sharp memory to beat your opponent. In this palooza, Concentration becomes a study of the subtle variations between colors—and an appreciation for their wonderful names.

What's the Palooza?

Create a memory game using colorful paint chips. Go to your local hardware store and make your way to the rack of sample swatches of paint. These paint chips usually come as sturdy strips of paper, each containing three, five, or seven different shades of the same color. Choose three to five different strips each of reds, oranges, yellows, greens, blues, and purples. Pick a strip or two each from the whites, grays, browns, and blacks. Make sure to grab two of each strip you pick.

Back at home, choose which colors to use for the game. Select five to seven distinctly different shades from each color family. For example, among the blues you might choose a midnight blue, a navy blue, a sky blue, a gray blue, a green blue, and a robin's-egg blue. Make your selection as varied as possible. For colors with fewer and more subtle distinctions, such as white and gray, you might want to pick only two or three unique shades. A single shade of black should be enough; perhaps it can act as a wild card, worth two matches instead of one.

Once the individual colors have been chosen from

among the swatches, cut them out, two copies each. While choosing and cutting out the color cards, players should take note of the differences between the shades of each color, as well as their often equally distinctive names.

When all the cards are cut out and assembled into a deck, shuffle and arrange facedown on a table in even rows and columns. And let Color Concentration begin! Take turns flipping over two swatches at a time. If there's no match, the player turns the cards facedown again, and the next person takes a turn. Whenever someone gets a match, they place it to their side and get to go again. When all of the swatches have been matched, whoever has the most pairs wins.

As with most games, the point is mainly to win. The long-term takeaway, though, is a new sensitivity to the nuances of color and an unavoidable appreciation for the difference between, say, a yellow the shade of "golden wheat" and one of "Mayan gold."

Extrapalooza

Monochrome Concentration

Once you have mastered the art of Color Concentration, you might want to try this even more challenging version of the game. This time, use twenty or so different shades from just one color family. Only a true color connoisseur can differentiate at a glance between "mandarin" and "emergency orange."

Busted

Whenever I'm in a play, I draw opening-night caricatures of the whole cast. But one year I decided to make busts of my castmates in character. I covered balloons with papier-mâché, and after they dried, I painted each one. They were fabulous, if I do say so myself. After that I was so inspired, I made papier-mâché busts of two friends as a wedding present. These very playful three-dimensional portraits are great fun to make with your kids—a papier-mâché palooza is a nice mucky activity that takes a long time, but it's so sustained and satisfying.

What's the Palooza?

Create an affectionate, whimsical bust of someone you know using "chewed paper"—that's American for papier-mâché. Your finished bust is a great gift to give the person you have portrayed—especially if you've managed to capture a particularly distinctive or beloved trait, like Grandpa's bushy eyebrows, Uncle Owen's ski-jump nose, or Mom's lopsided grin.

First set a plastic tablecloth on the table, or cover the table with newspapers and a sheet of waxed paper for your work area. Next, tear newspaper into strips approximately an inch wide by four inches long, until you have a good-sized pile. Tear, don't cut, the strips, because the ragged torn edges help the strips blend into each other. Now prepare a simple glue by making this flour-and-water adhesive:

Boil 5 cups of water in a saucepan.

In a bowl, mix ¼ cup of flour with 1 cup of cold water.

Mix with a whisk until smooth and completely free of lumps.

Who can play?
Ages 6 and up.

What do we need?
Plenty of newspaper, homemade adhesive (see recipe), pie tin, paintbrushes, balloons, plastic table covering or waxed paper, empty oatmeal containers, tempera or acrylic paints, one-pound-size plastic deli container (lid discarded).

Running time?
Two to three hours, or over a day or two, depending on conditions.

Budget?
$

Add the flour mixture to the boiling water.

Gently boil, stirring constantly for two or three minutes until the mixture thickens.

Remove from the heat and cool completely before pouring into a pie tin to use.

This will make fairly liquid glue. If you prefer a thicker glue that will dry faster, use one cup of flour to three cups of water for the cold flour mixture you add to the boiling water.

Now blow up a round or oval-shaped balloon, not too big, perhaps the size of a melon. Be sure to knot the balloon tightly so that no air escapes while the papier-mâché is drying. Set the balloon onto the open end of an oatmeal container. This will keep your balloon from slipping or flopping around while you work on it, and will also serve as the neck and pedestal for your bust.

Wet both sides of a newspaper strip in the adhesive and run it between your index finger and thumb to squeeze off excess paste. Starting from the bottom of the oatmeal container, paste a strip to the balloon, smoothing it down with your fingers to remove air bubbles. Repeat with the next newspaper strip, overlapping slightly on your last strip. Continue to paste strips one at a time over the oatmeal box and then the balloon, being careful to cover every bit of exposed balloon. Let this layer of strips dry completely before beginning the next layer.

How long it takes each layer to dry depends on the temperature and humidity of the room where you are working. You can speed the drying process by putting your bust-in-progress in a warm (not hot) room where the air circulates well. You can also set your bust outside on a dry, breezy day or use an electric fan, as long as you've secured it so it doesn't blow away!

When a layer has thoroughly dried, you can apply the next layer of strips exactly as you did before. Continue this layering/drying process until you have at least three layers. You can actually have as many layers as you like; it all depends on your patience with the process and how you intend to sculpt the features of your bust.

History of Papier-Mâché

Despite its French-sounding name, papier-mâché actually comes from China, where paper itself was invented more than 2,000 years ago. As long ago as 202 B.C., papier-mâché was used to make helmets, toughened by many layers of lacquer. Paper was an important link between the real and the spiritual world to the Chinese, so paper was used for spiritual, philosophical, and ritualistic purposes. One ritual involved burning paper as a means of sacrifice and purification.

Papier-mâché eventually spread to Japan and Persia, where it was used in mask making and festival activities. In the Middle Ages, papier-mâché spread as large numbers of imported papier-mâché objects became available in Europe. This in turn led France to start making its own papier-mâché and England did the same in the 1670s.

Once you have applied and dried your outermost basic layer, you can create facial features by molding them out of wads of gluey newspaper and affixing them to the bust. For instance, you can work a wad into the shape of an ear or a nose or eyebrows or lips or a beard. Just be sure the pieces aren't dripping wet with glue, or they'll have a hard time keeping their shape and staying put as they dry.

You can also cut out pieces of cardboard in the shapes of your facial features (or other features, such as a hat or sunglasses), affix them to your dry model with masking tape, and then apply another layer of paper strips over the whole bust. Let this last layer dry completely, and now you're ready to paint.

With a paintbrush, cover the entire bust with a base coat of flesh-colored acrylic or tempera paint. When this is dry, you can begin to paint the details on your bust, from rosy cheeks and lips to arched eyebrows to big grinning pearly whites. If you haven't already sculpted features like a hairdo or a beard or eyeglasses, you can just paint them on now. After your paint is dry, you can also add accessories like those little wire eyeglasses you can get at crafts stores, or googly eyes, or a beaded necklace or scarf. Or use real eyeglasses or hats from your coat closet. Now you have a bust that would make Beethoven proud.

Extrapalooza

Busted Hall of Fame

Start a collection of your busts. Create papier-mâché busts of everyone in your family and display them together in a place of honor. Or create busts of famous people. Look for distinctive features in their faces and exaggerate them on a bust, the way a caricature does. Make busts of your favorite ballplayers. Or create a Mount Rushmore of busts of *your* favorite presidents.

holiday
paloozas

Thankskeeper

Thanksgiving's got everything—lots of family, too much food, last whiffs of autumn and the hint of winter to come. Every family's got a history it brings to the Thanksgiving table. And a Thanksgiving journal is a place where kids can see themselves as a part of that history from year to year.

What's the Palooza?

Gather your family news and save your Thanksgiving memories in a journal you keep over a lifetime. A friend of mine began keeping a Thanksgiving journal some time ago, with detailed notes about the meal, including winner recipes, notes on dishes to avoid in the future, wines she served, and so on. After a few years, she started describing who was there, the activities of the day, and what she called "interesting developments"—bits of notable family news that had occurred since the last Thanksgiving.

One year her daughter asked if she could draw in her mother's journal a picture of the pumpkin pie she was so proud of making. The answer, of course, was yes, and in an instant the family Thanksgiving journal was born, a rich and wonderful account of who was who and what was what on Thanksgiving from year to year.

To start a Thankskeeper, get a scrapbook, an oversize blank journal, or even a sketching notebook. For the book's inaugural Thanksgiving, date the first page, then ask each person to write about and/or draw what they're thankful for. After you have collected thanks in the book from every Thanksgiving guest, you'll see that the mix of messages from young and old is a wonderful snapshot of where everyone is in their lives right now.

The children are in charge of the process. Spend time on your own entries and then make sure each guest contributes. One kid might be in charge of circulating the book, offering crayons or markers to even the adults—anyone knows how liberating a fresh box of Crayolas and a blank page can be in the hands of a world-weary grown-up. Someone else might be the day's photographer, snapping shots of each guest as they arrive, the cooks in the kitchen, Grandpa snoozing on the porch, Uncle Edward carving the turkey, and the whole group as they sit down to the table—the best photos to be pasted into the Thankskeeper. Someone can create a fancy French restaurant–style menu listing dishes and beverages served, which will also be pasted into the book later. Another can "interview" guests to collect news and gossip for the record. Or she can be the sports reporter covering the Backyard Bowl touch football game, noting who was on which team, big plays, final score. The photographer should cover this event, too!

The Thankskeeper involves everyone in a way that invests them in the events of the day, and asks them to pay attention to their own role in the family's Thanksgiving rituals. The keeping of the journal might become a permanent part of the Thanksgiving tradition itself, with each generation of children vividly and creatively memorializing the family experience. And what a wonderful portrait of a family it could become!

Tabletoppers

Collect interesting leaves on Thanksgiving morning, along with acorns, twigs and branches, seedpods or pinecones. Arrange a still-life centerpiece in which you can artfully nestle your candlesticks. If you don't live in an area that offers the bountiful gifts of deciduous trees, use what's native to your locale—palm fronds, citrus fruit leaves, desert stones, or native grasses. Bring the natural art of the outdoors to your Thanksgiving table wherever you live.

Extrapaloozas

The Art of Thanksgiving Dinner

For the culinarily inclined family, create an elaborate spread in your Thankskeeper describing and depicting the food that was served. Every dish is named and drawn in as much detail as a child can manage. Make special note of "guest stars," the dishes prepared and shared by guests. Tuck recipes between the pages, and your Thankskeeper becomes the first thing you turn to when you start to think about Thanksgiving.

Chef and author Jacques Pepin keeps beautiful self-illustrated scrapbooks of memorable meals he's prepared for family and friends. The pages are alive with

color and detail and really convey his love of food and company. It's a wonderful way to celebrate the art of a beautiful meal and the effort it took to prepare.

Come Give Thanks

In the weeks before Thanksgiving, create and send Thanksgiving invitations. The invites can be as simple as a postcard, as elaborate as individually drawn and decorated notes and envelopes, or clever computer creations. Request that each guest bring something special to include in the Thankskeeper, a small memento of a high point or interesting experience of the year—a program from the big swim meet, the stub from Dad's speeding ticket, a squashed penny from the top of the Empire State Building. Around the table after dinner, guests take turns telling the story behind the memento they're sharing.

Cranberry Orange Relish

----

2 pounds of fresh cranberries, washed and picked over for duds
1 pound of Granny Smith apples, peeled, cored, and roughly cubed
½ to 1 pound ripe Bosc or Anjou pears, peeled, cored, and roughly cubed
1 cup water
1 cup of sugar (or more, to taste)
Zest of 8 to 10 oranges
Juice from oranges

Combine cranberries, apples, pears, and water in a large stockpot. Bring to a quick boil on high, then turn down to medium low and cook for half an hour or more, stirring constantly until cranberry breaks down completely. Add small quantities of water while cooking if necessary. Add sugar and orange zest and combine well. Cook for 10 to 15 minutes more on low heat, adjusting with orange juice and sugar to taste. Let the mixture cool in the pot, then transfer to storage containers. Can be made up to four days in advance. Serve at room temperature.

Holiday Ad Hoc

I love family holiday traditions as much as the next person. But sometimes I think the traditions and holiday symbols become so familiar, we stop seeing the forest for the Christmas trees. This palooza gets you thinking about how to turn the holiday familiar into the fascinating, the ordinary into the avant-garde.

What's the Palooza?

Use stuff you've got around the house to reinvent the whole idea of holiday decorations. Pick one holiday object that's become so familiar in your home that it's almost invisible—a Christmas tree, a menorah, or a kinara—and make your own out of utterly unexpected materials. Don't think you've got to create something that will last a lifetime; just let this moment, this year, inspire you and worry about next year, well, next year.

Look around your house for a material that is common, distinctive, and never makes it within a country mile of your usual holiday arrangements. Playing cards and poker chips. Fat rubber bands like the kinds used around a bundle of broccoli. A cigar box. How about Q-tips? Eureka!

Gather all of your supplies: a cone-shaped Styrofoam base (available at craft stores), scissors, a big box of Q-tips, paint, and paintbrushes. Cut the cotton tip off of one end of each Q-tip. Then poke Q-tips, sharp end in, all over the Styrofoam base to complete your own unique Christmas tree. Make a nice, tidy pattern of even rows around the form or go wild and just stick them in freeform. When you've filled in the base with as many Q-tips as you'd like (the more the better), you can leave it all white, as is. Or you can "decorate" it, using equally unlikely materials, such as dental floss or

Who can play?
All ages.

What do we need?
Q-tips, foam cone, scissors, paint; marsh-mallows, popcorn; cans, paint, glue, Indian corn, bottle caps, and candles—or any other odd assortment of knickknacks and crazy tidbits.

Running time?
An afternoon.

Budget?
$

For many years, the Museum of Natural History in New York City put up a giant tree at Christmastime, decorated from top to bottom with animals and dinosaurs made out of paper in the origami style. Look for unexpected things you can make out of origami and transform your holiday ho-hum into something truly remarkable. Be wild. Be an origami original. Check out *Origami to Astonish and Amuse*, by Jeremy Shafer, and *Origami in Action: Paper Toys That Fly, Flap, Gobble and Inflate*, by Robert J. Lang. Both provide step-by-step instructions and offer plenty of cool projects for first-timers.

little Band-Aids or tiny elastics from your braces. Put a "star" on top, maybe a nutty star-shaped object made of toothpaste caps.

Hanukkah has its own familiar symbol, the eight-candled menorah. How to take the symbol and make it all new and all yours? Find eight small cans and one larger can (say eight soup cans and one coffee can). Clean them and take off the labels. Paint the cans whatever colors you like—all one color or multicolored, solid-colored or with jazzy patterns . . . you decide. Or don't paint them at all, and make the soup-can statement, Warhol-style. Fill the cans three-quarters full with sand and pop small tapered candles into the sand. Dig the candles in so they're different heights to break up the even line. Arrange the cans on a tray and set in an appropriate spot in your home.

Kwanzaa likes candles, too. Make a Kwanzaa kinara using Indian corn. Break the corncobs in half and snap or cut off the pointy ends so you've got seven small blocks of round corn (get help if necessary). Bunch them up and tie them together with a piece of raffia or ribbon. Or line them up and glue them together. Nail plastic soda caps open-side-up onto the flat surface of the corn with small nails or flat thumbtacks to hold the small tapered candles. Or how about you change the scenery every day and turn real food into candle-holders? Carve holes in seven apples with a corer, arrange on a plate, and put your candles inside the fruit. The next night, make your candleholders out of little pumpkins. Or baby eggplants. Or pattypan squash. Living light.

Whatever your holiday, the idea is to create an *objet* and conversation piece that gets people talking and thinking. It's not a revolution against tradition, just a revelation of fresh perspectives.

Extrapaloozas

Christmas Tree from Another Planet

Leave your delicate heirloom ornaments in storage this year. Instead, deck out your tree from top to bottom in something way-out. Buttons. Paper clips. Empty match-book covers. Movie stubs. Postcards. Foam peanuts. Strings of painted Cheerios. Or if you can't bear to forgo your traditional tree, dress a tiny tree and use it in your foyer or on a tabletop.

Collecting is Half the Fun

Designate Thanksgiving the official start of the Holiday Ad Hoc decoration hunt. Decide what kinds of things you'll need for your decorations—whether you're having a theme holiday or just rooting through the cupboards for inspiration—and make a list. Everyone has two weeks to collect the materials. Mark a box Collection Central for people to deposit items as they collect them. Give a prize to the person who collected the most—or the craziest—stuff. And remember: the most fun way to approach Holiday Ad Hoc is by being resourceful; use materials you already have, or can recycle, or collect day-to-day. Anyone can spend a bunch of money on decorations—it's the truly rich man who knows that the treasure was right under his nose all along!

ad hoc, adj.: Improvised and impromptu. In other words, made up on the spur of the moment, on the spot, and as you go along.

Celebrate This!

We know how to celebrate holidays, especially the usual suspects like Thanksgiving and New Year and Valentine's Day and the Fourth of July. But how often do we celebrate our family's own nutty rituals and inside jokes? This palooza says go ahead and do it! Celebrate your quirks and your habits, your passions and proclivities. Hey, you can celebrate your love of the color red, if that's what gets you blowing horns and throwing streamers.

Who can play?
All ages.

What do we need?
Imagination. And any other materials you deem necessary to the celebration of your holiday.

Running time?
At least one day!

Budget?
Free to $.

What's the Palooza?

Create your own holiday—about anything and on any day on the calendar. You can make it a holiday that requires nothing more than laughing every time you think about it—like Talk Like a Pirate Day (September 19), where you try to, well, talk like a pirate every chance you get, matey. Or you can make up a holiday only your family would understand, like King of the Westies Day, celebrating your West Highland terrier.

You can plan your holiday in advance—choose a day, mark it on the calendar—or you can let it happen when it happens. If you wake up and discover it's the first day of hayfever season and your family is sneezing their heads off, seems like that ought to be Gezundheit! Day. Hand out crazy-colorful tissues or handkerchiefs. Learn how to say "Bless you!" in twenty languages. You might have a floating holiday that isn't assigned a particular day, but is invoked as necessary—such as the Very Quiet Day, when Mom really needs a break from the usual household rumpus.

You can also look at the calendar and find a dead spot, when there are no birthdays or big holidays, and your family could use a dose of fun. The gray days of late January or the dog days of August come to mind. Take

Groundhog Day, the granddaddy of goofy made-up holidays, for example. This holiday has its roots in the German Candlemas Day, which marked the midpoint of winter. If the weather was fair on this day, the rest of the winter would be stormy and cold. If it was cloudy, the winter would pass more pleasantly. Back in Germany people watched a badger to see if he had a shadow (the measure of how fair the day). But with no badgers to be found by early German settlers in Pennsylvania, the groundhog was chosen as the replacement shadowcaster. Three hundred years later the groundhog, "Punxsutawney Phil, Seer of Seers, Sage of Sages," brings a bit of light to an otherwise dark patch on the calendar.

Whatever reason you establish a holiday, think of how to mark the day. Send funny homemade cards. Invent a special cookie or treat to be made every time you celebrate. Take a familiar song and recast it as the theme song of your celebration. Wear a special color to honor your day.

Your holiday will need a name, of course. You can play it straight and call it what it is—Barefoot Day or Orange Food Day, for example. Or you can play it with a curve, like my friend, whose family has a holiday called Woof! which is the annual celebration of all of their pets birthdays (at once), as well as a remembrance of beloved late pets. Some made-up holidays that may give you ideas for your own:

Anti-Labor Day. The doing-as-little-as-possible day, when you eat off paper plates, don't make your bed, and sing, "Hallelujah, I'm a Bum!"

Switching Over Day. This may the day in spring when you haul out the short sleeves and light jackets and stash away the sweaters and mittens. It's also the day in the fall when you do the opposite. Perhaps it coincides with the fall back/spring ahead of Daylight Saving Time. Part of the ritual here has got to be measuring the season's growth. How much longer have my legs become since last Switching Over Day? You can do the Hand-Me-Down ritual or mark the growth on a wall chart.

Odd Holidays

In case you were thinking of making up any of these holidays, someone has beat you to it!

National Nothing Day (January 16)

National Kazoo Day (January 28)

Get a Different Name Day (February 13)

National Honesty Day (April 30)

Yell "Fudge" at the Cobras in North America Day (June 2)

Hug Holiday (June 15 to 22)

Take Your Houseplants for a Walk Day (July 27)

National Mustard Day (August 5)

Middle Children's Day (August 13)

Bad Poetry Day (August 18)

World Hello Day (November 21)

Underdog Day (December 16)

National Whiner's Day (December 26)

Pass It On. The day when you dive into the bottom of those unplumbed depths of drawers, closets, garages, and attics and weed it all out, bag it up, and donate it to charity. After you've done all that, end it with a super treat-yourself treat, like gargantuan sundaes.

Diggin' in the Dirt Day. The day when the danger of frost is over and you plant those first seeds of the year. Make fancy little garden markers out of fat popsicle sticks. Draw a picture of what your garden will look like when your veggies and flowers come in. Sing "The Garden Song," made famous by Arlo Guthrie.

Talk Like a Pirate Day

September 19, 2002, was the first year Talk Like a Pirate Day was celebrated, the brain-child of two self-described "yahoos from Oregon." Mark "Cap'n Slappy" Summers and John "Ol Chumbucket" Baur were playing racquetball one day and realized it was much more fun to play while talking like pirates. That's when they decided there ought to be a Talk Like a Pirate Day, where everyone gets to talk like pirates all day long. They wrote an e-mail to humorist Dave Barry, trying to enlist him in their cause, and sure enough, he climbed aboard! Barry wrote a column about Talk Like a Pirate Day that was seen in newspapers around the country, and before they knew it, the scurvy dogs were being interviewed on the radio and TV about their wacky day. They have no illusions of seeing Hallmark cards devoted to their holiday—they understand that "silliness is the holiday's best selling point"—but it has been added to Chase's Calendar of Events, the bible of holidays and yearly events. Go to www.talklikeapirate.com to see what a made-up holiday really looks like!

Nutty Nutcrackers

The original choreography for *The Nutcracker*, set to Pyotr Ilich Tchaikovsky's magnificent score, was created over one hundred years ago by Marius Petipa and his assistant, Lev Ivanov. This palooza kicks off its shoes to update the classic choreography. Just a little.

What's the Palooza?

Listen to Tchaikovsky's magical holiday score, choreograph your own version of the ballet using steps from whatever forms of dance you like, and then dance it. With aplomb. Tchaikovsky's composition is remarkable for its storytelling and the many changes in mood, atmosphere, and tempo. Even if the story of Clara and her Nutcracker prince were not so familiar to us, we would be hard-pressed not to march around our living rooms when we hear the march from scene 3, or scurry like mice upon hearing the music from scene 8, when the Nutcracker battles against the Mouse King. Valery Gergiev's recording of the ballet includes the following scenes. Listen to them all, or skip around and then choose one or two favorites to dance to:

Overture

The Christmas Tree

March

Galop and Dance of the Parents

The Presents of Drosselmeyer

Who can play?
All ages.

What do we need?
A recording of Tchaikovsky's *Nutcracker*, costumes cobbled together from what's in the closet, and room to dance.

Running time?
Thirty minutes to an hour or more, as the music moves you. Sample recordings of the complete ballet run about eighty minutes.

Budget?
$

Grandfather Dance

Clara and the Nutcracker

The Nutcracker battles against the Army of the Mouse King. He wins and is transformed into Prince Charming.

In the Christmas Tree

Waltz of the Snowflakes

The Magic Castle on the Mountain of Sweets

Clara and Prince Charming

Character Dances Chocolate (Spanish Dance)

Character Dances Coffee (Arabian Dance)

Character Dances Tea (Chinese Dance)

Character Dances Trépak (Russian)

Dance of the Reed Pipes

Polichenelle (the Clown)

Waltz of the Flowers

Pas de deux, Intrada

Pas de Deux: Variation I (Tarantella)

Pas de Deux: Variation II (Dance of the Sugar Plum Fairy)

Pas de Deux: Coda

Closing Waltz, Grand Finale

Think about how you might act out a scene through dance. You're Clara or her brother, Fritz, at the party scene. Dance around the Christmas tree. Lift the presents one by one and wonder, What's inside? Swirl and sashay and flit about the room in excitement. Who can resist the "Galop and Dance of the Parents," and, well, isn't it obvious who needs to be dancing in the room for this number? Or, it's the "March." You're one of the many tin soldiers come to life in a dance to please the children. March and step and bow in time to the music, head held high. Your very best posture. Create a soldier's costume out of things in your closet—your winter boots for marching, an empty cardboard wrapping-paper tube for a sword, and your bathrobe belt for a sash.

Cast yourself as the Mouse King. Wear gray sweatpants and a sweatshirt. If there are other folks around, they can be your minions, whom you sneakily bring out of the woodwork for a battle with the Nutcracker. If not, dance and twirl, fence, jump, and dodge solo to the music. You need only an imaginary foe for your dance. Play the piece again and switch roles. Wear a red shirt or a red scarf and be the Nutcracker. How does the Nutcracker defeat the Mouse King? Is it an old-fashioned sword battle or a newfangled, *Matrix*-style slow-motion martial arts duel? What does the music suggest?

For the voyage through the kingdom of snow, you're a snowflake. Be light on your feet. Delicate with your hands. Wispy. How does a snowflake dance? Or modernize this section and choreograph the building of a snowman to the music instead. Does it work?

Then on to the Land of the Sweets and a mountain of candy. The character dances, or *divertissements*, are opportunities to show off your special moves. Try coffee grinders. Split jumps. Break-dance spins. What would your Spanish dance look like—salsa? How about your Chinese dance or Arabian dance? Hard to resist the

choreograph (kor-ee-o-graf), v.: To compose a sequence of dance steps to music.

divertissement (dee-vehr-tees-mahn), n.: Diversion. A suite of numbers inserted into a ballet meant to display the talents of individual dancers.

overture (o-ver-ture), n.: A single orchestral movement that introduces an opera, play, ballet or longer musical work.

révérence (rey-vay-rahns), n. Curtsey or bow.

repertoire (rep-er-twar), n.: Stock of musical or dramatic material that is known and can be performed.

Night of the Living Toys

Here are some other stories that feature toys that memorably come alive:

The Velveteen Rabbit, by Margery Williams

"The Steadfast Tin Soldier," by Hans Christian Andersen

The Magic Toyshop, by John Haber

The Indian in the Cupboard, by Lynne Reid Banks

The Return of the Indian, by Lynne Reid Banks

classic Russian dancing, but how can you put your twist on it? Do whatever the music makes you feel, adding an international flavor to your steps. Imagine the Sugar Plum Fairy greeting holiday guests on her twinkle toes. Or is she beating out some steps in her tap shoes? A grand entrance. A pirouette or shuffle step or two. *Révérence* for Grandma and Grandpa.

Extrapaloozas

Jazzy Cool Nutcracker

Listen to a recording of Duke Ellington's elegant and original reinterpretation of the Tchaikovsky classic, *Duke Ellington: Three Suites* (Sony). The "March" is a "Peanut Brittle Brigade," "Dance of the Reed Pipes" becomes "Toot Toot Tootie Toot," and "Dance of the Sugar Plum Fairy" is "Sugar Rum Cherry." Choreograph your own jazz dance—or any other kind of dance—to this music for a *Nutcracker* change of pace.

The Golden Dreydl

The Golden Dreydl: A Klezmer Christmas is the story of a young girl who wishes for a Christmas tree instead of her family's usual Hanukkah celebration. Listen to the audio recording of this work, composed by Ellen Kushner and Michael McLaughlin, and produced with the Boston Shrim Klezmer Orchestra (Rykodisk). Think of how you might reinvent the *Nutcracker* story to adapt to different cultures or customs. Could you create an urban/hip-hop *Nutcracker*, with totally contemporary characters? Modern dance maestro Mark Morris stages *The Hard Nut* every holiday season, a comic homage to the classic that is set in the swinging 1960s.

Washington Irving Halloween

Seems to me it's time we take back All Hallow's Eve from Freddie and Jason and Michael and give it back to the original night specter, the Headless Horseman of Sleepy Hollow. And while we're at it, let's lose the Silly String and shaving cream for some authentic Halloween fun.

What's the Palooza?

Make a little harmless Halloween mischief without ending up in juvenile hall. This palooza isn't meant to replace trick-or-treating (as if!) but makes for a great after-dark party on or near Halloween.

The Legend of Sleepy Hollow

Start with a reading of the mighty *Legend of Sleepy Hollow* by Washington Irving, either a shortened and abridged version on the night of your party, or the full-length original, read aloud at bedtime the few evenings before Halloween. The language is old and beautiful, the description of the goofy Ichabod Crane funnier than any Disney depiction, and the final scene of Ichabod's frantic attempt to escape "the goblin rider" will make your own heart thump.

Who can play?
Ages 6 and up.

What do we need?
Bale of straw, string, felt, yarn, googly eyes, scraps of fabric, old Barbie, GI Joe, or other doll clothes. Ingredients for doughnuts (see recipe). Clothesline and clothespins. Flashlights.

Running time?
Two hours.

Budget?
$$

The story ends with the mysterious disappearance of Ichabod Crane, and the marriage of Katrina Van Tassel to Brom Bones. What might a sequel to this story be? Would a vengeful Crane come back to haunt and torment the people of Sleepy Hollow, bitter and humiliated by his experience there? And if he does come back, is he alive or is he a ghostly figure? What would he look like as an angry, haunted man—how would his gangly features become more scary? Or maybe Crane doesn't come back at all, but Brom Bones and his mischievous gang are preyed upon by the Headless Horseman. Think of all the questions left unanswered in the original legend, and spin your answers into a new haunting tale. Prizes for the best new character, scariest ending, and so on.

Straw People

Instead of making full-size scarecrows, make little scarecrows, using a big fistful or so of straw for each. Stuff the straw into old doll clothes or make clothes out of felt, fabric, yarn, and glue. Use kinds of clothes that will make them funny—a biker scarecrow wearing GI Joe's

Headless Horseman

This game is a cross between the swimming pool game of Marco Polo, hide-and-seek, and flashlight tag—and can only be played in complete darkness, preferably outdoors. For safety's sake, be sure everyone understands the boundaries for this game—what areas they can and cannot use for hiding places. As with any nighttime game, be careful and don't run!

Every player gets a flashlight. The person who is it closes his eyes and counts to 20 while everyone else finds a hiding place using their flashlights. With hiders' flashlights off, and eyes still closed, the it person calls out "Headless" to which the hiders must respond "Horseman." Each time the hiders respond, the it person can turn on his flashlight for two seconds to try to locate a hider. He continues calling "Headless," listening for "Horseman," and having two-second bits of light until he finds a hider. The person who is caught first is then it.

Soul Cakes

Before there were Snickers and Kit Kats and Smarties to collect on Halloween, there were soul cakes. Long ago in England and Ireland, as people prepared their feasts and celebrations for All Saints' Day (November 1), children would go around the neighborhood knocking on doors and windows singing, "Cake for a soul . . . a soul for a cake . . . help the poor souls!" And the grown-ups, so pleased to see the children's concern for saints and holy souls, would offer little sweet treats.

These soul cakes were little round cakes with a hole in the middle just big enough to slip over a broom handle. The soul cakes were stacked on the broom handle and the broom set just outside the home. The little cake was also known as a "dough naught"—that is a little nothing (naught) made of dough. Doughnuts!

1 quart of vegetable oil for frying
2 cups all-purpose flour
½ cup white sugar
1 teaspoon salt
1 tablespoon baking powder
¼ teaspoon ground cinnamon
1 dash ground nutmeg
2 tablespoons melted butter
½ cup milk
1 egg, beaten

Heat the oil in a deep fryer to 375°. You can also use a heavy cast-iron skillet containing 4 inches of oil, heated to 375°.

In a large bowl, sift together flour, sugar, salt, baking powder, cinnamon, and nutmeg. Mix in butter until crumbly. Stir in milk and egg until smooth. Knead lightly with floured hands, then turn out onto a lightly floured surface. Roll or pat to ¼ inch thickness. Cut with a floured doughnut cutter, or use two round biscuit cutters of different sizes.

Carefully drop doughnuts into hot oil of deep fryer, a few at a time. Do not overcrowd, or the oil may overflow. Fry, turning once with tongs, for 3 minutes or until golden. Drain on paper towels. If you make them in a cast-iron skillet, cook as many as will comfortably fit in the skillet and still leave room to turn them. Cook until they brown evenly, turning two or three times, and drain on paper towels.

When the doughnuts are cool and drained of excess oil, serve on a platter—or a broom handle, your choice! Or string them on a clothesline well divided with clothes-pins, and have a doughnut nibbling contest. Hands behind your backs, first person to nibble his doughnut off the rope without dropping it wins.

Stingy Jack

Our present-day grinning jack-o'-lanterns have a dark and haunted past. The jack-o'-lantern has its origins in an eighteenth-century Irish folk-tale about a miserable cheapskate named Stingy Jack, who made the mistake of tricking the devil one too many times. When Jack died, he was turned away from the gates of heaven because of the miserable, mean, cheap life he had led. But he was also turned away from the other place, where the devil also refused him, sending Jack to spend a cursed eternity as a spirit in limbo. As he turned to begin his journey into eternity, the devil threw him a hot ember to light his way in the dark. Jack placed the ember in a hollowed-out turnip and set off to wander the world. According to Irish legend, you can glimpse poor Stingy Jack's spirit on Halloween, as he carries his turnip lantern through the darkness.

leather jacket. A prom scarecrow wearing Barbie's Cinderella gown. Make a hoedown outfit out of felt and fabric. Or a witch's outfit out of black felt and yarn. Decorate a Styrofoam ball for the head. Use googly eyes or big-headed pins, pipe cleaners, cloves, thumbtacks, or markers. Make the head scary, for ghoul's sake! Stick the sharpened end of a pencil in the neck and shove it down the middle of the dressed body. Make lots of different little scarecrows and arrange them in a tableaux. Or put them in your front window and light them eerily with flashlights.

Trick or Keats

English poet John Keats was born on Halloween, 1795, and though he didn't write a poem specifically about the haunted night, in "La Belle Dame Sans Merci," he wrote hauntingly of the ghosts who tried to warn a smitten knight—soon to be a ghost himself—about "The Beautiful Woman Without Mercy":

. . . I saw pale kings, and princes, too,
Pale warriors, death-pale were they all;
Who cry'd—"La belle Dame sans merci
Hath thee in thrall!"

I saw their starv'd lips in the gloam
With horrid warning gaped wide,
And I awoke, and found me here
On the cold hill side.

And this is why I sojourn here
Alone and palely loitering,
Though the sedge is wither'd from the lake,
And no birds sing.

My Funny Valentine

Enough of the drugstore-bought boxes of 45 cards your kids hand out to their classmates. This palooza tweaks certain Valentine's Day traditions for some memorable February 14 celebrations.

What's the Palooza?

Create the unexpected Valentine. Try any one or several of the following ideas, or come up with your own variations on the theme. The idea is to make it big. Make it unforgettable.

Not Your Grandmother's Doilies

It's not enough to just wear red this Valentine's Day. Tack paper doilies onto your shirt or dress, using double-sided tape. Decorate the front door top to bottom. Adorn the mailbox (does anyone ever send the mailman a Valentine?), refrigerator or kitchen cabinets, friends' lockers, a teacher's desk, Mom's steering wheel, Dad's favorite chair, even the remote control, with doilies. That's right. Doilies. But make them cool. "Tie-dye" the doilies using colored markers. Write single Valentine's Day messages in the center. Or put ransom-note Valentine's messages cut from magazine pages in the center. Or write a scrambled message by putting only a word or two on each doily. Valentine recipients have to unscramble the message by putting the doilies (words) in order.

Hidden Valentines

Make Valentines and hide them around the house. Or

Who can play?
Ages 6 and up.

What do we need?
Red construction paper or red poster board, white typing paper or tablet paper, paper doilies, corrugated cardboard, pushpins, markers, pencils or pens, and tape.

Running time?
One or two hours.

Budget?
$

doily (doy-lee), n:. A decorative lacy mat, usually made of lace, linen, or paper. Named after a man named Doyley, a London draper of the late seventeenth century.

make one special Valentine and provide clues to its whereabouts in the form of red hearts or ransom notes taped to the bedroom door, bathroom mirror, orange juice carton inside the refrigerator, coffee maker, and so on.

Singing Valentine

Sing Rodgers and Hart's classic "My Funny Valentine" to your intended Valentine with baleful exaggeration. Or find a recording of the song (Barbra Streisand, Sheryl Crow, Chuck Mangione, Miles Davis, Chet Baker, and many others have interpreted this song over the years) and wake the house up on Valentine's Day by playing it on the family stereo. Of course, any great love song can also be featured in this way. Search the family CD stacks for other selections.

Valentines with Impact

One great big giant heart in pink chalk on the sidewalk or in the driveway. One hundred hearts all over the house (Valentine recipients have to actively collect the 100 hearts). Use mural paper or butcher paper to stretch a very large Valentine message across the front door. Or say "I Love You" out loud 100 times over the course of the day.

Anacrostic Valentines

Use the first letter of the recipients name as the first letter for each line in the Valentine. Even Lucky the dog can get his own valentine:

Love your fuzzy tummy

Under my bed you hide

Can keep me company at night

Kisses from you are wet and slobbery

You are my Valentine

Tell Me a Holiday Story

I have a few friends who like to joke that if the Three Wise Men in the Christmas story had been Three Wise Women, things would have turned out very differently—"Three Wise Women would have asked for directions, arrived on time, helped deliver the baby, cleaned the stable, made a casserole, brought practical gifts, and there would be peace on Earth." That is funny, of course, but also makes us look at all the familiar characters and scenarios of our holiday stories and think, "Hey, what if . . . ?" This palooza is about playfully retelling your family's traditional holiday stories for the fun of it—and for the fresh perspective it sometimes gives us.

What's the Palooza?

Make up your own version of a traditional holiday story. Whether it's a southwestern Nativity tale, with Maria and Josef running out of gas and seeking shelter at a desert gas station, or a space-age Thanksgiving, with astronauts landing on the far shores of a distant planet and only having purple corn to eat, see how far from the original you can get while still staying true to the spirit of the story. This is fun to do when you're busy with your holiday traditions, like cooking and baking or decorating the tree or opening Hanukkah presents. Tell a new version every year!

Here are a few ways to think about rejiggering your holiday stories. Think about how you'll adapt the dialogue, the dramatic action, and the descriptions of the characters:

Who can play?
All ages.

What do we need?
Imagination.

Running time?
A few minutes to a half hour.

Budget?
Free.

I once wanted to become an atheist but I gave up—they have no holiday.

—Henny Youngman
(1906–1998)

Tell it as a very modern—even futuristic—story.

Make it a Western, with cowboys and sheriffs and bar-keeps for characters.

Tell it using funny rhyming. Or turn it into a limerick. Or rap it!

Make all the characters dogs. Or make them all kids. Or all girls. Or all elderly folks.

Give the characters monologues.

Make it a sock puppet story. Or tell it using dolls or stuffed animals for characters.

Tell a call-and-response type of interactive story where your audience plays a part. ("It was a cold, dark night." Response: "How cold was it?")

Extrapaloozas

Remembering Out Loud

The traditional stories aren't the only holiday stories worth telling. Families have their own holiday stories, which usually begin "Remember the time when . . ." You fill in the blank. When your two-year-old cousin pulled the self-cleaning lock on the oven while the

A Funny Thing Happened on the Way to the Manger

After many years of suffering through the same old nativity story acted out by the children at her church's Christmas pageant, a friend of mine decided there had to be another way to explore this familiar story. For instance, Mary never says anything in these productions; she just moves from scene to scene, making it clear she's being visited by an angel or riding a donkey or standing over Baby Jesus in the manger. But what is she thinking? What are all of these characters thinking? My friend challenged the children to write monologues for each of the characters (including the manger animals!) and to tell the story entirely from the characters' point of view through monologues. The result was a memorable, poignant, sometimes funny production that made the characters very real to the actors and audience alike.

Thanksgiving turkey was cooking, and by the time the turkey could be liberated from the oven, it was a dry, black rock? Or how about the Passover when a stranger really did knock at the door, just as the family lifted a glass to toast Elijah? Make an audio book of your family holiday stories. Or write them down, illustrate them, and make a Family Storybook. And don't just settle for the stories you already know; ask your relatives questions, get them to tell you stories perhaps you've never heard. Ask them to tell you about holidays when they were young. Our family stories are the thread that keep us together, so polish them up and tell them every time you gather to celebrate.

A Holiday of a Different Color

Use bits and pieces from one holiday to spruce up another. A haunted Christmas. An Easter harvest. Kwanzaa with fireworks. Purim with hearts. Write a song like "The Twelve Days of Summer" with hot dogs and pickles instead of partridges and pear trees. You know how the movie *Shrek* featured characters and creatures from many different fairy tales? Use the characters and symbols from all your family holiday stories and see what a crazy, crowded, unexpected story you can come up with.

April Fool

Wouldn't it be nice if April Fool's Day wasn't quite so much about pranks and tricks and making others look foolish, and was a little more about being nimble and playful and clever like jesters of old? This palooza tosses around ways to play with words that would make one of Shakespeare's fools proud.

Who can play?
Ages 9 and up.

What do we need?
Imagination.

Running time?
Five minutes to off-and-on all day.

Budget?
Free.

What's the Palooza?

Use all the words at your disposal to turn April Fool's Day into a celebration of wit, timing, and humor. Limber up your brain and ponder these eccentric little figures of speech, uses (and misuses) of language, and bits of twisted talk—then see how many ways and times you can sneak them into your patter on April Fool's Day.

Malapropisms

"He's the very pineapple of politeness," Mrs. Malaprop said in Richard Brinsley Sheridan's popular 1775 English play *The Rivals*. This was but one of the many nutty manglings of words for which this character is famous to this day. She should have said, of course, "pinnacle of politeness," but her most endearing and memorable trait is how she would use a similar-sounding word for the word she meant to use. *Malaprop* comes from the French *mal à propos*, which means inappropriate. That the word *malapropism* exists is a tribute to the Mrs. Malaprop's timeless humor. Here are a few more examples of Mrs. Malaprop's malapropisms (as well as the word she meant to use!) that will help you think of ways to play with words and phrases you use every day and turn them amusingly askew:

"... she's as headstrong as an allegory on the banks of the Nile." [alligator]

"I am sorry to say, Sir Anthony, that my affluence over my niece is very small." [influence]

"Why, murder's the matter! slaughter's the matter! killing's the matter! but he can tell you the perpendiculars." [particulars]

"I am sure I have done everything in my power since I exploded the affair." [exposed]

What can you do to turn around words you use every day? To Mom: "A nice plate of bricks and eggs would be tasty today!" To teacher: "When is our consignment due?" To Dad: "How late will you be at the orifice?" To your friend: "Do you want to come over and play scratch today?" Look at the very common things you say to people and search for words to play off, to replace with similar sounding words or variations on the word that make it sound silly. And play it with a straight face—*they* don't need to know that *you* know you're savaging the language!

Chiasmus

This is a lovely little trick that certain famous word lovers used whenever they got the chance. A chiasmus is, simply, a figure of speech in which there is a reversal in the order of words in two otherwise parallel phrases. The word *chiasmus* goes back to the ancient Greeks and their fascination with words and language. *Chi* is the letter "X" in the Greek alphabet, and the Greek word *khiasmos* means "crossing."

Take a familiar example in this line from President John F. Kennedy's inaugural speech: "Ask not what your country can do for you; ask what you can do for your country." It's a simple but effective reversal of words within the phrases. There's also Mae West's signature line: "It's not the men in my life, it's the life in my men." And perhaps the soundest bit of dietary advice ever given: "One should eat to live, not live to eat."

Chiasmus can be achieved by reversing complete

figure of speech (fig-ur uv speech), n.: An expression that uses language in a nonliteral way, such as a metaphor, or in a structured or unusual way, such as chiasmus, or that employs sounds, such as alliteration, to achieve a rhetorical effect.

phrases ("Some have an idea that the reason we in this country discard things so readily is because we have so much. The facts are exactly opposite—the reason we have so much is simply because we discard things so readily."—Alfred P. Sloan). Or chiasmus can come in the form of the simple reversal of sounds ("Why do we drive on a parkway and park on a driveway?"—Richard Lederer).

Try just once today, while speaking or writing, to turn what you're saying into a chiasmus. To the lunch lady at school: "Madame, I may be eating soup on the fly, but I don't deserve a fly in my soup!" Or a little advice for Mom at dinnertime (borrowing a little from our friend Will Shakespeare): "Match the pasta to the sauce, and the sauce to the pasta."

If you can pull off a chiasmus, you're in excellent company. Famous writers and thinkers who were fond of this form include John F. Kennedy, Shakespeare, Winston Churchill, Confucius, Benjamin Franklin, Ralph Waldo Emerson, Oscar Wilde, George Bernard Shaw, and many more.

Retired and Recycled Words

Have you ever wondered where old words go to die? Every time a new edition of a major dictionary is cre-

A Gift for Words

Shakespeare expressed his own love of wordplay, through Holofernes, the schoolteacher, in *Love's Labour's Lost*:

This is a gift that I have, simple, simple; a foolish extravagant spirit, full of forms, figures, shapes, objects, ideas, apprehensions, motions, revolutions: these are begot in the ventricle of memory, nourished in the womb of pia mater, and delivered upon the mellowing of occasion. But the gift is good in those in whom it is acute, and I am thankful for it.

ated, hundreds of old words (like *frutescent* and *impudicity*) are shown the door to make room for new words (like *phat* or *cheesed off*). They don't do this just to be mean; some words have simply fallen out of use (like *record changer*—the CD changer has literally forced the record changer out of business) or no longer apply in a modern context (*ten-cent store*—there used to be a ten-cent store in nearly every small town in America. Today we go to ten-dollar stores!)

Today would be a good day to air out a silly-sounding retired word. Take *snollygoster*. It just recently disappeared from the Merriam-Webster Collegiate Dictionary. A snollygoster is (was?) a "shrewd, unprincipled person, especially a politician." Gee, it's not like there are none of those around anymore! How about making *snollygoster* into a new word with a contemporary meaning? A *snoggo* can be a sneaky, apple-polishing teacher's pet. Or turn *snollygoster* into a verb that means to get tricked: "My sister *snollygogged* me into doing the dishes last night."

Go to www.worldwidewords.org and click on "Weird Words." Word lover Michael Quinion has collected a treasure trove of old, odd words to play with. Click on a word to learn about its origin and meaning. Then figure out how to use it or adapt it for yourself.

Nutty Names

For this one day, make it your business to assign crazy monikers to everyone you speak to. Maybe Mom is "Mama Mia" and Dad is "Father Time." Sister Sarah is "Que Sera Sera." And today the babysitter, Anne, goes by "Anna Montana." Or give everyone a military title, from Colonel to Rear Admiral to Quartermaster to Staff Sergeant. The problem with nutty names is that lots of times they stick—but that's the beauty of a nickname: it comes from nowhere and stays forever.

New Year's Fortune Cookies

Put aside all of those tired resolutions that you forget about by February and start the New Year with tasty good wishes.

What's the Palooza?

Make your own fortune cookies with New Year's wishes inside. First write your fortunes. Predictions of luck and happiness are particularly good for the New Year, or you can mix in some snippets of wisdom that the recipient can make use of all year long. Use the names of your family or friends in your fortunes. You can even use the cookies to make a gift-giving game for your family, by writing fortunes such as "Mom will pack your favorite lunch" or "Sarah will clean your room." You can also try mystery fortunes or joke fortunes.

Cut twenty pieces of paper into ½-inch by 3-inch strips. Print fortunes on pieces of paper using a ballpoint pen—fortunes written in felt tip marker could bleed when placed in the warm, moist cookie. You can also create them on a computer, of course. Set the fortunes aside and assemble all the cookie ingredients and equipment you'll need to make the fortune cookies.

Extrapaloozas

Holiday and Birthday Fortune Cookies

Make fortune cookies for any occasion. Add a few drops of red food coloring to your fortune cookie batter for

Fortune Cookies

1 cup flour
½ cup sugar
2 tablespoons cornstarch
½ teaspoon salt
⅓ cup oil
3 egg whites
½ teaspoon vanilla or 3 drops almond extract
3½ tablespoons water
Butter or nonstick cooking spray to grease the cookie sheet.

Preheat oven to 300°. Combine flour, sugar, cornstarch, and salt in a large bowl. Add oil, egg whites, vanilla or almond extract, and water to dry ingredients. Stir until batter is smooth.

Line a cookie sheet with foil and grease with butter or nonstick cooking spray. Drop a teaspoon of batter (no more) onto the cookie sheet. Gently spread the batter with the back of a spoon to a 4-inch diameter. Bake only 4 cookies at a time. Bake for 15 to 20 minutes, until the cookies begin to lightly brown.

Remove from the oven and immediately remove 1 cookie with a large spatula. Slide the cookie onto a clean towel. Place a fortune onto the center of the cookie and quickly fold in half, pressing the edges together to seal. Immediately fold cookie (sealed side up) over the edge of a bowl to form fortune cookie shape and hold for 30 seconds. Cool formed cookies in a muffin tin so they retain their shape. Continue with the rest of the cookies, working fast, as they harden fairly quickly. It may take some practice to get the cookie shaped just right, but it's fun to make mistakes when you're learning. If the cookies become too stiff to fold, return the cookie sheet to the oven for 1–2 minutes to soften. Or better yet, work with a partner to get the job done swiftly.

Makes about 20 cookies.

pink Valentine's Day cookies. Create conversation-heart-style fortunes like "Love ya, baby" or "Be mine." Mix in green coloring, and you've got fortune cookies for Saint Patrick's Day. Write Irish sayings such as "Wherever you go and whatever you do, may the luck of the Irish be with you." Or put the cookies to use for a limerick game. Put the beginning line of a limerick in each fortune cookie. The person opens his fortune cookie and has to make up a limerick with that starting line.

Fortune Cookies to Go

Decorate empty Chinese takeout boxes (available at paper and party stores) to hold your New Year's fortune cookies. Decorate the boxes with markers and glitter to make a sparkly container for the cookies. Use lots of red—the Chinese believe it brings joy and luck for the New Year.

birthday paloozas

Dig It!

The ancient Egyptians would parade the streets in masks, followed by dancers and tambourine players to honor Bes, the popular god who loved dancing and singing and who protected children from evil spirits. Children often ran alongside the parade, singing and clapping, while other townspeople shouted from the rooftops. The banquets of the pharaohs were also festive occasions and included elaborate feasts, circus-type entertainment, and plenty of wine and beer. Public ceremonies hardly occurred without music and dance. The Egyptians knew how to party!

Replicate the merriment with an ancient Egypt–themed birthday party.

Who can play?

All ages; see age appropriate activities.

What do we need?

Materials depend on the activities, decorations, and food chosen. Many supplies for this theme can be found around the house.

Running time?

Up to 2 hours

Budget?

$–$$$.

What's the Palooza?

Invitations

Design and make invitations using images from ancient Egypt. Go to www.metmuseum.org for ideas or look in books on ancient Egypt from the library. Draw pharaohs, clay pots, pyramids, vases, lotus flowers, mummies, scarabs, or hieroglyphics. Make the invitations look old and mysterious by tinting the paper brown with tea. Gently rub the paper invitations with a paper towel or clean sponge that is just moistened with tea.

Costumes

Encourage guests to come in costume! Browse library books for costume ideas. Think tunic, a sash, a headdress made from a simple cloth placed on the head and held in place with a headband, and lots of jewelry: beads, gold chains, coin belts, decorative wrist- and armbands.

Decorations

Turn the party space into a history museum. Make drawings of Egyptian images similar to the invitation motifs and display them. The birthday child can also use modeling clay to make vases or bowls for the museum. Make a bowl out of clay that stands on human feet, an example of which can also be seen at www.met-museum.org. Alternatively, you might buy inexpensive posters of Egyptian art at your local bookstore or look for Egyptian art posters online (www.art.com). Hang the posters around the room. Paint sheets with pharaoh and mummy faces and cover furniture with the sheets. You might keep the decoration to a minimum and allow the partiers to decorate with murals they have made as part of the wall-painting Egyptionary game (see page 236). Use blue and gold streamers and gold paper place settings from a party or dollar store. Make place cards for each guest using the guest's name, along with the name of an Egyptian god (see page 234). Guests may take on god like qualities for the duration of the party!

Games and Activities

The ancient Egyptians played games that are similar to some of our traditional favorites. Once the guests get into the theme, they will likely invent their own games on the spot. The following suggestions may also stir their imaginations.

Leapfrog (Ages 3–6). In this game, known to the Egyptians as *khuzza lawizza*, players form a line in crouched positions, and whoever goes first leapfrogs over everyone in the line to finally take a crouched position herself in the front of the line. It's more fun (and more Egyptian) if players repeat "Khuzza lawizza" when they reach the end of the line. When leapfrog comes to an end, ask everyone to repeat "Khuzza lawizza" ten times really fast.

Archaeological Dig (Ages 3–6, 6–9). In a sandbox or cooler filled with sand (available in multiple colors at art supply stores), bury a mix of "ancient" artifacts from different periods and cultures. Collect trinkets from museum gift shops or select unique (and unbreakable!) items from your shelves for partygoers to search for. Armed with plastic shovels, young archaeologists can sift through the sand to unearth clues to the past. Bury Egyptian-theme party favors or toys so guests can take their discoveries home with them.

Tug-of-war (Ages 6–9, 9–12). Divide into teams and play tug-of-war using linked elbows instead of rope. A version of this game is still played as sport in the Egyptian countryside.

Indoor games (Ages 6–9, 9–12). Put marbles on the

Egyptian Gods (for placecards)

Anubis: God of the dead. Shown often with the head of a jackal.

Bastet: Goddess often depicted as a cat. She protected women, children, and the sun's power to ripen crops. She was loved: It was not allowed to kill cats in ancient Egypt.

Bes: A jovial god who guarded children from evil spirits. Loves dancing and singing.

Hapy: God of the Nile. His arrival, marked by the river's annual flood, brought riches and fertility to the land.

Horus: Son of Isis and Osiris. Usually depicted as a falcon.

Imhotep: A real person and an architect who designed the first pyramid. Worshiped as a god.

Isis: Wife of Osiris. The perfect mother.

Nut: The sky goddess. She swallowed the sun at night, and it was reborn at sunrise.

Osiris: Isis's husband. God of the afterlife.

Ra: Sun god. Rolls the sun across the sky by day.

Sobek: Crocodile god who controlled the water of the Nile. Crocodiles were sacred animals in ancient Egypt.

Thoth: God of learning. Invented writing, arithmetic, and the calendar.

floor for an old-fashioned marble shooting match, or set out a Ouija board (Egyptian luck board) for older guests—both games date back to the days of the pharaohs.

Mummy Making (Ages 6–9, 9–12). Give each team of two to four players a few rolls of toilet paper and five minutes. The goal is for each team to create a mummy (though everyone will want a turn as mummy before it's over, so be ready with enough toilet paper). Decorate mummies with plastic trinkets and jewelry, scarves, washable marker hieroglyphics. Paint mummy faces with lipstick and eyeshadow. Take Polaroids of each team's creation and send the pictures home with the party favors or thank-you notes. Decorate frames or mounts for the Polaroids using cardboard forms purchased at a craft supply store or shirt boards from the dry cleaner.

Stones in the Nile (Ages 3–6). The lives of the Egyptians were centered on the Nile River and its surrounding desert. Re-create the Nile's silt in the backyard by filling a kiddie pool with sand and water. Place "precious" stones (plastic gemstones from a party or craft store) throughout the box and give strainers to the guests so they can search for them.

Hieroglyphic Treasure Hunt (Ages 6–9, 9–12). Obtain a key for translating hieroglyphics (go to www.members.aol.com/egyptnew/hiero.html or look in books in your local library) and write clues in the symbolic language. Give each team a key, and let them follow the clues to a final prize, perhaps the party favors or some more precious stones.

Egyptian Spa (Ages 6–9, 9–12). Turn the house or party room into an Egyptian spa. Make facials, ointments, and makeup as the ancient Egyptians did, using safe and natural ingredients such as honey. Find drawings of Egyptian women and try to re-create their exotic hairdos.

Pyramids (Ages 9–12). Use pictures from library books as models and guides and ask guests to build their own

ankh, n.: A symbol consisting of a cross with a loop for the top extension and a short crossbar, used in ancient Egypt to signify life.

silt, n.: Fine-grained sediment, especially of mud or clay particles at the bottom of a river or lake.

pyramids using sugar cubes and "mortar" made out of egg whites and confectioners sugar. Glue together ten rows of sugar cubes to make a square. Glue together nine rows of sugar cubes for the second level, then glue them on top of the square of ten. Glue eight rows of cubes for the next level, and so on, decreasing each level by one cube each time. Top the pyramid with a single cube. To make transport home easy, have guests mount their first layer of sugar cubes onto a sheet of cardboard.

Egyptionary (Ages 9–12). A game that incorporates charades and Pictionary using crayons, craypas, and mural paper. Divide the guests into two teams; for each round, assign one team a movie, sentence, or famous person to depict on the wall, and let the other team try to guess the picture. Or have one team member write a message in hieroglyphics for the rest of the team to decipher. The first team to decode their message wins the round. Play this game early in the party, so the murals can be used as decoration for the rest of the day.

Tomb Raider (Ages 6–9, 9–12). Create an ancient tomb complete with pyramids, tunnels, and mummies in a dark or windowless area of the house. Drape large cardboard boxes and tables with white sheets to replicate a pyramid; line up pillows to mark a pathway to buried treasure; mummify tall lamps or dolls with toilet paper and prop them against the wall. Hide party favors and candy throughout the tomb, and supply flashlights for the young explorers to uncover their treasure.

Music

While any Middle Eastern music sets the mood for this party, keep some lighter fare on hand as well. Steve Martin's "King Tut" and the Bangles' "Walk Like an Egyptian" both inspire spontaneous dancing.

Food

Replicate the type of food ancient Egyptians feasted on. Serve grapes, figs, dates, apples, and melons as starters, and follow the recipes below for more substantial dishes. Make a pyramid birthday cake by layering different-sized square cakes. Sprinkle brown sugar "sand" around the base.

Honey Omelet
4 eggs
1 cup milk
1 tablespoon olive oil
3 tablespoons honey
pepper

Mix eggs, milk and oil together, pour into frying pan that has been preheated with a little oil, and thoroughly cook on one side. Turn out onto plate, pour the warmed honey over the omelet, sprinkle with pepper, and serve hot.

Tiger Nut Sweets
Fresh dates (about ½ pound) are blended with a little water. Then add a little cinnamon and chopped walnuts to taste. Shape into balls, coat in honey and ground almonds, and serve.

Hummus
16 ounces chickpeas
2 tablespoons lemon juice
3 cloves garlic, chopped
5 tablespoons sesame seed oil
Salt

Cook and mash the chickpeas; add lemon juice, chopped garlic, and sesame seed oil, then season with salt to make this tasty paste to spread on bread, as popular in Egypt today as it was thousands of years ago.

Favors

Make goody bags using brown paper lunch sacks decorated Egyptian style. Fill the bags with rubber snakes and crocodiles and other Nile-dwelling animals, Egypt coloring books, wooden spinning tops, chocolate coins, temporary tattoos, ankh necklaces or beads, and the framed Polaroids of the mummy-making activity.

Slimed

No birthday party is complete without a few games. This palooza party is all about games—with a retro-game-show twist—that no one ever forgets. Pin the Tail on the Donkey never played like this.

What's the Palooza?

A game-show-themed birthday party in which each round is varied, teams are constantly rejiggered, and no one team actually wins or loses. Friends who did this party made it a double party for two eight-year-old boys whose birthdays are only days apart. Double the fun.

This party needs to take place outdoors, or inside with enough space to conduct games—and no parental stress when sliming takes place. My friends borrowed their church basement.

Invitations

Invite guests to a Slimed party. Make invitations that look like a clock or stopwatch on green cardstock or paper. Write game-show names where the numbers on the clock should be—Beat the Clock, Egg Drop Survivor, Name that Tune, Who Wants to Be a Millionaire. The invitation might read: "Sarah Smith, Come on Down! You're invited to a slick and slimy Game Show Birthday Party to celebrate Alex Brown's 9th birthday! Wear rough-and-tumble playclothes and come ready to win! Sunday, November 9 at 2:00 P.M. at Alex's house. Warning: someone (is it the winner or the loser?) gets slimed!"

- - - - - - -

What do we need?

Supplies vary, depending on the games you want to play, and the amounts depend on the number of children playing. Have a timer, stopwatch, or watch with second hand, and lively game-show-type music to play at the start of each game. You also need different-colored stick-on badges (at least four colors) to differentiate the teams. For Egg Drop Survivor, you will need bubble wrap, Styrofoam peanuts, shredded paper, or other loose packing material, masking tape, and a dozen raw eggs (in case of accidents while wrapping). For Beat the Clock, you need an orange, and a dozen empty milk cartons or stackable shoe boxes. For Name That Tune, you need a CD or cassette player and a CD or cassette sampler of songs the children are likely to know. For Who Wants to Be a Millionaire, you will need a list of at least twenty age-appropriate trivia questions and answers. For Slime, you will need a blender and slime ingredients, which can be made from water, cornstarch, green Jell-O mix, no-tears shampoo, oatmeal, and other fun stuff kids might like to mix together. Have a large drop cloth, plastic tarp, or other protective covering for the area to be slimed. Birthday boy and other team leaders (if not all the guests) should wear bathing suits, rain ponchos, or garbage bags with cut-out head and armholes for the sliming activity. You can also give them disposable painters' hats (available at most hardware stores). For the invitations: (S)lime green card stock or paper and markers. For decorations: Posterboard, markers, balloons, confetti.

- - - - - - -

Running time?

An hour and a half for the party; a day or two to prep with trivia questions and materials.

- - - - - - -

Budget?
$–$$

Decorations

Make elaborate marquee-like signs on posterboard for each game show. Other signs to decorate your game-show space might include "Winners!" or "Grand Prize!" or "Applause!" Liberal strewing of confetti is always a nice touch.

When guests arrive, give everyone randomly colored nametags, being sure to have an even number of players with the same color tags. Blues, reds, greens, and so forth, will be how you divide into teams for the games. For example, when you play Beat the Clock, divide into two teams by calling for reds and blues on one team; greens and yellows on the other. The color-coding of guests allows for an easy, controversy-free mixing of kids into different groups throughout the party so that no one group ever really gets ahead of another in competition. You can take any classic game show and adapt it as an event for your party; here are some game-show ideas you may want to try:

Beat the Clock

Team stunts against the clock. Divide into two or three teams. The first team to complete the stunt wins a point. The team with the most points wins the round. Here are a few suggestions for races and stunts:

Arrange yourselves in a single-file line alphabetically by last name. (Or make it trickier by saying it has to be alphabetically by the last letter in your last name.) First team to alphabetize wins a point.

Form team lines. Give the first person in each line an orange, which is held under the first person's chin. Without using your hands, pass the orange down the line person-to-person. If you drop the orange, or use your hands, the orange goes back to the start of the line. First team to get the orange to the end of the line wins two points.

Form team lines. Without talking, arrange yourselves in a line, single file, shortest person to tallest. First team to arrange correctly by height wins a point. Talking disqualifies a team from the chance to win the point.

Give each team five or six empty milk cartons or stackable shoe boxes and a blindfold. The team leader is blindfolded, and team members arrange cartons or shoe boxes in a circle around the blindfolded team leader, approximately three feet away from him. Teams must instruct or guide their leader to the cartons with verbal instruction only. "Three steps to the left. One baby step to the right." He must locate cartons and boxes and build a tower with them. First team to stack all cartons wins two points.

Name That Tune

Load at least twenty familiar songs onto a CD or an iPod. Choose popular radio hits ("Who Let the Dogs Out?"), or songs from current movies, or theme songs from classic movie sound tracks like *Beauty and the Beast*, *The Lion King*, or *Mary Poppins*, that the kids are likely to know. Form three or four teams and sit in a large circle. Open a can of tennis balls and put the empty can and balls in the center of the circle. Play the first tune. Any player who recognizes the song must grab a tennis ball and put it into the can before he's allowed to shout out the name of the song. Win a point for your team by being the first to correctly name the tune. Shouting out a tune without first putting a tennis ball in the can means you actually lose a point. Team with most points wins and adds the points to their team total.

Egg Drop Survivor

Form teams. Give each team bubble wrap, popcorn-sized Styrofoam packing peanuts or shredded paper, masking tape, and a raw egg. Give every team the same items to work with and the same amounts of each

---

Tips for Game Show Hosts

Look and act like a pro. When running this party, do your best Bob Barker/Alex Trebek/Richard Dawson imitation—wear a flashy outfit, bounce with enthusiasm, banter with the players. And conduct each game with authority. This means having every part of every game carefully mapped out to keep things orderly and moving along.

Have a script and rehearse. Have a step-by-step script for yourself and your helpers, and have all your props and trivia questions (and extras just in case) at the ready. Do a run-through of the party—including a test of any props or activities, to be sure they actually work—with your assistants.

Be prepared. Have one simple extra game in your back pocket, just in case you have a bit of time left before sliming at the end of the party. And have towels and wipes handy for after the sliming. Even if you cover every kid from head to toe in plastic wrap, they will manage somehow to get slime where it doesn't want to be. Of course, that's what they love about it, but still.

material. Ask the teams to build a cushion around their egg using any or all of the materials provided. Use a timer and give each team three minutes to fashion a protective covering for their egg. When time is up, a neutral party (a parent might do a good job here) climbs to the top of the stepladder and is handed one team's egg to drop from the tallest height he can safely get to on the stepladder. Each team's egg is put through successive rounds of drops from the stepladder. The team whose egg survives the longest wins.

Who Wants to Be a Millionaire?

Have twenty to thirty good, age-appropriate trivia questions prepared with point values assigned to each. Put questions in order of increasing point value. Form teams and arrange yourselves in lines by birthday, youngest to oldest. Teams are seated on the floor in lines. The party host asks trivia questions of the first person in each line. The player can answer the question alone, and if correct, win the point value of the question. Or he can ask for help from his teammates, and if correct, win half the point value of the question. If the player gives an incorrect answer, his team loses the point value of the question. The team with the most points at the end wins and adds points to team total. (Variation: Friends who did this party actually made a Powerpoint presentation for the questions, projecting images on the wall and using pictures of George Washington, geometric shapes, and so on, as items to identify. Try this if you have the space and enjoy making Powerpoints!)

Slime Time Finale

First make the slime. Set up a couple of blenders. Let volunteers take turns pouring ingredients such as cornstarch, water, tear-free shampoo, and so on, into the blenders with supervision (see recipe). Blend until frothy and slimy.

Form teams and have team leaders sit on folding chairs on a plastic tarp, facing their teams, wearing swimsuits, a rain poncho, or garbage bags. Party host asks trivia questions one at a time to each team. Every time a team gets a question right, the leader of the other team gets slimed. This means a parent takes a blender full of slime and gently pours a small amount of slime on the team leader. Every time a team gets a question wrong, their own team leader also gets slimed. Obviously, kids start to answer questions right or wrong just to see more sliming. By the end of the round, the parent who is doing the sliming has used up all the slime equally on the team captains.

Food

The basics. A few snacks that are easy to eat without utensils—pretzels, popcorn, and so on. Same goes for cake and drinks—nothing too complicated because this event will end on its high note (the sliming), and food truly is secondary to the hilarity of this party.

Favors

Little sacks filled with play money and erasers shaped like dollar bills. Or mini, key-chain-sized versions of games like Monopoly. Chocolate coins. Gold nugget bubble gum. Bite-sized Hundred Thousand Dollar Bars.

Slime Recipe

For each blender-full of slime, use up to 4 cups of liquid. Mix a combination of any of the following ingredients to make the wettest, gooeyest, drippiest slime you can:

Water

Shampoo (a good lathering, no-tears variety)

Conditioner (also no-tears)

Bubble bath (no-tears)

Yogurt

Green Jell-O mix

Cornstarch

Oatmeal

Popcorn!

I like to think of popcorn as the food equivalent of a giggle. This palooza party celebrates popcorn for the lighthearted, yummy bit of fun it is.

What's the Palooza?

An all-popcorn birthday party. Popcorn. It's a fun word to say, it's fun to eat, it's fun to work with—and it's the main ingredient for a lively, memorable party.

Invitation

Handmade, computer-generated, or store-bought invites that are shaped like old-fashioned candy-striped popcorn boxes overflowing with popcorn. Better yet, write the invitation information (who, when, where) right on an empty popcorn box: "A Popcorn Party! Come celebrate Susie Smith's birthday at a hoppin', poppin' popcorn party. . . ." Drop the box in guests' mailboxes or collapse the box, fold flat, and mail in an oversized envelope.

Costumes

None required, though adult hosts might wear scads of popcorn necklaces and refer to each other as "Pop" and "Corny" for the duration of the party.

Activities

Craft activities first, then come the games.

Rainsticks. Give each guest a small empty mailing tube with one end secured with painter's tape. Take a hearty handful of plain, unpopped popcorn kernels and drop it into the tube. Secure the other end with painter's tape. Decorate the tubes Native American style with markers. Then shake your rainstick at the sky and get out your umbrella.

Popcorn Necklaces. Set out bowls of plain popped popcorn. (If you pop it the day before, the popcorn will be less brittle and breakable than freshly popped.) Set out bowls of any or all of the following: licorice nibs (all colors), jelly beans, gumdrops, Life Savers, gummy rings, gummy fish, gummy worms, chocolate-covered or plain raisins. Give each guest a threaded needle (be ready with assistance as necessary) and show them how to thread the puffs of popcorn and treats (littlest ones may need to hand pieces of candy and popcorn to an adult to thread). Alternate between the popcorn and treats; create patterns of colors or shapes; do all gummies and popcorn or all red candies and popcorn or make sure

old maid, n.: An unpopped kernel of corn, too dry on the inside to have any pop left in it; usually found at the bottom of a bowl of popcorn.

you capture all the colors of the rainbow! When you've finished stringing your necklace, have a grown-up tie a knot connecting the two ends.

Popcorn Hands. Arrange about 12 cups of plain popped popcorn in each of three big bowls. Set out a bowl of 60 pieces of red licorice nibs or red jellybeans, and a bowl of various 6-inch bits of bric-a-brac like shimmery ribbon, yarn, lace, plastic chain, and so on. Give each guest a clear plastic food prep glove, have them blow into the glove to open it up, then put a red nib or jellybean in the end of each finger. Next, fill the glove with 2 cups of popcorn, not filling the glove too tightly and leaving room at the top to close. Close the glove with a twist tie, then cover the twist tie with a bit of ribbon, lace, or yarn. Place a plastic ring on one or two fingers. A creepy skull ring or a fabulous fake jewel ring is always nice. Or even a Band-Aid, for the injured popcorn hand.

Popcorn Pillow Fight. Needless to say, this game is played outdoors or not at all. Fill plastic grocery bags with the least expensive industrial-sized popcorn you can find. Tie closed with a loose knot of the bag handles. Give every guest a popcorn pillow and let them go at it as if it were midnight at a slumber party. When the popcorn flies—and it will—this game's over. The birds and critters will gladly clean up.

Popcorn Kernelbag Toss. This is just like a beanbag toss, but using bags made of small sweatsocks filled with plain unpopped popcorn kernels. Fill a dozen small white sweatsocks (decorated with markers to look like an ear of corn, of course!) with corn, and tie closed with a rubber band. Set up five buckets in a straight line. The buckets can be the same size, or get smaller (and therefore be a harder target to hit). Put different candies or little treats in each of the buckets, enough in each bucket for each child to get a treat, perhaps featuring treats and candies of increasing appeal as the buckets get smaller. Guests line up about two feet in front of the first bucket, and the first player tosses a bag toward the first bucket. If she misses the bucket, she goes to the back of the line. If she gets the bag in the bucket, she chooses a treat from the bucket and goes to the back of the line. Each time a player tosses, she is trying to reach the next farthest bucket from the one she last successfully hit. Players are highly motivated in this game, so you'll have to keep going until every player has hit every bucket and selected her treats.

Popcorn Race. This is also an outside game. Each player affixes a plastic cup to each foot. Before the party, prepare the cups by poking a hole in the center of the bottom of the cup and pushing a sturdy rubber band through the hole. Snag a large paper clip to the rubber band on the inside of the cup so it doesn't slip back through the hole. Players attach the cups on top of their feet, secured by the rubber band around their shoes. Break up the guests into two teams. Set up two buckets ten yards or so away, side by side, about five feet apart. Fill each player's two cups with popcorn. Players race to the bucket and, without using their hands, try to empty as much popcorn from each cup on their feet into the bucket. Obviously, popcorn will be trying to fall out on the way to the bucket, so players must race, but carefully! After depositing the popcorn, players race back to start and the next players in line repeat. The team with the most popcorn in the bucket wins.

Food

This is a great party to have in the middle of the afternoon, when whole meals don't need to be served, just snacks and birthday cake. Serve a frosted sheet cake decorated with a couple of rowdy popcorn clowns, ice cream, and popcorn/trail mix snacks.

Popcorn Clowns
1 cup butter
10-ounce bag of marshmallows
2 quarts plain popped popcorn
8 ice cream cones (pointed sugar cones)
M&Ms

How, Exactly, Does Popcorn Pop?

It's not the heat that makes popcorn pop, it's the tiny drop of water inside each kernel. The water is stored inside a circle of soft starch, which is surrounded by the kernel's hard outer surface. As the kernel heats up, the water inside expands and puts so much pressure against the hard outer surface that it explodes. As the kernel bursts open, the soft starch inside becomes inflated and bursts, essentially turning the kernel inside out. That's your popped corn!

Corny Jokes and Riddles

Why did the farmer stop telling secrets in the cornfield? Because the corn was all ears!

How is an ear of corn like an army? It has lots of kernels!

What did the salt say to the popcorn? Season's greetings!

What vegetable can you throw away the outside, cook the inside, eat the outside, and throw away the inside? Corn!

Gumdrops
8 eight-inch paper doilies
8 Styrofoam coffee cups

In a large heavy saucepan, melt the butter over low heat. Add the marshmallows and stir until melted. Set aside a small amount of this mixture in a dish to use for "gluing" candy to the clown. Gently fold popped popcorn into the saucepan with a soft spatula (so as not to break the popcorn puffs). Shape the marshmallowy popcorn into 8 balls, approximately 3 inches in diameter. Let them set on buttered waxed paper.

When your balls are set, add M&M eyes and nose to each ball using marshmallow glue. Cut a gumdrop into the shape of a mouth and glue it in place. Glue gumdrops on either side of the ball for ears. Glue M&Ms all over the ice cream cone (as few or as many as you like), then smear glue along the rim of the cone and press gently onto the top of the popcorn head. Don't let go until you're sure it'll stay put.

For the collar, fold the doily in half, half again, and half again. Then unfold and bunch up the center into a one-inch stem. Hold it like a flower by the stem and spread out the edges to form a ruffle. Cut the top three inches off the top of a Styrofoam coffee cup to form a ring. Center the doily in the ring, then place the clown on top of the doily.

Arrange two or three clowns on your sheet cake. You can write a birthday message on the cake, working around where the clowns will be. Or you can make each clown a little sign to hold, using a toothpick and small piece of paper, that says anything you like: "Poppy Birthday, Susie!" Or "Many Poppy Returns!"

Snack mixes can include popcorn, pretzels, cheesy goldfish, salty nuts, raisins, crunchy cereal. Set out different combinations in bowls. Serve beverages as necessary.

Favors

Fill an empty popcorn box with little trinkets and treats.

Drop a popcorn beanbag in each box, as well as the guests' popcorn hands and necklaces.

Popcorn Stories

End your party with a rousing reading of any one of these wonderful popcorn stories. Sandburg's is a favorite, and so is Tomie DePaola's.

The Popcorn Patch, by Edna Chandler
The Popcorn Book, by Tomie DePaola
Rootabaga Stories, "The Story of Jason Squiff and Why He Had a Popcorn Hat, Popcorn Mittens and Popcorn Shoes" or *Prose and Poetry for Young People,* "The Huckabuck Family and How They Raised Popcorn in Nebraska and Quit and Came Back," both by Carl Sandburg
The Popcorn Dragon, by Jane Thayer
Princess Rosetta and the Popcorn Man, by Mary Wilkins

He's gonna sing, folks. Now's the time to go out and get the popcorn.

—Bob Hope, *Road to Bali*

Clowning Around

What can I say? This palooza celebrates clowns for what they truly are—the life of the party.

What's the Palooza?

A birthday party where every kid's a circus clown.

Invitations

Make a mock employment ad: "Wanted: A few good clowns. Come to Andy's Big Top Birthday Party at his house on Saturday, February 4 at 2:00. Wear play clothes and bring a few good gags."

Decorations

Balloons! Brightly colored balloons everywhere. Put party hats on every stuffed animal in the house and pull them in a wagon like a circus parade. Make circus posters advertising acts featuring your guests as if they were performers: "Billy, the World's Strongest Man!" "Maggie, the Human Mouse!" Play Big Top music. Mom could dress as the Bearded Lady, Dad as the Ringmaster. Or vice versa.

Activities

Make Your Clown Hat. When guests first arrive, have everyone decorate a plain plastic hat. On a long covered table, set out hats, glue, glitter, pom-poms, scraps of fabric, plastic flowers, sequins, and other crazy or col-

Classic Whiteface Clown

orful trinkets in plastic bowls. Encourage conservative use of glue so the hats will dry quickly.

Dress the Part. Think about what kind of clown you want to be. First there's the classic whiteface clown, with a base of all white, eyebrows, nose, and mouth painted on in black or red, and smallish circles of red on the cheeks.

Auguste

There's also Auguste, the most comic clown face (like Bozo or Ronald McDonald). The base color is a pink or flesh color instead of white. The mouth is widely outlined with white, as are the eyes. Eyebrows and cheek color are added. Auguste is the most slapstick of clowns; his clothes are exaggerated and outlandish.

Finally, there is the Character or Tramp. He usually wears tattered clothes and a kind of weary, sad expression. There's pink or flesh color around the eyes, white around the lips, and a stubbly bearded look all over the cheeks and chin.

The Tramp

Put together costumes out a trunk full of pieces of clothing and props. Grown-ups help with the face painting. Use the white or pink face paint for a base and reds and blacks for the features—have black eye pencils (thick and thin) and plenty of fresh sponges on hand for individual applications. Everyone gets a red clown nose; crazy wigs would be nice, too.

High Jinks. Once in costume, form pairs or small groups to make up and perform short clown sketches. Get chased by a dog. Wait for a bus. Find a coin you've dropped. Think of small things that can be done and exaggerated to great effect. Clowns get big laughs for trying something (unsuccessfully) over and over, each time a little different. For example, try to open a prank can of nuts. It's too hard. Use a cloth. Put it between your knees and use both hands. Try your mouth (just pretending, of course) or banging it against your head (also pretending). Exaggerate your actions and make it bigger each time. When the jar finally opens, the snake pops out and scares you right out of your seat. Add pratfalls—skips, stumbles, and somersaults—then do the double take to see if anyone's watching. If you know how, do cartwheels. Juggle—especially if you don't know how! Take time to rehearse your skits, then perform for each other. Do a final skit with the whole group involved in an exaggerated tug-of-war. Make a video of the skits and play it back at the end of the party; parents coming in for pickup will love seeing the clownery on-screen.

Balloon Sandwich. This race calls for cooperation between clowns. Two players begin back-to-back at the starting line. Place a balloon between the backs of each duo. During the race the balloon cannot touch the ground, and no hands are allowed to touch the balloon, but the players must make it to the finish line without dropping the balloon. A popped balloon or one that touches the ground returns the team to the starting line. The first sandwich to get to the end wins.

Balloon Swords. Get long, skinny balloons and a balloon pump or an expert balloon inflater with superior lung capacity. A balloon sword is easy to make—and the ensuing balloon sword battle is a rollicking good time.

Blow up an extra-long balloon, leaving about 4 inches uninflated in the tail end, and knot it.

Fold the balloon about six inches from the knot end.

Classic Clowns

For inspiration, see classic clown performances in movies like *The Circus, The Immigrants,* and *The Kid* with Charlie Chaplin, *Inspector General* with Danny Kaye, or *The Greatest Show on Earth* and *Here Comes the Circus* with Emmett Kelly Jr. Look at Turk Pipkin's *Be a Clown* and www.ringling.com/ activity for more clown ideas.

Squeeze both parts of the folded balloon about two inches from the fold.

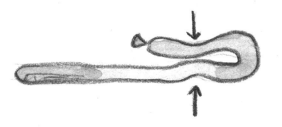

Twist the balloon two or three times at the place where you squeezed it, until the twist holds in place.

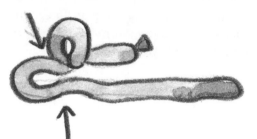

Fold the balloon again, as if you're making the second loop on your shoelaces, then twist again until the twist holds.

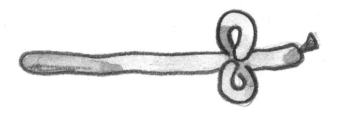

Finally, tuck the long part of the balloon between both handles. En garde!

Food

Offer popcorn in big bowls, animal crackers in those cute circus boxes, beverages (it's been said that clowns are partial to orange soda), and cake.

Tooty Fruity Gumdrop Birthday Cake. Make a layer cake out of your favorite cake mix and white or pink frosting. Set a plastic horn on the middle of the cake top, and tape a business-card-sized birthday greeting to the top of the horn: "Happy Birthday, Andy, You Clown!" Have the birthday clown cover the cake with gumdrops.

Favors

Fill empty popcorn boxes with bubblegum, kazoos, balloons, juggling balls or beanbags, bow ties, whoopee cushions, or punchballs.

Wiffle Ball Championship

For anyone who finds the crack of a bat a siren call, this palooza party will punch your ticket. This is an in-the-yard or in-the-park party, a nice bit of festive fresh air.

What's the Palooza?

An all-star party for the little slugger and his buddies. The Wiffle ball is light, so it can't be thrown or hit too far, and it's perfect for playing in tight areas—no regulation field necessary. That it was invented by someone's dad so his son could learn to throw curveballs . . . well, that just marries everything we love about America's pastime with everything we admire about American ingenuity.

Invitations

Cut softball-sized circles out of sturdy white paper, then decorate them with black marker to look like a Wiffle ball (eight vertical oblong perforations evenly spaced around the top half of the ball). Across the bottom half of the ball, write something like: "Please join the starting lineup for the Wiffle Ball Championship (and Timmy's 8th Birthday!) on June 6 at Miller Park. First pitch is at 2:00. Wear home uniforms (sneaks and playclothes)."

Uniforms

When guests arrive, divvy them up into teams and give them each a plain white T-shirt and fabric markers to adorn with their team names.

Name Your Team

Bandits
Beavers
Bees
Buckeyes
Comets
Diamonds
Dragons
Grays
Jammers
Kings
Knights
Monarchs
Mudcats
Muskies
Mustangs
Redhawks
Seals
Spiders
Swatters
Wings

Food

For snacks, serve popcorn and peanuts in ballpark-style paper bags or boxes. Or splurge and rent an old-style popcorn machine and dispense on the spot. Serve hot dogs on buns, with easy-to-use condiment dispensers at the ready, along with root beer or other drinks. For cake, serve white-frosted cupcakes decorated like a Wiffle ball or baseball. Have plenty of water handy, because popcorn and peanuts, as well as a rousing game of Wiffle ball can make you mighty thirsty.

Games and Activities

Name your teams and make your uniforms. Prepare your team assignments in advance—nothing's uglier than kids arguing over who's on what team. When guests arrive, sort them into their two teams, then have them choose a team name. This also can get a little bickery, but it will pass quickly. Give white T-shirts and blue permanent markers to members of one team, and a white T-shirt and red permanent markers to the other team. Put a shirt cardboard inside each T-shirt (so marker doesn't soak through the other side of the shirt) and, working on card tables or picnic tables, have players write the name of their team on the front of their shirts, and their own name and a favorite number on the back. Next have them take a plain white water bottle and do the same thing—mark it with the team name and the player's name and number. Fill the bottles with water to drink during the party, and then to take home with them as favors.

Have them put on their T-shirts, and take a Polaroid of each player in a batter's pose. Write the player's name and team across the bottom of the picture and save it to drop into his goody cup. Take team photos with a regular camera to incorporate into your thank-you notes later.

Play ball! There are as many versions of backyard Wiffle ball as there are freckles on a kid's face, and that's part of the fun of it. For your party, it's probably a good idea to stick reasonably close to the *real* rules of Wiffle ball, at least initially, to keep order on the field.

A Wiffle ball field is V-shaped rather than diamond shaped like a baseball field. Home plate is at the crux of the V, and the fair-ball playing field consists of everything inside the V. Use plastic cones to delineate the entire field, set evenly across from each other at spots along the V to mark where a ball is a single, double, triple, or home run. Try to have the width between home run markers at least 20 feet, and the distance between home plate and the Home Run Area at least 60 feet.

A full Wiffle ball team in the field consists of catcher, pitcher, double area player, triple area player, and home run area player. If you have more than five players on each team, arrange additional players evenly in the home run area.

The rules of Wiffle ball are similar to the rules of baseball, except there is no base running when someone gets a hit. Instead, the umpire (that would be a fair

Casey at the Bat

Be sure to have a copy of this classic poem to read at some point during your party. A favorite edition is *Casey at the Bat: A Ballad of the Republic Sung in the Year 1888*, written by Ernest Lawrence Thayer and beautifully, vividly illustrated by C. F. Payne.

and attentive grown-up) keeps track of the hits and outs, as well as the imaginary progression of base runners around the field. So, for instance, the first batter hits a ball into the single area (that's a single). The second batter hits the ball to the double area (a double), advancing the first batter to imaginary third base. The third batter hits a ball to the triple area (a triple) and two runs score (the runners that were at imaginary second and third). Like baseball, there are three outs per side per inning in a nine-inning game (which goes quickly because there's no baserunning). Three strikes or a caught ball in fair or foul territory are an out. No bunting, no bases on balls (walks), and obviously, there is no stealing of bases—there are no bases! In a complete inning, both sides must have an at-bat. Tied games call for extra innings.

Positions are assigned at the beginning of the game, and players bat in this order: pitcher, catcher, double area player, triple area player, and home run area player(s). That's it. Now let's play ball!

Sing It! Someone (likely an enthusiastic grownup) needs to lead off with the National Anthem before the game starts. And that same someone might as well call for a seventh-inning stretch and a little "Take Me Out to the Ball Game." It would be nice to prepare a little tape of the music to these songs to play in a grand and stately manner. Otherwise these favorites are eminently

singable a cappella. And maybe slip in a rousing reading of "Casey at the Bat"?

All-Star Challenge. If time allows after the game, let the players take a little target practice. Affix a big bull's-eye-type target to a tree, or hang a hula hoop from a tree by a rope at the top, and secure it with a rope to the ground at the bottom. At a distance of about ten paces (closer if necessary), give each player three throws at the target. The player with the most bull's-eyes (or closest to the bull's-eye) or the most throws that make it inside the hula hoop wins.

You can also play a quick game of home-run derby. Give each player ten at-bats (no players in the field). The player with the most home runs wins. Wiffle ball and bat sets as prizes for the winners would be nice.

Knock-Around Ball. Here's where the plastic Wiffle ball bat really comes in handy. Just before party quitting time, string your baseball piñata from a tree and give each guest a go at it. You'll see a lot of "swinging for the bleachers," so make sure everyone backs up. The candy carnage is collected and goes right into goody cups, which you're handing to them as they leave. Perfect timing.

Favors

With markers, decorate plain white sixteen-ounce plastic cups or baseball helmets ("Wiffle Ball Championship, June 6, 20XX, Timmy's 8th Birthday, Guest's Name"). Drop the Polaroid picture you took at the beginning of the party into the cup. Add a small handful of Bazooka Joe or Double Bubble bubblegum, a snack-size Cracker Jack, a pack of baseball cards, a whistle, and any other baseball-related goodies you like. Don't forget to send them home with their water bottles, too.

Wiffle Ball Tips

Always catch a Wiffle Ball with two hands because they're light and lively, which can make them hard to catch.

To catch, don't wait for a ball to fall into your cupped hands; instead, gently clap your hands around the ball when it's about a foot above your head.

To throw a Wiffle ball reasonably straight, throw it overhand, gripped with your index and middle fingers making a V over the ball, perforated holes facing up.

To hit the ball well, try to swing smoothly more than with force. The ball is light and can only travel so quickly, so a clean swing rather than a monster bash is more effective.

Ytrap Drawkcab (Backward Party)

Watching a movie run in reverse is always good for a laugh. So is a backward birthday party. Indulge in some absolute silliness with a palooza party that's topsy-turvy, back-to-front, and inside-out.

What's the Palooza?

A Backward Birthday Party, where all the traditional activities, foods, and decorations are turned inside out. It smacks of anarchy—which children love—but it's actually a well-organized, orderly affair, simply run in reverse.

Invitations

Invitations should be written backward: "Party Backward a to Invited You're" or truly backward so it can only be read in a mirror ("er'uoY detivnI ot a sdrawkcaB ytraP") These can be made by hand or on the computer. You can also write the whole invitation upside down. Or you can write your invitation as a thank-you note ("Thank you for coming to my party!")—and write your thank-you notes on invitations. Whatever the form of your invite, just be sure to include the important information like who, when, and where! And mention backward clothing requirement (below).

Costumes

As advised on the invitation,

everyone should wear things backward or inside out or buttoned crazily. One can always take this to the lunatic extreme, which is an especially fun thing for the hosts to do.

Decorations

Hang balloons by string from the ceiling. Hang a "Happy Birthday" banner upside down or backward, if you can read the backward message. Post an "Exit" sign outside your front door, and an "Entrance" sign at the back door. Arrange furniture, pictures, knickknacks, notes or magnets on fridge, and so on backward or upside down.

When they arrive, greet guests with a hearty, "Good-bye, glad you came!" Guests are given nametags with their names written backward, which are stuck on their backs. (Some people's names are so funny written backward, they're almost guaranteed to have a new nickname!) As everyone is arriving and getting their nametags, and so on, have every guest make a guess at how many Tootsie Rolls, gum balls, and trinkets are in

Make Your Own Ice Cream Mondays

This is an easy treat, and twice as tasty and fun because you make it yourself. Have chocolate, vanilla, strawberry, and mint chocolate chip ice cream out with scoops at the ready. Arrange chocolate sprinkles, rainbow sprinkles, small marshmallows, mini chocolate chips, gummy bears, peanut butter chips, chocolate sauce, whipped cream, and so on in separate bowls with spoons. Each child is given a big bowl and drops their choice of toppings into their bowl. Put one scoop of ice cream in a cone, then drop it upside down in the bowl. You can lift the cone and eat by dipping and redipping in your bowl of toppings. Or you can use the cone as a spoon to scoop bites of ice cream and toppings down the hatch.

the big jars. They write their guesses on a paper with their backward names. Don't tell them this, but the person who is furthest from the correct number wins the jar.

Food

Before any games are played, cake and ice cream is served! Hand out sheets with "Happy Birthday to You" lyrics written out backward. Birthday hats are worn under the chin, with the elastic string going around the head. For a birthday cake, set a big cupcake on a large dish and arrange the candles sticking out of the sides of the cupcake. Light the candles, sing (backward), blow out the candles—and *then* make a wish! The real treat for everyone is Make Your Own Ice Cream Mondays, which are upside-down ice cream sundaes. Or serve Frozen Hot Chocolate, a truly backward, counterintuitive treat if ever there was one. Next serve slices of pizza set point side down in a plastic cup. Drinks are slurped from small bowls.

Activities

The best way to play the games at a backward party is to take some familiar games and turn them around a bit. Pick and choose any of the following, depending on your time and space considerations. And as with any birthday party, be prepared for more games than you think you'll get to—it's painful to find yourself with time left on the party clock and nothing to do.

What Simon Doesn't Say. This game calls for, essentially, disobeying Simon. So if Simon says Sit, everyone stands. If Simon says Run, everyone stands still. If he says Touch your head, everyone reaches for their toes. The trick is, of course, processing what Simon is saying, and quickly figuring out what the opposite of that is. When someone accidentally does what Simon says, they're out.

Pin the Donkey on the Tail. This is just what it sounds like. Affix the tail to the wall, blindfold each player, and hand them the donkey to try to match up with the waiting tail.

Backward Charades. Each player gets the name of an exotic animal (or whatever you want your theme to be) stuck on his back, so everyone can see "who" he is but him. In turn, each of the other players tries to act out the animal. The person who gets the player to guess the correct animal is the next guessing victim.

Backward Challenge Course. Set up a challenge course that's made up of two sets of five stations and break the group into two teams. At each station, the player must pick up an object and carry it to the next station, where the next object is collected. All four objects must make it with the player to the fifth station. What's so hard about this? Let's see. The player has to go from station to station walking backward (no looking back). At the station, he must pick up the object without using his hands. And as he goes to the next station, backward, he

Frozen Hot Chocolate

A sweet shop in New York City called Serendipity 3 has become famous for this concoction. It is so sublime it doesn't matter that you can't really have something that's frozen *and* hot.

4 cups half and half
4 one-and-a-quarter-ounce individual packages of rich hot cocoa mix (your favorite brand in its chocolatiest, most indulgent variety)
8 tablespoons butter, cut into chunks
8 ounces best quality milk chocolate, broken into pieces
8 oz best quality bittersweet chocolate, broken into pieces
8 cups ice cubes

Heat half and half in a large saucepan over medium low heat until bubbles just begin to form around the edges and the mixture is heated through (2–3 minutes). Remove from heat, whisk in cocoa mix until blended. Add butter, milk chocolate, and bittersweet chocolate until smooth and blended.

Pour half the chocolate mixture into a blender container and add half the ice. Cover and blend on a high speed, pulsing as necessary to break up the ice (30 to 60 seconds). When the mixture is smooth, pour into individual mugs (it is hot cocoa after all!). Repeat with the second half of chocolate mixture and ice. Makes 12 one-cup servings.

Handy Words for Various Important Uses at a Backward Party

Abracadabra
Am-scray
Balderdash
Booby trap
Boondoggle
Bushwacker
Chowderhead
Clodhopper
Cockamamie
Fiddlefaddle
Fiddlesticks
Flabbergasted
Gobbledygook
Higgledy-piggledy
Hunky-dory
Jabberwocky
Kit and kaboodle
Lilliputian
Lollapalooza
Lollygagger
Palindrome
Poppycock
Ramshackle
Rigamarole
Thingamabob
Topsy-turvy

cannot put the first object down in order to pick up the next. Have stations set up at varying heights (table, chair, the ground) and have the objects be odd shapes and sizes that the person has to use his noodle to figure out how to pick up. Maybe a hula hoop, a roll of toilet paper, a pinecone, a playing card. At the fifth station, he deposits the objects, then puts an egg balanced on a plastic spoon in his mouth and carries it all the way to the starting line, backward. You can also turn this game into a relay, where a person is waiting at each station to receive an object from a teammate.

Scavenger Hunt. Take your basic scavenger hunt and turn it inside out. All the items on each list are spelled backward, so hunters first have to unscramble the list (each list is different). After the players find all the items, they have to use all of them in a Mad Lib to tell a silly story. After they create the Mad Lib, they have to hide the items in a prescribed area, and then the scrambled lists are exchanged, and each has to find the items that have been hidden. Give each player time to hide his items, and preferably each player's items are hidden in a different area.

Musical Chairs. Of course, we sit when the music starts, not stops. And each round, a chair is eliminated, but not a player. So at the end of the game, there's one chair left and all the kids are vying for it. This game should go near the end of the party. So should the next one.

Backward Tag. One person is chased by everyone who isn't It. This game can look like swarming bees—it's just the game to play while waiting for parents to pick up.

Favors

Anything nutty will do. Crazy straws. Groucho Marx glasses. Kazoos. Whoopee cushions. Paperback copies of *Amelia Bedelia*. Whatchamacallit bars and Dum Dum lollipops. Bazooka Joe bubblegum. Put it all in a paper lunch bag marked "Baddy Bag." And don't forget to say "Hello! Welcome!" when your guests leave your party!

Paper Chase

I've played these games with my kids since they were small—hiding clues on notes around the house, leading them on little paper capers that never failed to delight. For her sixteenth birthday, my daughter asked for a paper chase party that had her and her friends traipsing all over the campus at UCLA. At heart, this palooza is a treasure hunt, as much fun to invent as it is to play.

What's the Palooza?

An on-location paper chase birthday party requires a few things that most kids' birthday parties don't: first, it calls for high-level planning and participation on the part of parents, who need to research, write, and plant the paper clues. It also calls for a location with plenty of room to maneuver. A park, a mall—one friend used his whole small town for his kids' paper chase. The more area you have to work with, the more options you'll have creating sets of clues for two teams. Finally, you need adult supervision during the chase itself, preferably two adults per team, and perhaps an additional adult per team to act as a roving troubleshooter, moving ahead of the teams to make sure clues remain in place throughout the chase.

Location exploration. To create a paper chase, start by scoping out your location. I bicycled all over the UCLA campus choosing clue sites, and then again hiding the clues on the day of the party. Let's say your paper chase will take place at a big park, complete with wooded bike paths, picnic area, a playground, etc. Make a list of 12 to 20 clue sites you might use for two team chases.

Write clues. Then take your list of sites and begin creat-

Who can play?
Ages 9 and up.

What do we need?
Resources and references to create clues for the paper chase. Materials for any activity/challenges that punctuate the chase. Pizza, beverages, birthday cake; favors associated with the theme of your paper chase.

Running time?
One and a half hours.

Budget?
$

ing clues by thinking of ways to integrate the sites into the clues themselves; if one site is the foot of a certain hemlock tree, the clue that leads to that site can both describe the location of that site and require that the players be able to identify a hemlock. You can do the same for leaves, rocks, and other natural materials: give each team a couple of field guides to use to help solve their clues.

Write clues that are poems or riddles, mini–crossword puzzles, or word scrambles. Use lyrics from their favorite songs; refer to characters from their favorite books, movies, or television shows. Or write clues that require individual team members to contribute a different part to the solution. Write a clue in Latin or French or whatever languages they may be studying at school. Use a cryptic snip of Shakespeare they must decipher in order to solve the clue. Or maybe a series of trivia questions the answers to which add up to the clue.

Make it personal. Write a clue or two that shows you know them well—their interests, their quirks, what makes them laugh. Weave a little funny little reference to Beth and her mayonnaise sandwiches. Or to Steve and his lucky socks. And bring other people into the scheme if you can. Make the park ranger a clue site!
You can also create chase clues that make it part paper chase, part scavenger hunt. One friend of mine had a chase where a clue led the chaser to Burger King, where she had to get her picture taken with a Burger King employee. Scavenger hunt–type items to collect might be receipts, bags or wrappers, photos, or stamps—prove-you-were-there type stuff.

The more elaborate the clues, varied the sites, and interactive the whole experience, the more fun the hunt. The paper chase that each team follows ends up in the same final spot. One or two adults need to plant the chase clues shortly in advance of the start of the party. And one or two adults should accompany each team on the chase.

First team to get to the final spot wins. The prize should be funky and fun—a trophy constructed entirely of paperclips. Or commemorative T-shirts that say: "I Chased the Paper—and Won! Molly's B-day, 6/4/04." A picnic lunch, cupcakes with trivia questions attached with a plastic sword. Goody treats like minipuzzles or games.

Picture Paper Capers

Paper chases became an odd obsession in my house starting when the kids were very young. I drew picture clues that led them from spot to spot. A drawing of an iron, for instance, sent them scouring the house for the iron, where they found a picture of a bedroom slipper, and so on. It became a great rainy day ritual for us all, and as they grew older, the game became more complex, involving tricky picture and word clues, and finally, of course, the elaborate caper that ate UCLA!

Film Buffoons

Have you ever watched a musical and had an uncontrollable urge to burst into song? Or found yourself bellowing "Yo, Adrian!" after a screening of *Rocky*? For a great sleepover party, take your cue from those wildly interactive midnight showings of *The Rocky Horror Picture Show* or Sing-along *Sound of Music*. Choose a kid-friendly film like *The Wizard of Oz*—or I've been told (ahem) that *Footloose* or *Shrek* both make excellent film buffoon paloozas—and move the furniture back; there's going to be lots of singing and dancing and hamming it up.

Who can play?

All ages, depending on the film.

What do we need?

Video or DVD. Five-and-dime props, costumes, refreshments, and party favors suitable for your movie theme.

Running time?

An evening.

Budget?

$$

What's the Palooza?

Watching a movie while everyone gets to "be" a character, recite the classic lines, sing the big songs, or dance the big numbers. At a Sing-Along *Sound of Music* event (which inspired this palooza), before the movie begins, a master of ceremonies gives the crowd their props and cues for acting up the film. He tells everyone, "Sing about your favorite things! Cheer for Julie! Wave your edelweiss! Bark at Rolf (the telegram boy)! Boo at the bad guys! Join in earnest choruses of "Climb Ev'ry Mountain!" Themed props allow the audience to become part of the song-filled classic.

Start with these ideas to plan your own Film Buffoon party:

Invitations

Make your own out of blank index cards. Use a paper hole punch to make the edges look perforated. Write "Admit One to a Film Buffoon Birthday Party" and your where and when details. Buy a roll of real tickets from the party store and drop a few in the invitation envelope.

Decorations

Make homemade movie posters for your movie using pictures from books and magazines or the Internet. Make a big "Now Showing" movie theater marquee with your movie's title and stars. You can even make your own big "Hollywood" sign. You can also decorate using ideas from whatever movie you're screening, from big black spots everywhere for a screening of *101 Dalmations* to spaceship-like electronic panels made of cardboard for a screening of *Star Wars*. You can go as far as you want, dreaming up atmospheric touches for your film buffoon party.

Costumes

Dress like characters from your movie! You can tell your guests in advance to dress like their favorite character from the film, or provide simple costume fodder from which they can create their own look when they get there.

In Hollywood, if you can't sing or dance, you wind up as an after-dinner speaker.

—Ronald Reagan
(1911–)

Film Buffoon Film Ideas

No matter what you choose, this party is failproof because kids love movies! You may very well have your own odd favorite movie to turn into a great film buffoon party. Or any of the following, depending on ages of the guests, would work:

Annie	The Lion King	The Planet of the Apes
Beauty and the Beast	Mary Poppins	Rocky
Bye Bye Birdie	Music Man	Shrek
Cinderella	My Fair Lady	Snow White
Fiddler on the Roof	The Nightmare before	The Sound of Music
Footloose	Christmas	Star Wars
Grease	Oklahoma	Toy Story
Hello, Dolly!	Oliver	Willy Wonka and the
Help!	101 Dalmations	Chocolate Factory
The Jungle Book	Pee-Wee's Big Adventure	Yellow Submarine
The King and I	Pennies from Heaven	
The Little Mermaid	Peter Pan	

Activities and Games

Once guests have assembled, Mom, Dad, or a teenage sibling or friend is the emcee, explaining the "script" for interacting with the movie, assigning roles, and handing out interactive packets to each guest, which might include lyrics to songs, props, list of trivia-type details to look for while watching the movie, and so on. For example, props might include fake little white flowers standing in as edelweiss for *The Sound of Music* or light sabers (soft foam noodles) for *Star Wars*. The emcee can also plan a scavenger hunt as part of the viewing experience; for instance, everyone has to scramble to find something yellow every time "Yellow Brick Road" is sung or spoken in, while the emcee puts the movie on pause.

Everyone should feel free to be as boisterous as possible. No shushing allowed in this theater! Have a couple of snacky intermissions or game breaks—or keep the action going right through until the closing credits roll.

Movie trivia, movie charades, Pin-the-Tail type birthday games adapted to your movie's theme (Pin the Oil

A Holiday Film Buffoon

Screen *Rudolph the Red-Nosed Reindeer*, *A Charlie Brown Christmas*, or *How the Grinch Stole Christmas*—with all the film buffoon trimmings—for a memorable holiday party. Or screen all three for a wacky mix-'n'-match of activities and snacks and shout-outs. You can also screen longer classics like *A Christmas Carol*, *It's a Wonderful Life*, or *Miracle on 34th Street* for film buffoon fun. You'll have to draw straws, of course, over who gets to be Tiny Tim!

Scavenger Hunt Hints

Create a simple scavenger hunt that involves looking for actual objects—things of a certain color or with a quirky connection to a certain moment in the movie. So when Julie Andrews sings, "brown paper packages tied up with string," everyone needs to find a scrap of string. Don't tell guests in advance what they'll be looking for; instead, tell them you'll signal them during the movie with a whistle or a bell that it's time to scavenge!

You can also have them scavenge the film itself, looking for things in the movie (a broom, a comb or hair ribbon, a neckerchief, an egg, a snake). Have a long list of items (this requires your carefully screening the film in advance to create the list!) that you include in their interactive packet, and when they spot an item from the list on-screen, they can call it out and cross it off their list. You can also give each guest a different list of items to look for.

A Mary Poppins Party

A Mary Poppins Film Buffoon's party might include invitations that read like the ad placed for a nanny. Decorations could be cardboard brooms and chimneys and umbrellas. Guests could come dressed as a chimney sweep, or an old-fashioned nanny, maid, or prim English lady. There might be a sidewalk chalk-drawing competition, a kite-making activity, and spoonfuls of peanut butter, marshmallow, Jell-O, or other sweet treats (in lieu of sugar!). See "Spoon Lickers" palooza, page 349!

Can on the Tin Man!). Give prizes for best costumes or best scavenger hunter.

Food

Set up a theater-style concession stand with popcorn, candy, pretzels, beverages, hot dogs, nuts, chips, and dips. Provide toppings for the guests to put on their individual box of popcorn, such as cinnamon and sugar, raisins, melted butter, pizza seasoning, and parmesan cheese. Make or buy a birthday cake decorated in a way that plays off your movie theme—or have a big sheet cake that's decorated like a movie ticket.

Favors

Decorate popcorn-style plastic tubs with your movie theme, and fill them with any of the following: face paints or makeup sets, black "movie star" sunglasses, disposable camera, microwave popcorn packets, and bubblegum—or items even more specific to your movie theme.

Trip to Mars

You know as well as I do that no store-bought toy is as thoroughly wonderful to play with as a great big cardboard box. This palooza party is an amped-up, ramped-up, space-themed romp in a compelling configuration of simple cardboard boxes.

What's the Palooza?

Turn the typical party mindset on its ear and spend the week leading up to the birthday party building an amazing spaceship maze out of cardboard boxes and other recyclables. A family I know does a version of this birthday palooza every year. One year it's a spaceship, the next it's a funhouse, the next a jungle, and so on. They are creative and resourceful, saving all their interesting recyclables so as not to have to spend much money on the supplies.

The entire family needs to give themselves (and their party space) over to the process of designing and creating the spaceship for a couple of weeks of thinking, collecting items, and then, finally, on the weekend before the actual party, building the spaceship itself. Once the structure is completed, the family has a marvelous con-

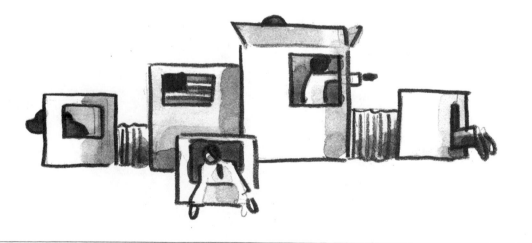

Who can play?

Ages 6–9.

- - - - - - -

What do we need?

For spaceship decor: Oversized cardboard boxes—lots of them—collected from appliance, electronic, and hardware stores. Styrofoam packing material of various shapes and sizes (the Styrofoam blocks that cushion a new television, computer, or DVD player, for example). Shirt cardboard or department-store gift boxes. Poster board. Plastic piping of various lengths and widths and/or the superwide cardboard tubing used for cement post-holes (both available at Home Depot). Packaging or duct tape. Box cutters. Sponges, bubble wrap, wax paper, aluminum foil, Christmas lights, textured filters or nontoxic insulation sheets (also available at Home Depot), or any other lightweight, interesting objects or materials that can be affixed to cardboard to become gadgetry in a homemade spaceship. Silver, black light, or glow-in-the-dark tempera paints. Colored markers. Rolls of disposable black plastic sheeting (again, Home Depot) to hang from twine to cover the walls and/or ceiling. Black-light bulbs in sizes that fit the lamps or overhead light fixtures in your party space. For invitations: Space-themed stickers and markers. For costumes: Large white garbage bags; sash-length pieces of yarn or twine. For music: Soundtracks from *Star Wars* and *2001: A Space Odyssey*, Mike Oldfield's "Tubular Bells," or Pink Floyd's "Dark Side of the Moon." For food: Little candies such as Sweetarts, M&Ms, or Skittles for astronaut "vitamins." Pizza and Tang for lunch. Cake decorated in Martian green. Ice cream. Party favors as suggested on page 276.

- - - - - - -

Running time?

Several weeks to collect materials. The spaceship may be built the weekend before the actual party, with family members helping and adding final touches throughout the week in advance of the party date. The process is the palooza. Take time to enjoy it. Suggested time for the party itself is 60 to 90 minutes.

- - - - - - -

Budget?

$–$$$, depending on how much material you can scavenge or recycle instead of buy.

struction in their living room—or whatever space best accommodates the party, and which you can reasonably put out of commission for a week or two—that your guests will be drawn to as if in a trance. The party itself is billed as "A Trip to Mars." Guests, aka astronauts, imagine, explore, and invent their own space-themed fun and games inside the wondrous cardboard maze.

Invitations

Invite guests to take "A Trip to Mars." Design and make

your own invitations using stickers or pictures of Mars, Martians, spaceships, and so on. Keep the invite list short and sweet for this palooza—this isn't the party you ask the entire second-grade class to attend; just the short list of best buds.

Building the Spaceship

Take half a dozen or more large appliance-sized cardboard boxes. Refrigerator boxes or washer/dryer boxes are ideal, as are boxes from office equipment and supply or hardware stores. (Avoid produce or food boxes from the grocery.) From a child's-eye view, arrange the boxes in your party space in an interesting way. Use tall boxes on their sides to create tunnels. Stack smaller boxes, open-ended at the top, to create vertical tubes or periscopes. Make crawl spaces with the boxes. Cut the corners and seams of the boxes, flattening them out to form large sheets of cardboard. Use the sheets as "roofs" or "walls" in the maze. Fasten the boxes and cardboard sheets together with packaging or duct tape. Cut circles in the cardboard walls and use plastic piping to connect box rooms, so that, for example, an astronaut in one box can peep through the piping to see and talk to a pal inside another box.

Decorate the insides and outsides of the box maze to look like the interior and exterior of a spaceship: Controls. Viewfinders. Solar panels. Windows. Buttons. Levers. Use black light paint and markers. Distinguish the rooms and crawl spaces. Cover one wall in bubble wrap, another in aluminum foil. Make a wax-paper ceiling. Strategically arrange Christmas lights. Use Styrofoam to make gadgets and instrumentation on the interior and exterior walls. Use shirt boards or gift boxes to make panel displays and instrumentation boards. Make signs inside the spaceship and label the instruments (see opposite).

Creating Mars

Outside the spaceship, you can create an enclosed area that is Mars. Use rolls of disposable black plastic sheeting to create this space. Hang the plastic on twine strung from the ceiling or window ledges. Or tent it from twine or wire that runs across the ceiling. Make the room dark and mysterious. Use red Christmas lights in safe and appropriate places to give it a Mars red glow. Cover the floor in bubble wrap. The idea is to create an atmosphere that is out of this world. Your Mars may have two polar ice caps (coolers of ice and juice boxes), a volcano and mountains (sofa cushions), and lots of craters (pillows in a circle). Post warning signs: "Live Volcano." "Deep Craters." "Danger."

Trip to Mars

If you build it, they will play. Now that the spaceship is ready, the Trip to Mars party is one giant playacting game of being in space. Think of it—there's a spaceship in your living room. The astronauts will know what to do!

When the guests arrive, pop a white garbage-bag tunic on each of them (you've cut head and armholes out of the bags in advance). Belt it with a little yarn or twine, and they'll look straight out of *Lost in Space*. Stick an astronaut's identification badge on their tunics (see astronaut names). The ID badges might also include space for vital statistics like, height and weight, heart rate, hair color, and so on. Set up the bathroom scale as a weigh station; use measuring tape or yardsticks to record heights; wear a stethoscope and carry a clipboard. Each astronaut records his own statistics. Set up astronaut "vitamin" trays or dispense small vitamins (little candies!) in disposable paper cups to fortify the astronauts for their launch and journey to Mars.

Once everyone is fit to go, trail the astronauts into the maze. Let them make up stories about what they find along the way. Suggest they play act a takeoff. A false start. A sea splash landing. Send out the space probe. What's out there? Have yogurt-covered raisins or chocolates kisses available in the habitation module, where astronauts relax, sleep, and eat. Assign astronauts to specific duties and rooms in the spaceship. You need someone to sit at the control panel. Someone to copilot. Someone keeps the record book. Another is in charge of the probe. Who's the computer engineer? Who's in charge of the robotics? Give them a few ideas

Space Ship Signage and Labels

Danger

Do Not Open

Antigravity Reaction Chamber

Probe Release

Moon Rock Storage

Mars Specimens Only

Alien Detection Unit

Habitation Module

Space Suit Storage

Fuel Cell

Extravehicular Mobility Unit

Manned Maneuvering Unit

Communication Central

like these as starting points, and then let them make it up and take it as far as they dare.

Parents or older siblings can also pretend to be Martians. Wear large men's T-shirts painted with glow-in-the-dark paint. Capture the astronauts when they land on Mars. Let the birthday child videotape the exploration and Mars landing. When everyone returns to Earth, sit them all down to watch the video.

Food

Go basic. Food is not the star in this palooza—Tang or juice boxes with straws, pizza, ice cream, cake. But you do want small candies, such as Sweetarts, M&Ms, or Skittles to be used as prelaunch "vitamins."

Favors

Glow-in-the-dark stars and planets for decorating a bedroom ceiling and freeze-dried ice cream (both available at Discovery Store). Milky Way bars. Polished rocks. A space-themed comic book. Goody container is a cardboard or plastic bucket decorated as a Moon Rock Collecting Receptacle.

Knights of the Round Table

King Arthur and his Knights of the Round Table timelessly enchant and inspire—my son and his friends enjoyed a rousing King Arthur palooza party that consisted of not much more than a homemade cardboard castle and cardboard shields and swords.

What's the Palooza?

A party fit for a king—and his loyal Knights of the Round Table. With the medieval theme and all of those knights and swords and games of skill and honor, who wouldn't have a good time?

Invitations

Make an invitation in the form of a parchment scroll. Tear an eight-by-ten-inch piece of butcher paper to make it look rough at the edges. Use a gothic font on your computer, or have a talented someone handwrite the invites in calligraphy: "A Call to Knights and Ladies to Celebrate a Birthday at the Round Table!" Roll your invitations and fasten them with raffia.

Decorations

Make a cardboard castle by connecting a few appliance boxes. Cut out windows and doors and make turrets out of wide cardboard tubing with cardboard roofs. Or cover your front door and the surrounding area with butcher paper and paint it to look like a castle. A "Camelot" sign would be nice. Make torches out of toilet paper tubes and firelike bunches of red tissue paper and arrange them around the house or yard.

Costumes

For the knights, make a simple tunic from a large brown or black plastic bag. Cut a hole for the head and two more for the arms. Slip the tunic over the head and tie yarn or twine around the waist as a belt. For the ladies, cut a hole in the bottom of a white plastic bag and slip it up to your waist to make a long skirt. Fasten the skirt to your waist with a sash of yarn. Take a piece of construction paper, roll it into a cone shape, and tape it together to form a hat. Decorate your hat with markers and even glue some flowing pieces of yarn to the top, which will hang down your back.

Games and Activities

Who Are You? Each of the Knights of the Round Table demonstrated some particular virtue, such as bravery or honesty, and each came to the banquet with his own story to tell. They often had special magical objects—

Arthur had his sword Excalibur, while others had magic coats of invisibility or impermeable shields to protect them. But all the knights also had a weakness—an enemy or terrible challenge to confront (like Kryptonite for Superman). Each guest creates a persona. Choose a knightly name, give yourself a virtue, an enemy or weakness, and a magic item. For example, "I am Kevin, Knight of Oak Lane. My heart is pure, I fear multiplication, and my power is in my magic baseball." Everyone is known for the duration of the party as their knightly selves.

Make a Crest and Shield. Parents prepare in advance a piece of cardboard (about eighteen inches square) for each knight to make a shield. Attach cardboard handles to the back with duct tape. Guests trim the shield into a special shape (a diamond or a circle) or just leave it square. Decorate your shield with markers. Choose one or two colors to be the signature colors of your heraldic design. Draw a crest that represents your virtue and your powers. Draw dragons or other mystical creatures. Parents also prepare small cardboard daggers by attaching a three-by-eight-inch piece of cardboard to a three-by-four-inch cardboard crosspiece. Have guests cover with tinfoil and tuck into their string sashes.

The Quest. The knights were always looking for the legendary Holy Grail, which had the power to heal the sick, ensure eternal youth, and provide good food to all who were worthy. The party knights go on a quest, hunting for the "Holy Grail" (small cups filled with two sacks of chocolate coins). Send them on a treasure hunt (outside is the most fun, but inside is fine too), with clues left in three or four places for each pair of guests. Use medieval-sounding language and script on the clues. As each clue is discovered, the knights must perform some feat of skill (a cartwheel, a tongue twister) before they can go on to find the next clue. Each clue leads to the next, until the Holy Grails are discovered. Each knight gets a sack of candy coins.

Juggling. Everybody gets to try their hand at being the court jester. Use Ping-Pong balls or beanbags and practice

Tales of King Arthur and Co.

Check out the stories and legends of King Arthur in these books and movies:

The Sword in the Stone and *The Book of Merlyn*, by T. H. White

King Arthur and His Knights of the Round Table, by Roger Lancelyn Green

A Connecticut Yankee in King Arthur's Court, by Mark Twain

The Sword in the Stone (Disney)

The Lion In Winter (MGM/UA)

juggling. Instructions for beginning jugglers can be found online at http://yoyoguy.com/info/ball/index2.html.

Lance Throw. This is strictly an outside game and should be the last game of the party, because it dissolves into a lot of sword fighting. Everybody gets a foam swimming noodle for a lance. Mark off the starting point in the yard with a stick. Guests take their best shot at throwing the "lance" as far as they can. The person whose lance lands farthest away wins. Or you can hang a hula hoop from a tree and have knights try to throw the lance through the hoop.

Slay the Dragon. Beat the stuffings out of a dragon piñata with a Wiffle ball bat.

Characters at Camelot

- - - - - - -

Bagdemagus: A Round Table knight and King Arthur's cousin; also kidnapper of Guinevere.

Bedivere: He cast the sword Excalibur into the lake after King Arthur was wounded.

Bors de Ganis: The knight who saw the Holy Grail but didn't retrieve it so he could return to the king's court to tell them about it.

Dagonet: A fool in King Arthur's court who was eventually made into a knight.

Galahad: A noble warrior and the purest of all the knights.

Gawain: King Arthur's nephew, who had many an adventure with the Green Knight.

Guinevere: King Arthur's queen.

Lady of the Lake: King Arthur received the sword Excalibur from this mysterious woman.

Lancelot: King Arthur's champion, who won many battles for the king.

Leodegrance: Guinevere's father and an early adviser to the new king; gave the Round Table to Arthur as a wedding present.

Merlin: The magician who set up the sword-in-stone contest that Arthur won to become king.

Morgan Le Fay: She had magical powers and healed King Arthur when he was brought to the magical Isle.

Perceval: The knight who found—and retrieved—the Holy Grail.

Food

Medieval knights had no utensils, so hearty finger foods for this party. Chicken wings or drumsticks, rolls, pears, apples, carrots, celery, and cheese cubes. Cider, ginger ale, and root beer to drink. Serve finger foods on platters and beverages in plastic goblets from the party supply store. Serve cupcakes decorated with heraldic colors and patterns, and ice cream sandwiches.

Favors

Treasure boxes full of gold nugget bubblegum, jacks, playing cards, Merlin magic tricks.

The Dragon of Wantley

Star of a famous Celtic ballad, the Dragon of Wantley was the dragon of all dragons. He had iron teeth, a stinger tail, and mighty wings. He ate trees and cattle and children, and, of course, breathed fire from his nostrils:

This dragon had two furious wings
One upon each shoulder,
With a sting in his tail as long as a flail,
Which made him bolder and bolder;
He had long claws,
And in his jaws,
Four and fifty teeth of iron
With a hide as tough
As any buff,
Which did him round inviron.

True Knightly Virtues

Mercy (toward the poor and oppressed— no mercy toward evildoers)

Humility

Honor

Sacrifice

Fear of God

Faithfulness

Courage

Extreme graciousness and courtesy to ladies

vacation
paloozas

Sunset Watch

Who says you have to go to a movie theater for cinematic magic? A good sunset can be as exciting and colorful as Disney—and you can write your own reviews.

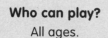

Who can play?
All ages.

What do we need?
A place with a view, portable chairs, refreshments.

Running time?
One hour.

Budget?
Free.

I have seen the sunset, stained with mystic wonders,

Illumine the rolling waves with long purple forms,

Like actors in ancient plays.

—Arthur Rimbaud
(1854–1891)

What's the Palooza?

This is a quintessential palooza: taking a simple, everyday moment and adding a dash of joie de vivre to turn watching the sunset into a Big Event. The idea is to celebrate a sunset by formalizing and acknowledging it as the brilliant bit of art it is.

Given the variability of weather, a Sunset Watch is more of a spur-of-the-minute idea. But once you've noticed a day with sunset potential, it takes scarcely any time to gather the troops and head west, young family.

Finding the best spot is part of the ritual. You might already have a family favorite location at home, but if you're on vacation, you can scout around in advance for a seat at nature's show. Then gather up the folding chairs or blankets, a few refreshments (popcorn!), some paper and writing instruments, perhaps a camera, and some warm wraps or drinks, depending on the time of year.

Once you've arrived, everyone settles in, facing the horizon, and starts watching intently. You might decide to have a no-talking rule, which heightens the sense of an audience waiting for a performance. You could place bets on exactly the moment the sun disappears, or shout out every variation of color you see.

Rating the sunset is a huge part of the fun. One family I know has a simple "On a scale of 1 to 10" system, but there are more elaborate scorecards to invent. How about points if:

The sunset has a nice preglow

You see the top or bottom of the sun touch the ocean

The sun's rays fan out and radiate

The sunset seems to be melting into the water or horizon

There is an afterglow

A boat, heron or other object is silhouetted against the sunset

You see a green flash (see page 287)

Whatever rating method your family chooses, keep track of the score, date, time, place, and who attended that Sunset Watch.

Another way to mark the occasion is to draw a picture or take a photo of the entire horizon from wherever you're watching the sunset. Then each evening mark the spot where the sun sets on the picture or photo for a visual record of the entertainment.

Extrapaloozas

Catch the Sun

Eskimos played a string game similar to cat's cradle to "catch" the sun and keep it from setting. You can try to catch the sun during your special sunset ritual by playing cat's cradle, in which two people make a series of string figure shapes with string and pass them back and

Safe Sunsets

There are plenty of old wives' tales, but the sun is safe to look at if you use a little common sense. The "rule of thumb" is that if your actual thumb, extended horizontally at arm's length, can cover up the sun while touching the horizon, then it's low enough in the sky to look at without harm. A few minutes makes all the difference, however, because the sun's brightness changes very quickly around sunrise and sunset. Another rough rule of thumb is to wait to look at the sun until twelve minutes before sunset or eight minutes if you're right at the equator!

Follow the Sun

There are as many ways of looking at the sun as there are different languages on Earth.

Egypt

Egyptians believed the sun traveled by boat, and at night Osiris, god of the underworld, had the boat pulled on an underworld river until it crossed the horizon and kept going toward the east. Their sun god was Ra, the creator of light and all things. Humans were born from the tears of Ra. The first known sun temple in Egypt, The Sphinx Temple, dates back 4,500 years. A western compartment in the temple was for sunset rituals. On March 21 and September 21 every year, the sun's rays fall perpendicularly on the right shoulder of the Sphinx before the sunset.

Greece

The Greeks believed their sun god, called Helios, drove the sun across the sky from east to west in his golden chariot every day. After sunset the sun sailed back across the ocean.

Greenland

Malina is the sun goddess of the Inuit people who live in Greenland. Her brother was the moon god Anningan, and they lived together until a terrible fight made Malina smear black grease all over her brother's face. Scared, she then ran away into the sky and became the sun. Anningan chased her and became the moon. Their constant chase is why the sun sets and the moon rises every day.

China

Ten suns took turns in the sky during the Chinese ten-day week, according to Chinese mythology. But one day they decided to appear together in the sky. The heat was so intense, the people asked the suns to fly solo, but they refused. The archer Yi was sent down from the heavens to reprimand the disobedient suns. Yi killed nine of the suns, and the one that remains is the sun in the sky.

forth. All you need is a piece of string, a few feet long, tied together at the ends to form a circle. If you're not already familiar with this old-fashioned game, see www.ifyoulovetoread.com/book/chten_cats.htm for photographic instructions, or the book *Cat's Cradle: A Book of String Figures,* by Anne Akers.

Rainbow Gazing

Rainbows are more elusive than sunsets, but if your timing is good, they are every bit as celebration-worthy. Be on the watch for light rain in the late afternoon or early evening, especially in spring and fall. Always position yourself with your back to the sun for the best rainbow sightings.

You're primed for a rainbow ritual and there's not a chance of one appearing in the actual sky, you can make your own in all kinds of ways. One of the easiest is to stand with your back to the sun and spray mist from a garden hose at different angles until you see a rainbow. Or fill a clear dish with water and set it in a sunny spot. Put a mirror in the water and lean it against the dish so that the sun's rays strike the mirror and reflect back out through the water to a spot on the wall. When the water is still, you'll see a rainbow on the wall.

Good Timing

You can look up the exact time the sun sets on any given day of the year in any location using this Web site: aa.usno.navy.mil/data/docs/RS_OneDay.html.

Le Rayon Vert

In his 1882 novel *Le Rayon Vert* (The Green Ray), Jules Verne describes an "ancient legend" in which anyone who has seen the Green Ray is incapable of being "deceived in matters of sentiment," so that "he who has been fortunate enough once to behold it is enabled to see closely into his own heart and to read the thoughts of others."

Although Verne made up the legend, you can catch the infamous green flash at sunset if certain atmospheric conditions are met. Then, the top sliver of the setting sun becomes bright green—but literally only for a flash of one or two seconds. To catch a green flash, it helps if you are in the right location as well as position. Your best vantage point is one where the horizon appears lower than your eye and the air is as clear as possible. An ocean sunset works well, but you can stand on top of a mountain for the same effect. In the beginning, it also helps to look through binoculars or even a slightly magnified camera lens. Once you know what a green flash looks like, it will be easier to spot one with your naked eye.

At the Beach

Although swimming and playing in the water at the beach can be a palooza in itself, here's one for those days when the creative urge strikes because all that sand begs to be turned into something besides a place to lay your blanket.

Who can play?
All ages.

What do we need?
A nice clean beach, a sand shovel, and a pail. Optional tools include shells, Popsicle sticks, plastic spoons and knives, Styrofoam cups, and small sticks.

Running time?
Half an hour to a whole, luxurious day.

Budget?
Free.

What's the Palooza?

Build a medieval castle using sand and any other treasures you can find at the beach. Check on the tide before building and pick a high and dry location to avoid your castle being swept away before you've even finished it.

Expert sand-castlers always start a structure with a very big pile of wet sand. Make a huge pile, which is to become the castle, and pack it firmly. Your castle is then actually "carved" out of the mound of wet sand rather than built from the bottom up. Work slowly from the top, carving little bits at a time. Form the basic shape of the roofline first—with turrets many turrets!—and then the walls. Shave sand off with plastic knives or a spatula, and work toward the center to minimize breaking edges.

If there are multiple stories in your sand castle, carve out another roof level with walls for the various floors. Carve out entryways and windows and mark them with smooth stones, shells, or tiny sticks.

A pile of rocks makes a rather grand entry, and seaweed adds nice landscaping touches. Dig a trench or moat around the castle and use a piece of driftwood for the drawbridge.

Even castles made of sand fall into the sea, eventually.

—Jimi Hendrix
(1942–1970)

Extrapaloozas

Imaginary Sand Creatures

Think of a family of sand creatures that will live in your castle. The surfside equivalent of fairies! Or aquatic Greek-style gods! Or sandbound space creatures! What's their story? Name them. How do they move and talk and swim? What do they look like? Draw them at home, and next time you come back to the beach, bring their house—and their story—back to life.

Flotsam and Jetsam Art

This is a beach palooza that goes against the grain! Create sculptures, characters, people, structures, animals, or anything else you fancy—here's the hitch—using everything but sand. What else is there? Flotsam and jetsam, like seaweed, shells, wood, beach glass, old flip-flops, lost sand toys, rocks, sticks, feathers.

Message in a Bottle

Write a message and put it adrift in a small bottle for someone else to find. Things to say in your message? Where you are, the date, the circumstances of your being on this particular beach, who you are, and whom you are with (first names only). Write a poem, story, or letter. Cork or otherwise seal the bottle and send it on its way.

flotsam and jetsam (flaht-sum and jet-sum), n. phrase: The wreckage of a ship and its cargo found either floating upon the sea or washed ashore. Also refers to useless trifles, and odds and ends, as well as penniless vagrants, drifters, and tramps.

Travel Brochure

Anyone who has ever made vacation plans based on the promise of a glossy travel brochure will appreciate how alluring they can be! Teeming with lush photos, suggestions of thrilling activities and fabulous restaurants . . . well, who wouldn't get on the next train to paradise? This palooza asks your kids to create a travel brochure of your next vacation destination. When they're done, you may be the one paying for the holiday, but they'll surely be the ones invested in it.

What's the Palooza?

Make a travel brochure about the place you're going to visit on your vacation. Travel brochures have attracted tourists to areas for years with their pretty pictures and promises of an unforgettable vacation. You'll find out what's so special about your vacation destination when you investigate the place to create your own travel brochure.

Start by going to a travel agency and collecting a few travel brochures to use as a model for your brochure. You will see right away that the brochures are created to sell a destination to a tourist. The mix of attractive photographs, enthusiastic headlines and copy, and useful information about the destination are what draw you in. To make your own brochure, you'll need to find out all you can about your vacation spot. Use the following list of questions to gather information and to get a feel for what you can expect when you get there. Peruse the travel section of the library or bookstore or go online to find the answers to these questions and to discover what's really cool about the place you will visit. If you're traveling out of your own country, find out:

What is the native language?

Does it have a big population or a small one?

What are popular local dishes?

What is the weather like?

What animals call the region home?

What currency is used?

What are the largest cities in the country?

Is there a king or queen, a president, or a prime minister?

What types of music are native to the region?

What historical events took place there?

What special attractions—museums, concerts, natural wonders—are the must-sees?

Going someplace not so far away or foreign? Find out things like:

What's the area code?

Are there any sports teams that play there?

What's the weather like?

What are the local food specialties?

Do any famous people come from this place?

Have any historical events or scandals taken place there?

What's the state's motto? Flower? Any other official state items?

How many miles from your house to your destination?

In your research, keep an eye out for any attractions the area has to offer. Look for the wackiest ones you can find—that Paul Bunyan statue, an alligator farm, a giant ice cream cone—to include in your brochure. Be sure to note any museums, amusement parks, or sports arenas in the area that you'd like to visit.

> *The traveler sees what he sees, the tourist sees what he has come to see.*
>
> —Gilbert K. Chesterton
> (1874–1936)

For an in-depth look at virtually any vacation spot, consult online references such as www.fodors.com, where you can search by destination, or www.travelroads.com, where you can search by activity—from mountain biking to camping to fishing to ballooning—to learn about the many ways you can spend your vacation in paradise.

Once you've gathered info about your destination, cut out photographs from magazines or print them from travel Web sites; for example, choose images of beaches, monuments, natural beauty, or nightlife that make this destination unique. Armed with colorful pictures and bursting with important tidbits about the vacation spot, assemble your travel brochure.

Fold a piece of paper in vertical thirds. Make a big, bold brochure headline across the front page. Give it a catchy or crazy slogan for your brochure cover—"What's Boston Without Tea? Free!" "Memphis Where The King Still Reigns!" "Gilroy, California—The Place with the Best Garlic and the Worst Breath!"

Arrange and glue each picture, leaving room for a caption and some text about the attraction you're writing about. Include fun facts you've discovered about the area. Use descriptive words to make the brochure pop with personality—breathtaking views, tantalizing aromas, rolling hills, crashing waves, amazing attractions,

Ephemera

Everybody seems to collect something. Travel brochures are a group of collectibles that fall under the category of *ephemera*, defined as anything short-lived or temporary. In the world of collecting, ephemera are usually documents that weren't meant to be long-lasting. Items such as travel brochures, letterheads, tickets, menus, postcards, advertising materials, and programs are all cataloged under the collecting umbrella of ephemera. Luckily, people have rescued and collected travel brochures over the years, and there are a few places you can look at some of these golden oldies. Check out www.travel-brochuregraphics.com for examples of beautiful travel brochure graphics from the 1920s and 1930s.

Also look at *See the USA: The Art of the American Travel Brochure,* by John Margolies and Eric Baker. This book shows how American travel brochures touted everything good (and sometimes not so good) about American states to draw tourists.

and majestic mountains. Have the cover of your brochure highlight one of these features or some funky attraction you've discovered that you've just got to see.

Finally, be sure to take your homemade travel brochure with you on your trip. Use it as a checklist of things to see, places to eat, fun stuff to do. And don't forget to take pictures of the places your brochure reminded you to visit!

Extrapalooza

Eat at Joe's

Maybe your family hasn't decided where it's going to go on vacation—but you have a choice destination in mind! Create a brochure to convince your family that that's the place to be. Thoroughly research your destination. Put together the most selling headlines, images, and descriptive copy you can. Note places and activities of special interest to every member of your family.

Hands-On Adventure

Set the touristy parts of your vacation up to be a creative checklist of things you want to see and do to keep interest levels high and observations skills sharp.

What's the Palooza?

Design a travel journal specific to your destination, one that directs, guides, and documents the adventures of your trip. The idea is to work up a checklist of sights, sounds, artworks, and experiences you're likely to encounter on the trip and a variety of ways to record them in the travel journal. So, for example, if you're planning a trip to the San Francisco area and you know beforehand what some of the highlights of your trip will be, create pages devoted to those spots in your notebook. This means you'll need to do some research in advance. Use the guidebook you've no doubt already purchased to help you come up with activity ideas.

For example, if you're sure to go to Chinatown, make a page in the notebook for your Chinatown afternoon and include a place to write down the date, time, and day of the week of your visit. Write instructions similar to the following on your Chinatown pages:

Stroll Grant Avenue and find a store that sells silk hats with long ponytails attached. Try one on and get someone to take a picture of you wearing the hat. Paste the picture here when you get it developed.

Stand in front of the Old Chinese Telephone Exchange

Building on 743 Washington Street. Or go across the street for a better view. Make a sketch of the building with its three-tiered pagoda here.

Have lunch in a Chinese restaurant. Use chopsticks. Write down what everybody in the family had for lunch. What was the best thing on the table? Collect the fortunes from everyone's cookies and paste them in here. Label whose was whose.

Go by Sang Sang Fish Market. Look in the tanks and find a fish that you like. Sketch it here. Be sure to label your drawing. What kind of fish is it?

Part of the fun in going anywhere is being able to prove that you've been there. And what better way to remember "what I did on my summer vacation" than to document the best parts all the while you're doing them? The notebook's checklists add some structure to the tour and actively engage everyone participating. At Cannery Row, "Find the bust of John Steinbeck. Make a rubbing of the brass nameplate. Insert the rubbing here on this page." After riding a cable car, "Look for and buy a postcard of a cable car. Paste it in here." Or, "Take in views of the Golden Gate Bridge. Make a sketch of the bridge here."

The instructions can also be more general, especially if you don't have time to research specifics beforehand. Make pages for general activities that can be done no matter where you visit. Just vary the tasks, the more hands-on the better. Think, too, of ways to bring souvenirs into the pages of the notebook. Some activity suggestions that work no matter where you are:

Try foods the area is known for. Rate them either: Delicious. *Comme çi, comme ça.* Yuck!

Make rubbings of gravestones, statue nameplates on statues, or art labels.

Sketch skylines and/or shorelines.

Draw the tallest or most unusual buildings.

Draw animals you encounter on a nature walk or at the zoo.

Collect and Keep in Your Notebook

Admission receipts

Autographs (concierge, tour guide, waiter, cabdriver)

Brochures

Business cards (from hotels, restaurants, and other establishments)

Maps

Matchboxes

Menus

Names (and autographs) of other tourists you meet along the way

Postcards

Subway or ferry tokens or passes

The true traveler is he who goes on foot, and even then, he sits down a lot of the time.

—Colette, *Paris from My Window*

tourist (tour-ist), n.: Someone who visits places away from home for pleasure.

vacation (va-ca-shun), n.: Period of time devoted to rest, travel, recreation or relaxation.

Design and draw your own architectural structure (bridge, museum, department store).

List artworks.

List natural wonders.

Write a poem about a person, place, or thing you encounter.

And jot down these kinds of notes:

What was the high point of the day? The low point?

What interesting people did you meet or observe? Who, where, when, and what were they doing?

What was the weather like? Indicate the weather each day by drawing pictures of sun, rain, clouds.

Once home, you've already got a great start on the vacation memory book. Develop any remaining film and paste in all the photographs you made specifically for the journal. Use markers and colored pencils to decorate any blank pages in the book. Cut up attraction brochures and maps and paste your favorite parts into the journal. Label everything. Decorate the outside of your journal with favorite pictures or a collage of bits of memorabilia. Then show friends and relatives all the places you've been and the things you've done.

Good Books

These travel book series are great to use when creating a hands-on journal for your trip because they focus on important things you must see, as well as interesting and obscure things you'd better not miss. There are the *Eyewitness Top 10 Travel Guides* to nearly fifty destinations in the United States and abroad. Each guide breaks down facets of a visit into top-ten lists that help you make your own gotta-see lists. Also check out the *Insider's Guides,* which are just that—the quirky inside scoop on what you really want to see when you visit more than sixty destinations in the United States.

Gypsies

Some of the best vacation times I've ever spent with my kids were long, unscripted drives from Los Angeles to Montana, with a little bit of camping, a little bit of exploring odd, off-the-map places. The kids picked the route, the diversions, the restaurants, the campsites. When I plan our free time, they feel trapped. When they map it out, they feel free. This palooza is really just a where-the-wind-takes-you state of mind.

What's the Palooza?

Take some time—even if it's just an afternoon—to see and do things that aren't on a schedule, visiting places that aren't a "destination," tasting foods that aren't your usual fare . . . with kids in charge of exploring the opportunities and then choosing what happens. This is an experience everyone has to give themselves over to—people can go a lifetime without exercising those muscles that let them act on impulse. Great memories come from these kinds of spontaneously unfolding times, from rambling road trips to a few hours honking around a town or city you've never visited before.

Use your tools. Start with a general idea of where you want to end up, either a specific final destination (the annual rodeo in San Antonio) or a looser one (the coast, up north, a big city). Get out maps and look at how you might get from where you are to where you want to go. Use a highlighter to sketch out possible routes. Then take a closer look at those routes and identify the possibilities for fun along the way. See a town with a great name? Put a star next to it. Does your route come close to something irresistible like a cavern? Star it. Use guidebooks and online resources to find wacky museums, hole-in-

Who can play?
All ages.

What do we need?
Maps, guidebooks, a journal and camera. Provisions (food, clothes, etc.) for however long and wherever you are on the road.

Running time?
An afternoon, a weekend, a whole vacation.

Budget?
$–$$$

the-wall restaurants, racetracks, minor league ballparks, little-known natural wonders, and more.

Make a list. Take every item you've starred on your map, every place you've discovered in your research that's even remotely interesting, everything you've thought you might want to do, and make a list, approximately in order of where they'd appear on your route. Think about how long it would take to get from one place to another, or how long visiting a place might take. Your list should be as long as you can possibly make it. You're not going to do everything on it, just what you decide to do when you're out there doing it. But the longer your list, the more ideas you have to play with.

Make rules. So your trip isn't a total free-for-all, make a few simple rules. Maybe you want to take turns being in charge of the day. Or one person chooses what happens in the morning, one person chooses the course of the afternoon. Or one person chooses activities or sites, and one person chooses where to eat or sleep. Everyone has to defer to the person choosing how to spend time. No griping. No mutinies.

Do it. Sleeping until noon may seem like a good way to spend unstructured time, but it's not the point of this palooza. You have to be on the road to see the world, so make a commitment to a time to get started, when you might need to stop for lunch, when you might call it a day. Beyond that, though, you're a leaf on the wind, so enjoy!

Take note. Have one person be in charge of keeping the family journal of your gypsy journey. Describe what you saw, where you ate, people you met. Take pictures. Keep mementos. Write down the inside jokes, theme songs, or ongoing oddities of your trip.

Obviously, not every vacation can be free-form. But if you try it once, you discover that even the most destination-driven, activity-oriented vacation is better with a little dose of come-what-may.

Extrapaloozas

Have a Banana

Go out for an afternoon with no plans at all and see what happens. One of my favorite gypsy days was spent with my daughter and her very best friend Anna, whom we fondly call Anna-Banana. We decided to just get in the car and drive to Pasadena. We had no schedule, no plans, no time to be home. We stopped to get a mocha and stumbled on the most amazing trash art exhibit. We had such a loose and wonderful time, it was like a whole relaxing vacation in one afternoon. And that day we decided that an afternoon going wherever the road takes us should be called a "banana." Have one!

Surprise Day

Let one person choose everything that happens to the whole group for a day, from meals to outings and activities—without anyone else having any idea what's in store. Perhaps one Sunday every other month, one person investigates the opportunities, plans and leads the day, and makes all the decisions. Surprise your family with unusual, enjoyable activities—chocolate pancakes for breakfast, flying balsa-wood airplanes in the park, treasure hunting at the flea market, dim sum in Chinatown. Other than enlisting the help of a driving/cooking/paying grown-up, don't tell anyone where they're going until they get there.

I travel not to go anywhere, but to go. I travel for travel's sake. The great affair is to move.

—Robert Louis Stevenson
(1850–1894)

A good traveler has no fixed plans and is not intent upon arriving. A good artist lets his intuition lead him wherever it wants.

—Lao-tzu
(570–490 B.C.)

Gates of Heaven

No matter where you go on vacation, from the tiniest tucked-away town to the world's greatest cities, there are amazing cemeteries that reveal extraordinary details of the times and culture and people who lived there.

Who can play?
Ages 6 and up.

What do we need?
Paper (white newsprint paper or tracing paper), chunky crayons (outer paper removed), soft paintbrush, soft clean cloth, masking tape, empty paper towel tube, pen or pencil, notebook or journal.

Running time?
An hour or an afternoon.

Budget?
$

What's the Palooza?

To get the grave's-eye-view of the place you're visiting, go to a destination cemetery one of the all-time great resting places of some of history's most notable figures. Or go to a tiny six-stone churchyard cemetery in a town with no name and get the same wonderful sense of history and humanity. Gravestones everywhere tell of love and loss, of journeys and bravery and good luck and bad luck. Read the epitaphs. Look for symbols or fancy stonecutting styles. When you find something that catches your eye—perhaps an unusual word or an ornate decoration set yourself up to make a gravestone rubbing.

First rule of rubbing is Do No Harm. There may be people at the cemetery who are paying their respects, and behaving with decorum is much appreciated. Stick to paths where there are paths, speak quietly, don't run, and so on. And only take rubbings from gravestones that are undamaged, smooth, and clearly carved. If a stone is crumbly, cracked, or not solidly planted in the ground, skip it because you may cause accidental damage when making your rubbing. If there is a caretaker or manager from whom you can ask permission to make a rubbing, by all means do. And plan to make just one rubbing per outing—you don't want to wear out your welcome!

To make a rubbing, clean dirt and debris off the stone with a soft rag or dry, soft paintbrush. Tape your paper securely to the surface of the stone. Make sure the paper extends beyond the edges of the area to be rubbed. Begin in the center and make gentle strokes with the broad side of your crayon. Cover the whole area lightly and evenly, go back to the center, and repeat. Try to keep your strokes uniform in pressure so you won't end up with some parts darker than others. Step back and look at your rubbing to make sure all the details are sharp and clear. Carefully remove the tape and paper from the stone, making sure no tape is left behind. You may want to mark on the back side of your rubbing the name of the cemetery and any information on or about the gravestone The name, dates, epitaph, location of the stone, the type of stone. Then roll your rubbing up and store it in your paper towel tube or slip it flat between the pages of your notebook.

Always police the area to be sure you've collected any scraps of your paper or tape, and any other bits of litter you may encounter—try to leave the cemetery in a little better shape than when you got there. You may also want to be sure to bring water with you and to visit the restroom before going to a cemetery, which is most unlikely to offer comfort facilities for visitors.

Extrapaloozas

Cemetery Journal

Keep a journal of your cemetery adventures. Keep notes on the name and location of the cemeteries. Record interesting facts, such as the oldest marker or intriguing names and epitaphs. One young friend of mine who lives in New England likes to visit only very old cemeteries, and he notes every Revolutionary War marker in his journal. Keep your gravestone rubbings in your journal, or photos of great stones you have seen. When you've gone out of your way to visit a cemetery where a

Great Cemeteries of the World

Arlington National Cemetery, Arlington, Virginia

Gates of Heaven, Valhalla, New York

Hollywood Forever Cemetery, Los Angeles, California

Bonaventure Cemetery, Savannah, Georgia

Westminster Abbey, London, England

Père Lachaise Cemetery, Paris, France

Santa Croce Cathedral, Florence, Italy

Alexander Nevsky Monastery, Tikhvin Cemetery, Saint Petersburg, Russia

Cemetery Poetry

Read "An Elegy Written in a Country Churchyard," by Thomas Gray and "The Quaker Graveyard in Nantucket," by Robert Lowell.

famous person is buried, make a page of your journal devoted to that person.

Write Your Own Epitaph

In order to leave a lasting impression of their own choosing, sometimes people prepare their own epitaphs for their gravestones. Some years before his death, Thomas Jefferson wrote his own epitaph, and instructed the stone carver it should contain "not a word more." His epitaph read: "Here was buried Thomas Jefferson, author of

Common Gravestone Symbols and What They Mean

Anchor: Hope or "at rest."

Angel: Agent of God, guardian of the dead.

Bed: Deathbed.

Book: Faith.

Circle: Eternity.

Cross: Symbol of Christian religion.

Cypress tree: Mourning or death.

Dove: Peace.

Gates: Entry into heaven.

Hands: A symbol of farewell.

Heart: Love and devotion.

Horse: Strength, courage, or swift passage of time.

Hourglass: Passage of time.

Ivy: Immortality or friendship.

Labyrinth: Eternity or the inward path.

Lamb: Innocence.

Lamp: Immortality, knowledge of God.

Laurel: Literary or artistic fame.

Lily: Purity.

Lion: Courage or strength.

Obelisk: Eternal life.

Rocks: Steadfastness.

Rose: Innocence and purity.

Scythe: Passage of time and death.

Shell: Pilgrimage.

Skull: Mortality.

Snake: With its tail in its mouth, eternity.

Sundial: Passage of time.

Sword: Justice or fortitude.

Torch: Immortality.

Tree: Life, renewal or immortality.

Urn: If draped and empty, means death; if flaming, means new life.

Wheat: Fruitfulness.

Willow: Grief and mourning.

the Declaration of Independence, of the Statute of Virginia for Religious Freedom, and Father of the University of Virginia." Didn't he forget something? Apparently he didn't count being president of the United States as one of his most memorable accomplishments!

The late Mel Blanc, the famous voice of animated characters Bugs Bunny and Porky Pig, to name two, requested an epitaph that reads simply, "That's all, folks." And William Shakespeare, not wanting anyone—ever—to disturb his grave, wrote: "Good frend for Jesus sake forbeare, To digg the dust encloased heare! Blest be the man that spares thes stones, And curst be he that moves my bones."

Some of the best and funniest epitaphs are short rhyming poems like Shakespeare's. Write your own epitaph in this style. "He wasn't mean and his room was clean." Or describe your accomplishments like Jefferson did: "Johnny Smith, inventor of six ways to avoid doing homework and teaser of sister, Jill." Or invent a visual epitaph, like ancient mathematician Archimedes did: his was decorated with a sphere inside a cylinder of equal diameter, and inscribed with the ratio of their volumes. He considered this ratio to be the greatest of all his mathematical discoveries. Your visual epitaph might be a basketball or your trusty trombone.

Cemetery Locator

There are many cemetery and gravesite locators on the Internet, but one of the best is www.find agrave.com, which you can use to search for the famous by name, location, date, or claim to fame. You can also search its listings of nearly 5 million gravesites of the non-famous.

epitaph (e-pi-taf), n.: A commemorative inscription on a tomb, monument, or gravestone marker; often a brief poem or other writing in praise of the deceased.

Good Books

Budding cemetery explorers wanting to learn more should look at *Going Out in Style: The Architecture of Eternity*, by Douglas Keister, which examines the art and architecture of cemeteries. There's also *Corpses, Coffins and Crypts: A History of Burial*, by Penny Colman, a terrific and lighthearted book for older kids about burial customs of many cultures, including photos, literary quotes, graves of famous people, great epitaphs, and gravestone carvings. And for the real cemetery sleuth, there's *Your Guide to Cemetery Research*, by Sharon Carmack, which is a great resource for anyone interested in the incredible information you can collect in a cemetery.

Drive Time

Being strapped into a car for any length of time is no picnic for kids (or for adults, for that matter), but keeping them palooza-ed can make the time fly.

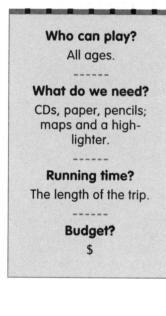

Who can play?
All ages.

What do we need?
CDs, paper, pencils; maps and a highlighter.

Running time?
The length of the trip.

Budget?
$

What's the Palooza?

Make time pass as easily as the miles do on a road trip.

License Plate Literacy

Have a presidential election using the license plate game. The object of the game is to "win" electoral votes by being the first to spot a state license plate. For instance, the person who spies a California license plate gets 55 electoral votes. The passenger who finds a plate from Kentucky will get 8 electoral votes. The person who gets the majority of electoral votes (270) wins the election. It may take a few car trips to win the election, so keep track of who found what states, and the votes they've collected, in a glove-compartment notebook you keep for all your license plate games and sightings.

Keep an eye out for vanity plates. See if you can figure out what they mean and note the best ones in your notebook. Make up your own vanity plates for each passenger an indecisive dad might get 2B R N2B, or a kid with discriminating tastes might get PKY ETR. Use vanity license plate language to describe yourself physically BRN III (brown eyes) or SML MOM (small mom).

Also look at the letters on a license plate and try to think of a word that has all those letters in it. For example, out of a plate that reads WCH 749, you can make "which" or "watch." You don't have to use the letters in order; out of Z94 U3B, you can make "buzz." Take turns, keep track of everyone's words, and the person who comes up with the biggest license plate word wins. It's like the game of Boggle on wheels!

Car Repair

There are so many cars on the road, you can't help but notice all the dings and dents. Turn it into a game by making everybody a mechanic. Keep your eyes peeled for all types of vehicle—damage scratches, dents, wobbly

Electoral Votes by State

Here is the list of states and the number of electoral votes each is assigned. May the best person win—by a clear majority, of course!

Total: 538; Majority Needed to Elect: 270

State	Votes	State	Votes
Alabama	9	Montana	3
Alaska	3	Nebraska	5
Arizona	10	Nevada	5
Arkansas	6	New Hampshire	4
California	55	New Jersey	15
Colorado	9	New Mexico	5
Connecticut	7	New York	31
Delaware	3	North Carolina	15
District of Columbia	3	North Dakota	3
Florida	27	Ohio	20
Georgia	15	Oklahoma	7
Hawaii	4	Oregon	7
Idaho	4	Pennsylvania	21
Illinois	21	Rhode Island	4
Indiana	11	South Carolina	8
Iowa	7	South Dakota	3
Kansas	6	Tennessee	11
Kentucky	8	Texas	34
Louisiana	9	Utah	5
Maine	4	Vermont	3
Maryland	10	Virginia	13
Massachusetts	12	Washington	11
Michigan	17	West Virginia	5
Minnesota	10	Wisconsin	10
Mississippi	6	Wyoming	3
Missouri	11		

Our battered suitcases were piled on the sidewalk again; we had longer ways to go. But no matter, the road is life.

—Jack Kerouac
(1922–1969)

wheels, crooked radio antennas, and peeling paint. Listen for mechanical problems like a loud muffler or a squealing belt when a car turns a corner. Keep score to see who can find the most car problems on a trip.

It's important for mechanics to know their cars, so start noticing how many different kinds of vehicles you see. Instead of seeing just an SUV, sedan, sports car, or truck, note the company who made the car (Ford) and the model (Mustang). See how many different models you can find for each car company. Try to spot old or exotic cars. Do you know which cars are domestic and which are foreign?

Navigator

Learn how to read a map and be the trip navigator. Before a trip, get out a map or maps that cover your route. First, become familiar with the symbols on the map. You can print out a list of symbols from http://mac.usgs.gov/mac/isb/pubs/booklets/symbols/roads.html. You can also go to Mapquest, a Web site that can help you choose and map out your route (www.mapquest.com). Trace out the route to your destination on a road map with a highlighter and figure out how many miles you'll travel with the mileage scale. Mark a few key locations that you'll pass through, as well as any important changes in route or direction, so you can confirm at a glance that you're following the route you've mapped out. Nothing's nicer or more valuable to a driver than having a capable navigator who can tell him what roads to take and point out different sites along the way. It's like being a copilot!

Use the map to create a record of your road trip as you go along. At rest stops or during breaks, note the things you've seen along the way. Make little notes beside the roads you've traveled about what you've seen. The map can become a part of your scrapbook of your trip.

The Waiting Game

Any film or television actor will tell you, it's one part acting, three parts waiting. A film set in particular can be a torture chamber of waiting—so I've gotten very good at the waiting game.

What's the Palooza?

Hordes of people and endless lines can drive even the most eager vacationer to the brink. Passing the time can be a fun and memorable part of the experience if you just know how to play the waiting game.

Memory Detective

Choose an area (a cluttered table, waiting area, or coatrack) or a person, examine it carefully for a minute, then turn away and try to recall at least ten details about the subject. If after a minute, you cannot recall ten details, look again for no more than five seconds, then turn away and try to get to ten. Each person is given a chance to observe and recall a different subject. The person who remembers the most correct details wins.

Assassin

Assassin is a game of cloak-and-dagger. The cloak is your timing and wit, and the dagger is a wink of your eye. The object of the game is twofold. The assassin tries to "kill" all the other players without getting caught, and the other players try to identify the assassin before they are killed.

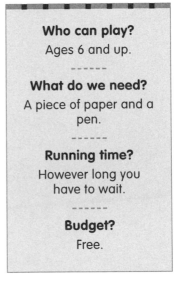

Who can play?
Ages 6 and up.

What do we need?
A piece of paper and a pen.

Running time?
However long you have to wait.

Budget?
Free.

Divide a piece of paper up into as many pieces as people playing and mark one piece of paper with an "X." Fold them up and mix them up in a pocket or hat. Everyone chooses a piece of paper, looks at it, then hides it away in their pocket. The person with the "X" is the assassin. In order to eliminate the other players, the assassin must slyly wink at them one at a time without being caught by any of the others. Once a person has been winked at, five seconds later they must announce, "I'm dead," and they're out of the game. If one of the other players sees (or thinks she sees) the assassin wink and kill, she announces the identity of the killer. The accused must show his piece of paper as proof that the accuser is right or wrong. If the accuser is wrong, she's dead; she drops out of the game but so does the accused, so new papers are drawn among the remaining players and play continues. If she's right, she wins. The assassin wins if he successfully eliminates all of the other players before being fingered as the assassin.

How to avoid getting caught if you're the assassin? Don't let anyone see you winking, of course. Choose just the right moment in conversation when no one is looking and attention is elsewhere to make your deadly move. And swiftly turn your own attention elsewhere—leaving the scene of the crime, as it were—so there is nothing to connect you to the incident. And how to avoid being killed if you're not the assassin? Keep your eyes darting constantly, to lessen the assassin's chances of catching your eye. And be alert—most victims are killed when they let their guard down and start daydreaming.

Botticelli

Botticelli is a guessing game. Choose a person to be It (coin tosses, rock/paper/scissors, draw straws). Whoever is It thinks of a person whom all players would have occasion to know, but only reveals to the players the first letter of the subject's last name. For example, the It person is thinking of George Washington, so he says "W." The other players try to find out who this "W" person is by earning direct yes-or-no questions about the "W" person that they can ask the It person. (Direct questions are basic Twenty Questions–style, like "Are you living?" "Are you male?" "Are you American?" to narrow down the possibilities). To win the chance to ask a direct question, the players must stump the It person with questions of their own about *other people* whose names begin with "W." For instance, you can ask the It person, "Were you a popular cartoon character in the 1950s?" If the It person doesn't know you're thinking of Woody Woodpecker, then you have earned a direct question, and the It person must answer truthfully. If the It person knows the answer is Woody Woodpecker, the player doesn't get to ask her direct question.

The George Washington round of direct questions (should players earn enough opportunities to ask!) might look something like this:

"Are you living?" *No.*

"Are you male?" *Yes.*

"Are you American?" *Yes.*

"Did you live in the twentieth century?" *No.*

"Nineteenth century?" *No.*

"Eighteenth century?" *Yes.*

"Were you in the arts or entertainment?" *No.*

"Were you an inventor?" *No.*

"Were you in politics?" *Yes.*

"Were you president?" *Yes.*

"Were you known as 'the father of your country?'" *Yes.*

By this time the questioners will have found out the identity of the "W" person. Anyone can attempt to earn a direct question or make a guess at any time during the game. Whoever guesses the "W" person is the next to be It.

Essences

Essences is another guessing game. The person who is It thinks of a person that is someone that all players might know. The player on Its left begins by asking the

It person, "If I were . . ." questions about the chosen person. For example, if John Wayne is the name to be guessed, the questions might go like this:

"If I were a food, what would I be?" The It person might answer: *A sizzling steak.*

"If I were a color, what color would I be?" *Leathery brown.*

"If I were a car, what kind would I be?" *A Mustang.*

"If I were a plant, what would I be?" *A tumbleweed.*

"If I were a piece of clothing, what would I be?" *A ten-gallon hat.*

Any player can make a guess at any time, but if she misses, she must sit out a round of questioning. The first player to correctly guess the chosen person wins and becomes the next It person.

Try narrowing down the pool from which the It person can choose a person for guessing. Make it just sports figures or cartoon characters or movie actors, for instance. This makes it both easier and more difficult to win. While you've only got one category of people to guess from, the possible similarities they share just being in this category make choosing your questions harder. For instance, if you've already guessed it's a player on the Patriots football team, there are plenty of them to choose from, and narrowing it down can be tricky. Shoot, it could take all day!

Table Time

"Against boredom, even the gods struggle in vain," Friedrich Nietzsche said. Add to boredom a stomach growling with hunger, and things can get ugly. This palooza consists of a tasty handful of creative games—beyond Dots and Hangman—that'll keep the natives from getting too restless.

What's the Palooza?

I'm reminded of the funny game played by the father and daughter characters in Richard Russo's novel *Empire Falls*: they love to look for oddly worded signs. Here are short games to play while waiting for a table or food at a restaurant.

Who can play?
All ages.

What do we need?
Paper, pencil or pen, and a piece of a newspaper or magazine.

Running time?
Ten minutes—or as long as it takes before you're able to eat.

Budget?
Free.

Group Doodle (All ages)

Everybody adds to each other's doodle. Each person starts a doodle on a piece of paper. It can be anything a geometric shape, a flower, a heart, or a squiggle. Pass the papers to the person on the right. That person adds another doodle to the picture, then passes it along to her right. The papers make their way around the table until the food comes.

Word Detective (Ages 6 and up)

You choose a word, and the others have to guess/find the word. Tear a random section of text as big as the size of your hand from a newspaper or magazine. Choose a word that is found somewhere on this scrap of paper, and don't tell what it is. Give the piece of newspaper or magazine to the first player. That player asks you a question about the word and takes a guess based on your answer. If she guesses wrong, play moves on to the next person at the table. Whoever guesses/finds the word first wins. Some sample questions might be:

maître d' (ma-ter-dee), n.: Short for *maître d'hôtel*, or master of the house.

Is it a noun? A verb? An adjective?

Is it a person, place, or thing?

Is it in the subject or predicate?

Does it describe a feeling, thing, or action?

Is it a physical action, such as running or jumping?

Is it a passive action, such as reading or writing?

Is it a color?

Is it the name of something?

Is it a number?

Guess the Animal (All ages)

One person begins to draw an animal, and the others have to guess what animal it is. (This is a great one to do at those restaurants with paper tablecloths.) Start by drawing a single body part of an animal, something that is common to lots of animals, like the eyes. Then start entertaining guesses. As you move along, draw parts that won't give it away too soon. For instance, the legs of a giraffe can look similar to those of a horse, but the long neck is a sure giveaway. The person who guesses the animal correctly first gets to start the next round.

A variation of this game is to guess a person's profession. Draw a stick figure to start with. Others have to guess their profession by whatever accessories you give to the stick figure. A cap, a briefcase, a uniform, and finally a plane reveal a pilot. Draw accessories that can be associated with any of several different professions first pens, clipboards, caps then zero in on the specifics that'll be real clues.

Paper Person (Ages 6 and up)

Everybody gets to contribute to a picture of a person. Fold a piece of paper into fourths lengthwise. The first person draws a person's head on the top fourth of the paper, then makes little marks to guide the next person to draw where the neck should go, or legs, and so forth. Go all out on the detail—give it a hairdo, distinctive eyes, lips, teeth, maybe a hat. The more detail you give your part of the person, the funnier the final product. After you're done with the head, fold that portion over so it's hidden from view. Pass it to the second person, who draws a torso on the second section of the paper, again with plenty of details (necktie, T-shirt slogans, stethoscope!), and folds it over when she's done. The third person draws the legs and folds her half over. The fourth person finishes up by drawing the feet (sneakers, cowboy boots, ballet slippers, clown shoes). Open up your picture and see what sort of discombobulated person you've all created. Add to the excitement by having more than one picture getting drawn at a time.

A Waiter by Any Other Name

When you're eating international, your waiter may be impressed to be addressed in the cuisine-appropriate language.

Dutch: *ober*

French: *serveur*

Finnish: *tarjoilija*

German: *kellner*

Hungarian: *pincer*

Icelandic: *thjónn*

Italian: *cameriere*

Polish: *kelner*

Portuguese: *camareiro*

Spanish: *camarero*

Swedish: *kammartjänare*

And if you find yourself dining in Vatican City, you can call your waiter (in Latin, of course) *"cubicularius"*!

Doggerel

They say every dog has its day, so pick one and celebrate! Maybe you're lucky enough to have a dog who's waiting at the window when you get home, a dog who steals your pillow, a dog who doubles as a vacuum cleaner. Or maybe there is no dog, and your kids have to get by on watching *Homeward Bound* with a stuffed pooch. Either way, what better way to spend a day than to devote it to our best friend?

What's the Palooza?

Who can play?

All ages with supervision, especially with cooking and mask-making activities.

What do we need?

Posterboard or sturdy paper, markers or crayons, glue, two pieces of string or ribbon, 15 inches long. Also see ingredients for dog biscuits, opposite.

Running time?

All day or any smaller amount of time for individual activities

------

Budget?

$

It's Doggie Day, complete with a dog's-eye view of the day, homemade dog biscuits, some new tricks, and creating dog portraits.

A Mutty Morning

Greet the morning with a lazy, dog-inspired stretch called Down Dog. Start on all fours, with your toes curled under. Slowly straighten your legs, lift your bottom in the air, and extend your arms out in front of you, almost pushing away from the floor. Let your head hang down and slowly breathe in and out a few times. Bend your knees and come back to all fours, then sit back on your heels. A big, sloppy yawn often follows.

Spend a little more time on all fours, seeing your house and family from your dog's point of view. Follow your pooch to the kitchen to see what's for breakfast. A nice piece of cinnamon toast cut it into the shape of a dog bone for you; the usual for your dog. The usual, that is, until you make him some tasty homemade dog biscuits. These are cinchy for you to make, crunchy and tasty for doggy to eat.

Doggy Biscuits

- - - - - - -

Ingredients

1 cup all-purpose unbleached flour
1 cup whole wheat flour
½ cup coarse yellow cornmeal
½ cup instant nonfat dry milk
1 teaspoon brown or granulated sugar
½ teaspoon garlic powder
pinch of salt
1 large egg
½ cup shredded sharp cheddar cheese
¼ cup grated Parmesan cheese
¼ to ½ cup (or more) hot chicken, beef, or vegetable broth
nonstick spray (such as Pam)

Equipment

Large mixing bowl, wooden spoon, measuring cups and spoons, pastry cloth, rolling pin, cookie sheets, bone-shaped cookie cutter, cooling racks

Preheat oven to 250° F. Spray your cookie sheets with nonstick spray.

Mix dry ingredients (flour through salt) thoroughly in a large bowl. Mix in egg, cheeses, and broth to make a dough that is heavy but not sticky. Add a bit more flour, one teaspoon at a time, if the dough is too moist, or more hot broth by teaspoon if the dough is too dry.

Turn the dough onto a floured pastry cloth and knead up to 10 times until the dough is elastic, then let it rest for 5 minutes.

Flour your surface lightly, then roll out the dough to ½ inch thick with a rolling pin. Cut bones with the cookie cutter (if you don't have a bone–shaped cookie cutter, a gingerbread man cutter will do!) and transfer to the cookie sheets. You can place the bones close together because they will not spread. Bake for one hour, then turn cookie sheets around (180°) and bake for another half hour. Remove biscuits from the oven, let them rest for a minute, then transfer to cooling racks to cool completely. Store in a wide-mouthed jar or a ziplock bag.

Teach Your Dog to Read

This trick will amaze your friends and family. Think about what tone of voice you use that makes your dog wag her tail. Some dogs respond to the way you say, "Do you want to go out?" or "Do you want a treat?"

One dog I know starts wagging like mad when you ask in a certain way to see his fuzzy belly. Practice using this tone of voice saying things other than what you usually say to make his tail wag.

Now teach your dog to "read" by holding up a sign saying "Wag Your Tail" while saying your dog's name in that magic tone of voice. Practice a few times throughout the day, and when dinnertime rolls around, you will be ready to astound your family with your highly literate dog.

Pooch, P.I.

Let your dog find his inner Sherlock Holmes. Have someone distract him while you hide his treats (maybe bits of your tasty homemade dog biscuits?) around the house on a low bookshelf, halfway under an ottoman, on the seat edge of a hard chair. When your dog returns, ask "Where did they go?" and watch as he sniffs out his snacks. Some dogs are better sleuths than others, so offer help as necessary, of course.

Play Hard

On Doggy Day, plan to play as long and hard as your dog wants to. Give him his ball and throw it until he's fetched out. Wrestle or chase him until he cries uncle. He'll be thrilled with the undivided attention. And after all that exercise, he'll be happy to curl up on the couch with you to enjoy a cinematic ode to dogs, like *Old Yeller, Homeward Bound, Lassie, 101 Dalmatians, Cats and Dogs, Beethoven,* or *My Dog Skip.*

High Art

Many an artist has indulged a love of dogs in his art. Some feature dogs as props or background; some create knowing, loving portraits of dogs. And some just have fun. William Wegman and his agreeable and photogenic Weimaraners come to mind. Who can forget his portrait of his beloved Fay as Little Red Riding Hood?

Think of all the ways you could immortalize your pooch. A formal portrait, in the Old Masters style. Crayons or markers on paper, of course. Or perhaps a

Dog Dictionary

Dogberry: A comical constable in Shakespeare's *Much Ado About Nothing*, best known for confusing and misusing words. Perhaps he should meet Mrs. Malaprop for coffee? A foolish, blundering official is known as a Dogberry.

Dogcatcher: A person employed by the dog pound to find and impound stray dogs and cats.

Dog-cheap: Very inexpensive.

Dog-ear: To fold down the corner of a page of a book to mark one's place.

Dog-eat-dog: Destructively or ruthlessly competitive.

Dogface: Nickname for an enlisted man, especially an infantryman, in World War II.

Dogged: Persistent in effort, stubbornly tenacious.

Doggery: Doglike behavior, especially when surly.

Doggo: British slang for out of sight. To "lie doggo" is to stay under the radar.

Doggone: Darn. As in, "Doggone your crazy scheme!"

Doghouse, in the: In disfavor or disgrace.

Dog in the manger: A person who selfishly keeps something that he does not need or want so that someone else may not use or enjoy it.

Dog Latin: A mixed up jargon imitating Latin.

Dogleg: A route, way, or course that turns at a sharp angle.

Dogma: A strenuously adhered to opinion, doctrine, or belief.

Dog nail: A nail having a head projecting to one side.

Dog paddle: A simple swimming stroke used to keep afloat involving paddling both arms and kicking the legs underwater in a crouched position.

Dog's age: Quite a long time.

Dog's letter: The letter "R," especially when representing a trill.

Dog star: The bright star Sirius in Canis Major.

Dog tag: A small metal identification tag that hangs from a dog's collar; also the two identification tags that hang from a chain around a soldier's neck.

Dog-tired: Utterly exhausted.

Dog tune: Slang for a second-rate song in jazz and popular music.

Dogwatch: A nautical term for either of two two-hour watches, from 4 to 6 P.M. and 6 to 8 P.M. Also journalism slang for the period after the regular edition of the paper has gone to press, during which reporters on duty must await any new developments that would warrant an extra edition.

Sculpey clay version of your dog in a familiar pose. You can capture the spirit of your dog using all kinds of materials, from Play Doh to balloons to Legos to pipe cleaners. If your dog makes a good model, create a series of portraits—*Fido #4* and *The Nap*—in crayon. Or take a series of photos of your dog that portray the essential him. Frame and hang or display your likenesses to remind you every day why they call him man's best friend.

Extrapaloozas

Dog or No Dog

If you don't—or can't—have a dog but love 'em anyway, have a Doggy Day without the dog. Make dog biscuits and lavish attention and treats on a relative's or a neighbor's dog. Decorate your room or the house with stuffed dogs and create dog art to display all over. Go to a dog pound or pet store and talk to the dogs—they need the company and the affection. Enjoy a dog movie or read a dog book. And smile, knowing you're the fairy godperson in some lucky dog's life!

A Day in the Life of Your Dog

Use a video camera to create a documentary from your dog's point of view. Or take photos of what you think your dog sees. Set them up in the order he encounters them over the course of a day—his bed, his food and water bowls, that pesky cat, the toilet bowl, the door-knob, the carpet, the worn sneaker, the spilled orange juice, the freshly mown grass. . . . Write voice-overs or captions in your dog's "voice," expressing what, until now, only his canine thought balloons could say. This is very funny, off-kilter photography and commentary that will make you appreciate the world the way your dog experiences it.

doggerel (do-ger-el), n.: Loose or irregular verse, often comic or burlesque, giving the impression of having been quickly and casually composed.

Animal Talk

Sure, our pets have a lively and effective repertoire of earnest stares, wagging tails, nagging meows, and impatient yelps. But imagine everything they'd say if only they could talk. I shudder to think how quickly they could take over my house—the world?—given the gift of language.

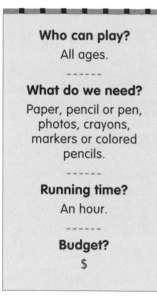

Who can play?
All ages.

What do we need?
Paper, pencil or pen, photos, crayons, markers or colored pencils.

Running time?
An hour.

Budget?
$

What's the Palooza?

Write a script for your pets—what they might say if only they could! (If you have only one pet, write it for your pet and the neighbors' pets, or if you have no pets, write a script for your friends' or relatives' pets or even for your favorite animals at the zoo.)

It's fun to think about what your animals would say to you, but think about what they'd say and do to each other, if given the chance. For instance, what are they doing while everyone is at work or at school in your house? Does the dog jump on the bed and turn on the television set? Does he make long-distance calls to his littermates back in Iowa? What kind of arguments would break out over who gets Dad's recliner and who gets the remote?

Make up comic dramas that take place in your house while you're away (sort of the way the toys cavort in *Toy Story*). How would they bicker over who's the boss or who's the smartest? Who answers the phone when it rings? When things go wrong—and they always do—who runs for cover and who saves the day? Plot a simple, funny scene, then consider how your animals would talk.

Think about what you already know about your animals and their personalities. Might your nervous little lapdog who can't bear to be alone have a voice that is squeaky and thin? Does your high-strung Dalmatian speak only in rapid-rhyming couplets? Does the neighbor's broad-chested bulldog talk like he grew up on the streets of Brooklyn? And the snooty Persian cat? Does she talk with a vague foreign accent? And does your goofy Lab/Irish setter mix jump from subject to subject as if he can't decide which is his favorite?

So you've thought of your scene and the personality profiles of your characters; now give them some dialogue—the simpler the scene, the better. Pretend your cat and dog are doing the family grocery shopping. The dog's a lovable, oblivious goof. Your cat's a skittish detail freak.

Dog: Do you think we should get some of that cereal the boy likes, with the little sugary marshmallows?

Cat: Are you crazy? What do you think makes him chase me, put me under that orange crate, and pretend I'm the only exhibit in his zoo? The sugar, dummy! No, no sugary cereal.

Dog: What about that fruit punch he likes?

Cat: Fruit punch? Ha! It's about ½ percent fruit and 99½ percent sugar. Like I said before, no sugar!

Dog: Okay, no sugar. But we're supposed to pick up some toothpaste, too.

Cat: Toothpaste. What a laugh. Like the kid ever brushes his teeth. Sure, we'll get the toothpaste. But if he ever uses the stuff, I'll eat my shorts.

Your scene will show what your cats and dogs and other creatures know about you and what you know about them. Let your imagination take a full run with what your animals might be saying to each other if (a) they could and (b) you weren't listening.

> ## Good Books
>
> ------
>
> We've all seen the wonderful movies featuring talking animals—*The Incredible Journey, Milo and Otis, The Lion King, Babe, Homeward Bound.* But before there were talking animal flicks, there were superbly imaginative talking animal books. These books are must-reads for any animal lover: for younger readers, *The Wind in the Willows* by Kenneth Grahame and "Rikki Tiki Tavi" by Rudyard Kipling, and for slightly older readers, *Charlotte's Web* and *Stuart Little* by E. B. White, *The Jungle Book* by Rudyard Kipling, and *The Chronicles of Narnia*, by C. S. Lewis.

Extrapalooza

Sunday Funnies

Create a panel comic strip starring your pet. Use photographs of your pet or drawings to illustrate a simple sequence. Write dialogue or thoughts in little balloons over his head. To convey the mini-plot of a comic, carefully select the details you illustrate in order for it to work in a four- or five-panel comic. Does your dog drive the mailman crazy? You might show your dog spying through the mail slot in the door as the mailman comes up the sidewalk. Then the mailman looking around to be sure the dog isn't there. Then the mailman smiling to himself as he slips the mail in the slot. Then the dog's snarling head popping through the mail slot just in time to take a big bite out of the mailman's behind. What might the dog and the mailman be saying to themselves in the thought balloons? Have some fun with the panel comic format, and your pet might become the next Garfield!

Koko Talks

Scientists have long been fascinated by the ways in which animals communicate with each other and with humans. By far the most famous "talking" animal is Koko, the gorilla. When Koko was a baby, Francine Patterson began to teach her American Sign Language. Koko ended up with a working vocabulary of over 1,000 signs and understands approximately 2,000 words of spoken English. Koko "can convey to us feelings that her wild counterparts cannot," says Dr. Patterson. Koko has even invented her own words for things; a ring is called a "finger bracelet,'" a cigarette lighter is a "bottle match." Read *Koko's Kitten* by Francine Patterson about the sweet relationship between Koko and her pet kitten, All Ball. You can also go to http://www.koko.org/kids club/ to learn more about Koko the amazing talking gorilla.

Cat Yoga

Sure, there's the Cat pose from traditional yoga, a reasonable and gratifying imitation of a cat enjoying a post-nap, back-arching stretch. You can call it yoga, or you can just call it being a cat. Kitty-loving kids will easily identify all of the other artful, restorative poses that punctuate every day of their cat's life.

What's the Palooza?

Every cat has its own favorite poses it moves through during a day. The belly-up, arms extended, sun-worshiping stretch. Curled up in a ball like a fiddlehead fern. Elegantly at-attention like an Egyptian statue, which brings to mind the common sphinx pose. There's also how they look when tucked in for a half-nap, with arms curled underneath them as if wearing a muff. Every cat has its variations on these cat classics, and some—the real yogis—have one-of-a-kind poses that obviously make them feel at one with the universe. One big-bellied cat I know reclines as if in a chair, legs splayed like Buddha.

To begin to identify your cat's yoga poses, watch Kitty sleep. Look at the curled-up sleep position, the stretched-out sleep position, the asleep-with-one-eye-open sleep position. When these positions are identified, name them! Round Cat. Long Cat. Careful Cat. And then draw them or take a photograph of the cat in each position. Throughout the day, watch for the action positions—ready to pounce, batting a toy, chasing its tail, or spooked and scooting down the hallway sideways. Also look at the way your cat watches things, or the position of his body when he's on high alert, or the curve of his body as he rubs against your legs.

Once a good handful of poses have been identified, named, and drawn or photographed, spread the images

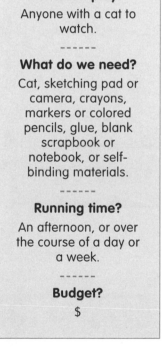

Who can play?
Anyone with a cat to watch.

What do we need?
Cat, sketching pad or camera, crayons, markers or colored pencils, glue, blank scrapbook or notebook, or self-binding materials.

Running time?
An afternoon, or over the course of a day or a week.

Budget?
$

out on the table and arrange them the way they might appear in a book. Perhaps the watching and thinking poses first. Maybe the action poses next. Then wrap it up with the sleepy poses. Turn the front pages of your blank scrapbook or notebook into the title and dedication pages. Then glue the images to the blank pages in the order you have chosen for your poses. Title the images of the poses with the names you have given them, or title them and include a short description of how a person might actually get into that pose himself! (Lie down on your side in a patch of sunshine. Curl into a tight ball with your top arm wrapped around your knees and your bottom arm stretched above your head. Purr.) Decorate your book's cover with an extra photograph or drawing, title and sign it.

Cat Yoga is a fun way to see your cat in a whole new light—who knew such wisdom and tranquillity lived right there in your house? And a child's Cat Yoga book ends up being a sweet celebration and keepsake about Kitty.

Extrapaloozas

Cats and Other Critters

You may have just one cat to inspire you. Or you may have all kinds of animals to bring in on the yoga fun. Dogs, of course, are endlessly expressive with their bodies. And they actually like to get on a yoga mat, if given the

Great Words from the World of Yoga

- - - - - - -

amrita	dristi	manas	samana	vairagya
asana	hatha	maya	smriti	vata
ashtanga	indriyas	pingala	sthira	vikriti
ayurveda	ishta devata	pitta	sukha	vinyasa
brahmana	kapha	prakriti	tantra	vrttis
dosha	langhana	prana	udana	vyana

opportunity. Lizards and snakes have wonderful, almost sculptural aspects to their stillness, as well as to their movements. Small animals such as hamsters, gerbils, guinea pigs, and

rabbits can be an inspiration in their nervous tranquillity.

Maybe you have lots of allergies and no pets at all. A trip to the zoo with a notepad and camera can yield a whole world of animal yoga ideas.

Practicing Cat Yoga

Put on some comfortable clothes, turn on some soothing music, and lead mom or dad through poses in your Cat Yoga book. Do everything you would do in a real yoga class: move slowly and deliberately through the poses; breathe purposely; be conscious of your posture. Look for ways to connect the poses, creating sequences. End with a few moments of quiet—and *namasté* ("I bow to the divine in you") to your student and your cat!

Lions and Tigers and Bears, Om My!

Real yoga—asanas, vinyasas, pranas, and all—is loaded with inspiration from the animal kingdom. Many poses are modeled after and named for animals (translated from the original Sanskrit), including Cat, of course, and Down Dog. Others include Lion, Dolphin, Fish, Butterfly, Cobra, Locust, Camel, Crow, Cow, Peacock, Pigeon, Eagle, and Dead Bug. Cat and Down Dog are easy and fun to try; others, like Peacock— well, don't try this at home!

A-Maze Me

A boy I know decided to make a maze for his guinea pig for a science project. He spent long afternoons absorbed in constructing an elaborate maze, only to discover that his rather portly guinea pig, Crash, had no intention of enjoying the maze; he parked himself at its opening and wouldn't budge. If only Crash had been a hamster! A maze or tunnel adventure is always met with energetic enthusiasm by a hamster.

Who can play?
Ages 6–12.

What do we need?
Large piece of cardboard for a base (at least 2 x 2 feet), 10 paper-towel tubes, 5 empty cube-shaped tissue boxes, 4 empty oatmeal cartons, scissors, nontoxic tape, playing cards, nontoxic glue, butcher paper, non-toxic markers. A hamster or gerbil.

Running time?
A few hours.

Budget?
$

What's the Palooza?

Make a cardboard castle maze out of household materials for your hamster or gerbil. Arrange the four oatmeal cartons upright on the four corners of your cardboard base. Discard the plastic lids. These cartons will be your castle anchors. Cut holes to fit cardboard tubes in the back and left sides of the front right carton, in the front and left sides of the back right carton, in the back and right sides of the front left carton, and in the front and right sides of the back left carton. (Get help cutting, as necessary.)

Cut holes to fit cardboard tubes in the front and back of two upright tissue boxes and place the boxes between the front and back anchors on both sides. Connect the front and back anchors to the tissue boxes with four paper-towel tubes. Use little bits of tape to secure the pieces you've connected.

Next cut holes to fit cardboard tubes on the sides and front of one upright tissue box, and on the sides and back of another upright tissue box. Cut holes in the front and back of a fifth upright tissue box that is situated in the middle of the castle. Connect the right and left anchors to the tissue boxes with four paper-towel tubes. Connect the back and front tissue boxes to the middle tissue box with paper-towel tubes. Secure all connections with tape.

Carefully cut an opening in the front of the front, center tissue box that will be the entrance to your castle. And now you have a castle maze for your hamster, complete with "rooms" with openings on top that let you see how he's progressing (and so he can breathe!). You can leave the castle just the way it is, or make it fancy by covering the pieces with butcher paper and using markers to make it look extra castle-like. You can affix little flags to the anchors and add other authentic, castle-like touches.

Warning: Don't make your castle so fancy and fabulous that you can't bear to part with it. While your hamster will certainly enjoy exploring the castle for hours, eventually he'll start to nibble and gnaw on it—that's more than half the fun for little Hammy.

Extrapalooza

Queen of Hearts, Jack of Diamonds Castle Maze

Decorate the larger pieces of the castle with face-out playing cards (preferably the face cards) to create a colorful, royal look for your hamster's playground. Here's where those old decks missing a card or two will come in handy. Hide little hamster treats throughout the rooms of his castle to make him feel like a king.

The Truth about Herr Hamster

The word hamster comes from the German word *hamstern*, which means "hoard." Though originally from North Asia, Russia, and China, the most common hamsters available today are descendants of six hamsters discovered in Syria in 1930. How's that for six degrees of separation?

   In their natural environment, hamsters live underground in burrows, with different compartments for nesting, food, even for matters of personal grooming. This probably explains why your hamster enjoys moving from room to room in his spacious castle. In the wild, hamsters are also known for running up to five miles every night collecting food in the desert. Which explains why your hamster at home is such a bundle of unspent energy—and so happy to have his castle maze.

Bird Theater

Birders are a lovably loony bunch—and I count myself among them. There are 850 species of birds in North America alone—and some of us want to meet each one of them personally! This palooza puts you on a first-name basis with the birds you see every day near your home, and is likely to introduce you to many more.

Who can play?
All ages.

What do we need?
Imagination, a bird feeder, birdseed, and a good field guide. Notebook and binoculars, optional.

Running time?
Off and on over a week—or a lifetime!

Budget?
$

ornithology (or-ni-tho-lo-gee), n.: The study of birds.

What's the Palooza?

Create a soap opera starring the feathered folks who live outside your window. If you take the time to look carefully at the few birds you see every day, you'll see they're each very different from the other, and not just in the color of their feathers or the shape of their beaks. Some are shy and quiet and politely wait their turn for a grain of seed. Others are loud and bossy and seem to take over the feeder, or make it their business just to annoy the other birds. A lot like some kids in the lunchroom at school, right?

Set up a feeder right outside your window, or in your backyard, not far from a window where you can watch clearly. Try to set it in a somewhat sheltered location because birds much prefer a dry, well-maintained feeder. Keep the feeder stocked with wild-bird seed for a week and make a point of checking out the action every morning and at least one other time of the day. You'll quickly recognize the "regulars," the birds who live somewhere nearby and can be counted on to visit your feeder whenever there's food!

By now you've noticed the different looks and personalities of the birds at your feeder: that big blue jay who fearlessly divebombs the feeder, scattering the little wrens to the wind; the showy but cautious cardinal; the dawdling doves; the raucous caw-caws. And of course you've seen the nervy squirrels vying for their fair share of the feeder booty. Name your backyard critters—Big

Red, the strong silent cardinal. Donna and Doris Dove, who coo back and forth while they peck, as if gossiping over a cup of coffee. Stella, the sassy starling. Then create an over-the-top daytime drama starring your backyard friends: *As the Bird Turns* or *The Feathered and the Fabulous.*

Invent overlapping story lines involving your main characters. Stella doesn't know it, but Donna and Doris are plotting to get her fired from her job at Starbeaks. Big Red secretly loves Stella, but can't tell her because he's too shy. Will Bill the Blue Jay sweep Stella off her feet before Big Red can proclaim his love? Will Donna and Doris's plan backfire and cost them their own jobs at the Coffee Klatch? Who's the handsome stranger who flies into town and causes such an uproar at the feeder? Name your bird feeder as if it's a hotel or an estate or even a town. Your story will become even more interesting when you're imagining it happening at the dilapidated Chateau Rien or the gossippy village of Sleepy Acres.

Get your family involved in watching the birds and imagining what's happening and what they're saying. It's an irresistible game, and once you start, you'll find you'll never stop looking outside for them and wondering what happens next in your backyard soap.

Extrapaloozas

What Are These Birds?

Use a field guide to identify the species of birds you see. Start by noting the basic shape and color of each bird, as well as its beak, wings, and feet. When you flip through the field guide, you will probably see a few birds that remind you of your bird, so use the maps to narrow down whether the bird in the book would be

> *A bird doesn't sing because it has an answer, it sings because it has a song.*
>
> —Maya Angelou
> (1928–)

hanging out at a bird feeder in your part of the country. The more you know about what your birds really are, the more delicious detail your backyard soap opera will have. A great family field guide is *Smithsonian Handbooks: Birds of North America,* by Fred Alsop III. *A Field Guide to the Birds of North America,* by Roger Tory Peterson, is a terrific pocket field guide to use spotting birds when not at home.

Life List

Start keeping a list of the birds you see and can identify in your backyard. Birdwatchers call this a "life list." Note the species of bird, the day you spotted it, and where you saw it. You might also add a little drawing of the bird next to your notation. Beware: Once you start a life list, it's hard to break the habit of trying to add new birds to your list. The average birder tops out at around 350 of the 850 species found in North America, but the truly obsessed plan their vacations and travel around opportunities to add even more birds to their life list. You can set up an online life list at www.birdzilla.com.

food
paloozas

Literary Dish

Much of literature is infused with intoxicating references to food, often times so tempting that it's hard to wait until the end of a chapter to grab a snack. While Hemingway writes of salty oysters and Proust has his buttery madeleines, children's books are also spiced with fanciful foods. When kids see that it's possible to make incredible foods—green eggs and ham, anyone?—spring from the page and onto the table, they just might try a new dish or two. Creativity is key here, so don't be afraid to let the literary dish run away with the spoon!

Who can play?
All ages, with a little kitchen supervision.

What do we need?
Anything in the refrigerator, from pickles to peanut butter!

Running time?
Ten minutes for some concoctions, up to an hour for the aspiring chef.

Budget?
$

What's the Palooza?

For the youngest eater-readers, *The Very Hungry Caterpillar* by Eric Carle inspires a mini tasting menu. If tots find themselves feeling like the caterpillar with an insatiable appetite, they can follow him on his Saturday food scavenge. Taking small tastes of a smorgasbord of berries, cheese, pickles, salami, muffins, and cherry pie prevents anything akin to the caterpillar's Sunday-morning stomachache. On a cold, snowy day, everyone can contribute to Little Bear's big black pot of birthday soup. The chef might replace his hat with the cub's space helmet (perhaps an old metal strainer), and guests can enjoy a hot meal alongside favorite (stuffed) animal friends.

Charlie and the Chocolate Factory by Roald Dahl is full of sweet ideas for older kids to explore. Recipes for simple fudge or candied fruit are easy to locate, and green oompa-loompa food coloring adds to any dessert. Concoct recipes for Wonka's wacky inventions, such as "toffee-apple trees" (first cousin of the candy apple), "hot ice creams for cold days" (some hot sauces, perhaps?), and "fizzy lifting drinks" (carbonation is the key). Fans of Shel Silverstein will also find inspiration for new recipes in many of his poems. Read Silverstein's "Eighteen Flavors" as a starter and choose a mix of flavors to experiment with in creating a new dessert.

In Judi and Ron Barrett's *Cloudy with a Chance of Meatballs*, the town of Chewandswallow experiences deluges of dinner and buttered toast breakfasts. The meals described in this whimsical book aren't on a plate, rather they swirl around the air like the weather. *Cloudy*-inspired meals don't come from recipes; instead ask a child to imagine what his meal might be, meteorologically speaking. Kids can create their own food forecasts out of their ordinary meals. Storm clouds of scrambled eggs, smoothie sleet, and a butter-and-jam tornado. For mashers and stirrers, an ice cream and chocolate sauce cyclone.

Extrapaloozas

Cheesed Off

The Stinky Cheese Man, by Jon Scieszka, prompts an easy food-shopping activity: find a local gourmet grocery store and get to know the cheese man. Let him introduce you to a new seriously stinky cheese every week.

Riddles for the Griddle

Dr. Seuss's books seem to have been written with the kitchen explorer in mind. Flip through any one of his fantastical books for new recipe ideas. Think red-fish-blue-fish sugar cookies. Or potato-chip pork chops. Seuss's book of riddles, *Oh Say Can You Say*, is also a double delight for the tongue.

Roald Dahl's Revolting Recipes

Recipes from many Roald Dahl favorites— *The Twits, Matilda, Charlie and the Chocolate Factory*—are collected in *Revolting Recipes* and its sequel, *Roald Dahl's Even More Revolting Recipes*. Complete recipes are included for edibles such as Candy Pencils you can eat in class to Stink Bug Eggs (mostly they're deviled) to Mr. Twit's beard food (mashed potatoes, hard-boiled eggs, mushrooms, and mini hot dogs).

Mama Mia

Italy is one of those places that just wedges itself in your imagination, no matter how old you are. Who wouldn't want to be picking lemons under the Tuscan sun, boating along Venice's winding canals, or racing a Vespa through Rome? Turning your dining room into an Italian restaurant is the next best thing to being there.

Who can play?
All ages.

What do we need?
Ingredients for an Italian dinner (pasta, tomato sauce, garlic bread fixings).

Running time?
One evening.

Budget?
$

What's the Palooza?

A full Italian dinner to celebrate that boot-shaped land. Set the mood with classic Italian music like "O sole mio." Be warned that someone will probably join in as Enrico Caruso belts his heart out on the stereo. Watch *Roman Holiday* or *Summertime* as you're preparing dinner to get you feeling like you're in Rome or Venice. Choose roles: one can be the waiter Luigi, someone else is the bossy Chef Salvatore. The cooks can wear red aprons and chef's hats made of paper (roll a white piece into a cylinder, staple, fold another piece in around the edges to create a ballooning sphere, staple it to the first roll).

Italian meals often can be thrown together using stock pantry ingredients: tomatoes, pasta, dried basil, olives, good bread, garlic, parmesan, and San Pellegrino or seltzer. The fun is in chopping and dicing, stirring (and spilling), tossing and spinning. One never-fail dinner is spaghetti with tomato-basil sauce. Put canned plum tomatoes and a splash of olive oil in a blender and season with garlic and basil to taste. Toss onto a plate of steaming pasta.

Dim the lights in your dining room, or if you're going alfresco, on the porch. Set a red-checkered tablecloth and candles stuck in old Chianti bottles. Then arrange fresh wildflowers as a centerpiece and write the day's specials in white chalk on a blackboard. Or, have "Luigi" announce the day's specials with a white napkin draped over her arm. For appetizers, set out bowls of olives and slices of bread with vinegar and olive oil for dipping. Everyone has to speak with Italian accents (extra points for expressive hand motions and use of real Italian phrases). Using Italian proverbs like *"Non si vive di solo pane."* (English translation: One does not live by bread alone) earns double bonus points.

For dessert, enjoy bakery-bought cannolis or tiramisu. Close your eyes, sip espresso (adults only!), listen to Caruso, and you can almost hear the hum of Fiats in the Roman street below.

Garlic Bread

½ stick butter, softened
1 cup parmesan cheese, grated
5 cloves garlic, chopped
3 tablespoons fresh parsley, chopped
½ teaspoon oregano
1 loaf fresh Italian bread (or French baguette), cut lengthwise from the side

Preheat the oven to 375°F. Mix butter, parmesan, garlic, parsley, and oregano in a small bowl. Spread butter and herb mixture onto both halves of the loaf of bread. Slice the bread so that individual-sized portions are easy to break off the loaf. Wrap bread in aluminum foil and bake for 20 minutes. Remove from foil and place under the broiler to brown for 2 to 3 minutes. Serve at once.

Extrapalooza

Around the World

Vary the location. Go Moroccan, make couscous and lamb, and sit on cushions on the floor. Decorate your dining room with bright fabric and copper lanterns. Drink mint tea in glass cups. Or try Thai. Stick bamboo in a vase and serve pad thai, dumplings, and Thai iced tea. Work your way around the globe.

Pasta Shapes

True gourmands know their Italian pasta shapes as well as their fun-loving names:

casarecci: Short lengths of rolled and twisted pasta.

cavatelli: Small shells that resemble tiny hot dog buns.

conchiglie: Resembles conch shells.

farfalle: Resembles bow ties or butterflies.

fusilli: Shaped like screws or springs.

gemelli: "Twins" in Italian; short rods twisted together in a spiral pattern.

gigli: "Lilies" in Italia, shaped like flowers.

lumaconi: Giant snail shells.

maltagliati: "Poorly cut" in Italian; describing various pasta scraps.

margherite: "Daisies" in Italian, but shaped more like ridged shells.

radiatori: Resemble small radiators.

torchio: Resemble torches.

Iron Chef

At some point, a kid has to figure out that dinner is more than just showing up at the table with reasonably clean hands. Inspired by the crazy-popular Japanese cooking show of the same name, this palooza gives kids a vigorous, hands-on introduction to what goes on behind the scenes when making a meal—namely, creativity, planning, and a little elbow grease.

Who can play?

Ages 6 and up, with supervision as necessary.

What do we need?

Cookbooks, basic kitchen utensils and equipment, and ingredients.

Running time?

An afternoon.

Budget?

$–$$, depending on ingredients.

What's the Palooza?

Have a friendly culinary competition where each chef creates a single dish using a theme ingredient. Choose a theme ingredient. Simple and versatile theme ingredients such as eggs, tomatoes, fruit, cheese, pasta, chicken, or chocolate allow for a broad choice of dishes to make. The theme ingredient may also be seasonal, for instance, zucchini in the summer (zucchini bread, zucchini quiche, or fried zucchini perhaps) or pumpkin in the fall (pie, of course, or maybe pumpkin ravioli or pumpkin soup).

Hunt for recipes in cookbooks you have at home, or in kid-friendly cookbooks and recipe Web sites, to find a dish you'd like to make. Each chef needs to make a list of ingredients he'll need. Check off what's already available in your cupboard or refrigerator and you're left with what has to be purchased. These will be the items on your the grocery list (make sure you know how much you need of each ingredient). Now see if everyone can hitch a ride to the grocery store.

Once all of the ingredients are on hand, it's time to organize all the utensils and equipment you'll need. You may need to work in shifts, if there isn't enough equipment or space to go around. Review your recipes and gather the spoons, knives, mixing bowls, measuring cups, pots, pans, and whatever else is needed for preparation, so they are handy.

Have plenty of empty cups or bowls available for measuring and setting aside ingredients, because it's easiest to prepare each ingredient of the recipe before putting them all together. Perhaps the first ingredient is one cup of chopped tomatoes. Cut and measure the tomatoes before moving on to the next ingredient. You may want to check off each ingredient as you move down the list.

Once all the ingredients and equipment are ready to go, move on to the directions. Children's cookbooks often have pictures that show how something is done. Make sure to ask questions about any techniques or cooking terms you don't understand. Mom or Dad would be happy to demonstrate—you can probably even enlist them as chopping-and-measuring assistants.

Clean as you go. Once a bowl or utensil is used, it can be quickly washed and ready to put away or be used for some other part of the recipe. Washing one bowl a couple of times during cooking is a lot easier than piling up two or three bowls that need to be washed when you're done. Cleaning as you go allows you to enjoy what's been prepared, rather than dreading the mess in the kitchen when you're done.

Now you stir, sauté, simmer, stew—or whatever your recipe asks you to do. Follow each instruction carefully and pay attention to the cooking times in the recipe. Use a timer to remind yourself when your dish is done, or use it several times while cooking to remind yourself when you need to move on to the next instruction.

When all the cooking is done, each chef makes the presentation a production. Use a nice serving dish and set out your creations with garnishes. Always present what you cook with just a hint of a flourish, to honor the effort and creativity it took to create as well as to honor the people you are serving.

The judges—the folks chowing down on your dishes—can vote for the best dish or just do the smart thing and say nothing more than, "Mmmmmm, it's all so good! I can't decide!"

Naming Your Dish

The dish may not be new, but the name sure can be. Give your dish some of the glory it deserves. Good old spaghetti and meatballs can be transformed into Stella's Pile, Italian Style! Here's a sampling of some of the all-time great creatively named dishes:

Ambrosia Salad

Angel Food Cake

Apple Brown Betty

Deviled Eggs

Devil's Food Cake

Hermit Cookies

Hoppin' John

Pigs in a Blanket

Red Flannel Hash

Red Velvet Cake

Sloppy Joe

Extrapaloozas

Reverse Iron Chef

Start out with a recipe and search the kitchen for the ingredients. Consider it a kitchen orientation. You'll figure out how your kitchen is set up and where to locate things. Finding the mustard in the refrigerator might be a surprise, but you'll know where to look the next time. Choose a recipe and try to find your ingredients in the cupboards and fridge. Once everything is assembled on the table or counter and you make your dish, you have to remember where you found everything so you can put it back.

Iron Chef Stone Soup

The classic story of Stone Soup is a cooking lesson it itself. A peddlar with a "magic stone" tricks some villagers into sharing bits of food they have to make a hearty, delicious soup. Iron Chef Stone Soup is made in the same spirit—with a basic soup recipe and whatever ingredients you have on hand. This is at the heart of truly innovative and creative cooking.

Iron Chef Stone Soup

1   stone, big and smooth, so it won't get lost in the soup
1   tablespoon. butter or vegetable oil
1   medium onion, chopped
2   celery stalks, trimmed and chopped fine
1   large carrot, cut into rounds
3   medium potatoes (unpeeled, and cut into quarters)
1   large garlic clove, pressed
6   cups chicken, beef, or vegetable broth (or a combination of broth and water)
Any combination of the following, adding up to 5 cups:
    diced zucchini, or diced large yellow squash
    diced large corn kernels, fresh or frozen
    mushrooms, diced large
    cooked tubettini or ditalini, or other soup pasta

chicken or beef, cooked and cubed
    firm tofu, cubed
Salt and freshly ground black pepper to taste
Grated Parmesan cheese
Croutons

Scrub the stone thoroughly with soap and hot water, rinsing well. For an extra cleaning, you can drop it in a pot of water to boil while you prepare the rest of the soup.

In another large pot, melt the butter or heat the oil, then sauté the onion on medium-high for 2 to 4 minutes. Stir in the celery, carrot, and potatoes, sautéing for 6 to 8 minutes. Add the garlic and sauté for about 30 seconds, then add the broth/water. Using a spoon, fish the stone out of the other pot, add it to the soup and bring to a boil. Add your combination of vegetables and/or pasta, and cook another 8 minutes or until the veggies are cooked the way you like them. You can also add a cup or two of cooked, cubed chicken or beef or firm tofu to make it an even heartier meal. Season to taste with the salt and pepper, then ladle the soup—minus the stone—into individual bowls and sprinkle with cheese and croutons.

Let the Search Begin

Remembering the dishes you like to eat, look for three or four things from the cupboard or fridge that go together. Hook up some pasta with butter and cheese. Mix whatever salad greens and vegetables are in the vegetable drawer with dressing, leftover chicken cut into cubes, and croutons made from slices of bread. Make a stir-fry with tofu and whatever vegetables you've got in the fridge, served over rice. Make an easy Thai peanut sauce using peanut butter, scallions, soy sauce, garlic, and ginger and top some spaghetti. In any cupboard or fridge, there's always something that goes with something that can be a meal.

Happy Hunting

Check out these kid-friendly cookbooks and Web sites for recipe ideas:

Emeril's There's a Chef in My Soup! Recipes for the Kid in Everyone, by Emeril Lagasse

Children's Step-by-Step Cookbook, by Angela Wilkes

Betty Crocker Kids Cook! By Betty Crocker Editors

www.kidchef.com

www.allrecipes.com, Kids links

At the Table

Dinner in America has become something of an eat-and-run experience. Our families are lucky to sit down to dinner at the same time, never mind set a lovely table and linger over a meal with lively conversation. This palooza gets them thinking of how they can put their own stamp on it. Who knows, the whole gang might start to linger!

Who can play?
Ages 3–6, 6–9.

What do we need?
Construction paper or posterboard, crayons or markers, clear contact paper; plates, silverware, napkins, and glasses.

Running time?
One hour.

Budget?
$

What's the Palooza?

Set a lovely table. Whether it's Sunday dinner with all the fixings or Chinese takeout, you can set the table to make the meal an occasion.

Start with what goes where: the placement of the plate, the fork to the left of the plate, the napkin to the left of the fork, the knife to the right of the plate, the spoon next to the knife, and the glass at the upper right hand corner of the plate. To keep these hard-to-remember details in mind, make a template place mat to use at every meal until you're familiar with what goes on at the table.

Take a piece of construction paper or poster board about the size of a regular place mat and set the three utensils, plate, and glass where they belong in the setting. With a pencil, trace each piece of the setting onto the place mat to make the template. Remove the items and draw over the pencil tracing with markers or crayons. Each piece can be elaborately decorated (curlicues on the silverware, florals on the plates), colored in with solid colors, or labeled "spoon," "plate," and so on. Cut two sheets of clear contact paper slightly larger than the size of your template, then seal the template in the contact paper to make it a place mat that can be actually used at the table. You can also take your placemat to a copy shop with a laminating machine to seal it.

Find out how settings differ for breakfast, lunch, dinner, and a formal dinner. Talk about how the napkins can be set in different areas of the setting, the use of place cards, and how additional silverware is used in a formal place setting. Find out what fork, knife, or spoon to use for each part of the meal or the types of glasses used for different beverages.

Extrapaloozas

Napkin Folding

Napkin folding is an art that can take the place setting from ho-hum to woo-hoo! From the simple accordion fold cinched with a napkin ring to an elaborate swan fold, folded napkins can become your specialty and can change at every meal.

While cloth napkins are traditionally used for napkin folding, dinner-quality paper napkins can work just as well. Party stores carry an assortment of large, sturdy paper napkins in an array of colors that are perfect to use for folding.

An easy-to-learn folded napkin is the Candle. Take a cloth or large square paper napkin, lay it on a table, and fold it in half to form a large triangle, open tips facing up. Fold up two inches of hem from the bottom. Flip over and begin to roll tightly from one side all the way to the other end. Tuck the end corner snugly into the hem.

Check out www.freenapkinfolding.com for some easy instructions on a handful of napkin folds, or *Decorative Napkin Folding for Beginners*, by Lillian Oppenheimer and Natalie Epstein, for more folds to try.

Place Cards

My wife once asked me to make place cards for a dinner party only half an hour before the guests were to arrive. I made a quick Pollock-

A Question of Manners

Make up a quiz of sticky, tricky table manners questions and make it an after-dinner around-the-table family game. What do I do when I drop my napkin or a utensil? Where should I put my napkin while I'm eating? Can I eat any food with my fingers? Do we pass or serve food from the left or the right? A great source for questions— and, of course, the answers—is *You've Got Manners: Table Tips From A to Z for Kids of All Ages,* by Louise Elerding.

like painting on paper and let it dry. Then I cut it up and made place cards out of the pieces. The guests loved them. Place cards help organize the table so everyone knows where to sit. For larger gatherings, write down the guest list and make place cards using the blank side of an index card, folded in half, for each guest. Decorate all the place cards in the same style or make individualized cards for each person. Coordinate the colors of the place cards to the table settings or decorate with holiday images for special occasions. You could even write simple riddles on each place card so that the guests have to guess who's who and who is sitting where: "I'm a redhead with a chalky, talky job." That's Aunt Susie, the school teacher.

Once the place cards are done, draw a picture of the table and make an official seating chart for the occasion. Where should the hosts be seated? How should guests be arranged boy/girl or according to interests, for example to encourage interaction, conversation, and so that the company can be enjoyed to the fullest? Finally, set out the place cards according to plan and watch everyone settle in to a lively meal.

Simple Centerpieces

Anyone can arrange a bouquet of flowers in a vase in the middle of the table. While that works just fine for a decorative centerpiece, find out a creative way to decorate the table beyond the ordinary. Take a familiar container—a clear shallow bowl, for instance—and fill it with something unusual. Marbles or stones or shells can anchor a chunky candle. A few interestingly shaped sticks and twigs embedded in a bowl full of moss make for a tabletop forest.

A Monk's Supper

A friend of mine first described this palooza to me. She said it was an activity she did as a Girl Scout, but I really can't imagine that the Girl Scouts ever awarded a merit badge for sheer uncontrollable laughter.

What's the Palooza?

Have a formal dinner, complete with elaborate menu and music—but no knives, forks, or spoons. The idea is to substitute offbeat utensils such as eggbeaters, potato mashers, or spatulas for ordinary silverware and attempt to eat a complicated meal. That in itself is enough to keep everyone entertained. But what makes this a true palooza, the pièce de résistance, is that, like any serious, self-respecting monk, no one can talk or make a sound during the entire dinner. Everyone must take a vow of silence, just like monks do!

The harder the dishes you make are to eat, the funnier the Monk's Supper is. So think chicken à la king,

Who can play?
All ages.

What do we need?
Ingredients and equipment to make whatever dishes are featured on your menu. Crazy utensils for eating the meal. Simple garments and rope belts for monk's costume.

Running time?
One hour for supper, plus the time it takes to prepare the meal. Definitely set a time for the meal itself to end, say 7:30 sharp.

Budget?
$

pasta with meatballs, or perhaps shepherd's pie. Avoid mashed potatoes or other soft food that can be scooped easily. With older kids, the meal can be stretched out with multiple courses.

To create the proper mood, everyone dresses like a monk. Your look doesn't have to be totally authentic. A hooded sweatshirt, or a piece of rope tied around the waist, is enough to suggest monkness. Set the table with the wacky non-forks, knives, and spoons of your choice. Root through the kitchen utensil drawer for the most awkward fork substitute you can find. You may want to cover the table with a vinyl or washable tablecloth and set out nice low candles. Find some parchment or butcher paper and write the menu in your best calligraphic script. Add Gregorian chant music in the background, or ring a bell to signal everyone to the table, and you're ready to sup. Set a fixed time for dinner to end at which time ring the bell again. Oh, and remember: Don't say a word or make a sound. If you can.

Extrapalooza

Tables Turned

If older and experienced enough, kids do the cooking and serving and the grown-ups are the monks. A simplified version of the Monk's Menu might be:

    Baked herbed chicken
    Rice
    Frozen peas
    Ice cream

Hold on to your wire whisks and let the messy fun begin.

Tidy Time

I was always a terrible failure at getting my kids to clean up. Once we were on vacation in Montana, and each of my two younger kids had brought a friend. So I created a clean-up routine where there was a different kitchen captain every night. Well, it was a disaster. They would make each other do the most awful jobs; you can imagine every minute childhood grudge being nursed. I've been searching for a better way to make cleaning up fun, effective, and civil ever since. And this palooza is the result.

What's the Palooza?

Who can play?
All ages.

What do we need?
Cleaning supplies, music, alarm clock or timer.

Running time?
Thirty minutes.

Budget?
Free.

Invent your own Mary Poppins-y, Cat-in-the-Hat-like cleanup game. What did Mary and the Cat have in common? They turned everything into a game and added a "spoonful of sugar" to the mix. No mention of the words "cleaning" or "chores"—just a matter-of-fact plunge into a rollicking game of, well, tidying up.

Name your game. If it's about cleaning as much as you can in a certain period of time, maybe it's called Beat the Clock. If it's about a concentrated assault on a particular room, it might be The Invaders. You can name each job. Dustbusting. The Big Sweep. Under the Bed. Or you can name each person doing the job. Dr. Dishwasher. Lieutenant Laundry Folder. Or make up very elaborate and official titles, maybe the Executive Vice President in Charge of Dustwhacking and Hyper-hygiene or a Chief Operating Officer for the Elimination of Irrelevant Material. Creating nutty names for everything about your game makes it uniquely yours.

Sometimes a certain job just needs doing. The dishes or laundry, for instance. How to choose who does what? Keep a big jar with the names of each member of the family written on a different Snapple cap or wine cork.

Children have never been very good at listening to their elders, but they have never failed to imitate them.

—James Baldwin
(1924–1987)

The Jobsmeister (a position that is assigned to a different family member weekly, for obvious reasons) reaches into the jar and pulls the name of the person on duty for the job. That person's name is subsequently removed from active duty for two turns, to limit chances he might randomly and accidentally end up doing dishes, laundry, and vacuuming all in one day! If it's a whole morning's worth of work that needs doing, make a list of the jobs, and pull names for each job until all are assigned. If you're a small family—maybe it's just two of you—keep returning your names to the jar until you've divvied up all the jobs.

Sometimes an effort to get things in general order is required. Use your jar of names to make assignments to each room that needs attention. Do a quick inventory of each room with every soldier, making a short, simple, manageable list of no more than five very concrete things to do. TV or living room? Stack magazines and put them on the shelf. Collect toys and return them to their owners. Put crayons and paper away. Arrange pillows on the couch. Set the stove timer for fifteen minutes; by the time it goes off, no matter how many of these items actually get done, the general appearance of things is much improved!

When things get out of hand in a room—the kitchen after an afternoon of cooking or baking, a bedroom after a rainy day of play—the idea of putting everything back in shining order can be daunting. Break these jobs down into smaller pieces and make funny assignments. Pick up and put away only toys with eyes! Put away all things made of paper! Clean this one square foot of counter until it sparkles!

Spoon Lickers

Inspired by Carl Sandburg's "The Wedding Procession of the Rag Doll and the Broom Handle," this palooza turns spoon licking into a main event, instead of just the lick you steal after mixing a batch of brownies.

What's the Palooza?

Carl Sandburg's deliciously inventive short story, "The Wedding Procession of the Rag Doll and the Broom Handle and Who Was in It," describes a wedding parade like no other:

> Who marched in the procession? Well, first came the Spoon Lickers. Every one of them had a tea spoon, or a soup spoon, though most of them had a big table spoon. On the spoons, what did they have? Oh, some had butter scotch, some had gravy, some had marshmallow fudge. Every one had something slickery sweet or fat to eat on the spoon. And as they marched in the wedding procession of the Rag Doll and the Broom Handle, they licked their spoons and looked around and licked their spoons again.

And so shall we. Line up a procession of cups and fill them with tasty spoon foods and dunker-ins. Peanut butter, chocolate frosting, and Marshmallow Fluff work well together, for example. Use three cups filled, say, a third of the way, with one ingredient each. Fill another three cups with dunker-ins such as granola, mini-chocolate chips, and gummy bears. Ideally, the spoon-licking procedure will go something like this: Dip one spoon into the peanut butter and have a lick. Dip a second spoon into the chocolate frosting and have a lick. Dip a third spoon into the Marshmallow Fluff and have a lick. Try to avoid a spoon-licking free-for-all, at least in the

beginning. Aim for a method to this madness. Describe the activity as a tasting, of sorts. Each food/flavor is discerned and appreciated and rated for its own spoon-lickability.

Then begin the dunker-ins. Dip the peanut butter spoon back into peanut butter and then into mini-chocolate chips. Lick. Double-dip the same spoon back into peanut butter, mini-chocolate chips, and finally granola. Lick. Heavenly. Add marshmallow fluff to the mix. After a while it will be impossible to resist double- and triple-dipping and the switching around of ingredients and spoons: "Mom, I'm going to try Marshmallow

Spoon Bread

Of all the eating utensils in your kitchen, spoons are the best. They're cozy, they're curvy, they fit right in your mouth. That's why we love spoon bread. It's cozy, too, and certainly spoon-lickable. Here's how you make it:

2 cups milk
1 cup cornmeal
1 teaspoon salt
Black pepper to taste
4 tablespoons butter
4 eggs, separated
1 cup fresh or thawed frozen corn

Pour milk into a saucepan and bring close to a boil. Add the cornmeal, stirring constantly. Continue cooking and stirring until the mixture is thick and smooth, for about one minute. Do not let the mixture get too thick. Add the salt, pepper and butter and remove from the heat.

Beat the egg yolks until light and yellow and add to the cornmeal. Add the corn. Beat the egg whites until stiff and fold into the cornmeal.

Pour into a well-buttered casserole and bake in a 375°F oven for about 35 minutes, or until the spoon bread is browned on top. Serve hot with butter.

Fluff first this time with just the gummy bears. Then I'm going to dip the peanut butter into Marshmallow Fluff."

If there's more than one spoon licker at the table, use disposable spoons and toss after each dip-n-lick. For germ control.

Extrapaloozas

Spoon Licker's Parade

Read Sandburg's story in its entirety and have a kitchen parade that includes Spoon Lickers, Musical Soup Eaters, Tin Pan Bangers, and others. Invent other characters based on kitchen supplies for the parade. Name them. You'll find the tale in *Rootabaga Stories* by Carl Sandburg.

Savory Spoon (or Fork) Licking

A piece of cheese or a cube of crusty bread on the end of a plastic fork dipped into a cup of marinara. Or a cube of chicken dipped into a cup of Thai peanut sauce. Fondue for spoon lickers!